WRITING/TEACHING

Published by the University of Pittsburgh Press, Pittsburgh, Pa. 15261
Copyright © 2000, University of Pittsburgh Press
All rights reserved
Manufactured in the United States of America
Printed on acid-free paper
10 9 8 7 6 5 4 3 2 1

Permission to reprint poems and other works may be found on
the last page of this book.

Library of Congress Cataloging-in-Publication Data

Kameen, Paul, 1949–
      Writing/teaching : essays toward a rhetoric of pedagogy / Paul Kameen.
           p. cm.
      — (Pittsburgh series in composition, literacy, and culture)
Includes bibliographical references (p.) and index.
      ISBN 0-8229-5723-X
      1. American poetry—20th century—Study and teaching. 2. Gender
identity in literature—Study and teaching. 3. Sex role in
literature—Study and teaching. 4. Race in literature—Study and
teaching. 5. Teaching teams. 6. Dialectic. 7. Teaching. 8. Socrates.
9. Plato. I. Title. II. Series.
      PS306 .K36 2000
      808'.0071—dc21

                                                    00-008410

This book is dedicated to the memory of my friend
Jim Fahey: "Kansas wheat/tan and dry"

CONTENTS

PREFACE

For a number of years now many of us—college and university professors in such diverse disciplines as composition, cultural studies, and rhetoric—have been arguing for a reconfiguration of the relationship between teaching and research. Conventional wisdom construes research as taking place prior to and independent of teaching. In this arrangement, it is inevitable that the classroom will be prefigured as a site for the dispensation of already-constituted knowledge rather than as a site for the construction of new knowledge. This book offers one way—a simple reversal of that temporal sequence—for upsetting both the dominant hierarchy and its most immediate epistemological consequences. In other words, the various texts that follow here, and the knowledge(s) they proffer, originated in the classroom. They—both as text and as knowledge—are the product of teaching, which came first. And they offer a general testimony on behalf of the classroom as a legitimate arena for the production of important knowledge. Whether or how these texts serve as "research" will depend on one's assumptions about what its features and effects should be. But I can say this: There is nothing in this book that would or could have found its way even into written form, let alone into the public realm, were it not for my work in the classroom, which fully preceded and prefigured it.

The first half of the book is a group of essays written during, after, and entirely about a specific graduate course I team-taught with my colleague Toi Derricotte. That these essays could not exist without my having taught that course is self-evident. I tried for some time to find an available generic term for them that would familiarize them to a reader—make it easier to read them as I preferred them to be read. The name I came up with to explain to the seminar what sort of "personal" writing our course was inviting—ideological autobiography— remains, with all of its limitations, the one I prefer. I wanted at the time to call attention to the fact that the "stories" we might end up telling to one another in the public forum of the seminar had a very express political purpose, arising from and constituted by the larger context of the course, which was going to pre-scribe their narrative lines. They were intended to function not as memoir but as pedagogy. In a general sense, then, the essays that compose the first half of this book seek to reenact the discursive world that we all inhabited in the seminar; in a narrower sense, they represent some of what I came to know concerning the "subject"—in both of its applicable senses—of this course through the experience of teaching it.

This was a course part of whose agenda was to elicit personal stories from its participants. So in this case I happened to be writing down on a regular basis what the syllabus was inviting/compelling me to think about. But every course I teach, every course any of us teaches, makes us think in equally complex ways about equally consequential matters. Usually, we just don't write them down along the way, while they are occurring to us. There are reasons why we don't that involve more than just the time it takes to do so, which is a considerable deterrent, I admit, in a typically busy semester. One of those reasons is that we are conditioned by our professional experience to believe that texts of this type are not scholarly and are, therefore, not publishable. They are *merely* personal, applicable only to our own immediate, local situations. That I had no intention toward publication when I began writing these texts is what, ironically, allowed me to write them. I was in the midst of my work on the essays that make up the second half of this book when I turned to the texts again with a growing belief that they had something to say back to and about the same pedagog-

x

ical dynamics I was struggling to get at through my readings of Plato. I remember asking myself why I felt that texts of this sort had any less right to enter the public domain than did my essays on Plato. I decided finally that they did belong there. And that, further, my two projects belonged together between the same covers because they were both sustained efforts to foreground teaching in its relation to research and were, in that respect, fundamentally commensurable.

The second half of the book, this series of essays on Plato's dialogues, is derivative from my teaching in quite a different way. I have read enough about Plato to know how what I do here might fit in—or not—with what other scholars, in philosophy and rhetoric departments for example, are doing. But I read that scholarly work for the same reason I read Plato in the first place: to help me think about certain issues pertinent to teaching—particularly the teacher-student relationship—that trouble and intrigue and hound me, and have for many years. Plato became for me some time ago one field where I could play out my reasoning about matters that have immediate import for my daily work in the classroom: how I configure a version of myself to operate there; how I configure the practices that determine the effects this version of myself has there; how I configure those other people who join me there under the general rubric of "students;" how I configure the sort of change(s) that will be transacted through our various interactions. The dialogues that I write about here I have read over and over, with increasing perplexity and delight. What I do with Plato may not always be what philosophers or rhetoricians tend to do with Plato. It is, though, what a teacher, this teacher, does with Plato. And what Plato does with him.

Just before I started the final revision of this manuscript, I was commissioned to write a multibook review for *College English*. One of those books was Kathleen Blake Yancey's *Reflection in the Writing Classroom*, near the end of which she describes herself as having played three primary roles in its composition: "first, always as teacher; later, more tentatively as researcher . . . ; later still, as writer. . . . Here, I've made the choice to bring the teacher, the researcher, and the writer into dialogue within the public view, to animate one inside of the others, each in terms of the others."[1] I admire Yancey's method in this regard, and I share with her a desire to rechart the customary distinctions among our various professional roles. I'm especially interested in bringing teaching and writing into productive dialogue: thus the book's title, with its slash marker and offsets to suggest that I see these two modes of textualization—teaching and writing—as always symbiotic in their interrelationship, one defining and reshaping the other in a chronic pattern of revision. Admittedly, the figure of the researcher can never be very far removed from a book written by a professor for an academic audience; a book part of whose express intent is to blur customary distinctions between the personal with the *scholarly*, a book whose second half is laden with academic apparatus. But through it all, I am writing "first" *from the position of the teacher*, a phrase I'll elaborate in the interchapter between the book's two halves; and I'm writing "always" *for* other teachers—teachers who, like me, are concerned about the way we accrue and exercise our authority; about the intellectual lives of the students with whom we are engaged; about who is being changed and how in the classrooms we animate; about, really, the day-to-day effects of our pedagogical work.

ACKNOWLEDGMENTS

I didn't realize until later that the writing was the easy part. It was only through gifts of grace and good people (often the same thing) that this book was brought to bear. I want to thank David Bartholomae for his amazingly unwavering support of this project. I want to thank Kathryn Flannery, who encouraged me to keep going and advised me so wisely along the way. I want to thank Mariolina Salvatori, who read and reread with such great care and patience, always with an eye to what was best for me. I want to thank James Seitz, who responded so usefully to an early version of the book. I want to thank Gwen Gorzelsky, who provided support and insight to guide my final revisions. I want to thank Elizabeth Kameen, who convinced me that you didn't have to be an English professor to enjoy what I was trying to do. I want to thank Jean Ferguson Carr, who helped to shepherd the book through the intricate review and publication process. I want to thank Stephen Carr, who helps me to think about so many of the things that concern me here. I want to thank Matthew Willen for his contributions to "Socratic Method and the Absence of the Student." I want especially to thank, and applaud, Toi Derricotte and all the participants in the Race and Gender in Twentieth-Century American Poetry seminar—especially Liz Ahl, Eve Alexandra, Robert Casper, Paul Hamann, M. E. Kubit, Maria McLeod, Karen Themstrup, and Kathleen Veslany, whose work I use in the book. Without their imagination and vitality the first half of this book would not have been possible. I want to thank Ann Berthoff, who opened a way. I want to thank my parents, Paul and Elizabeth, who are always echoed in my voice. I want to thank my wife, Zoe, and my children, Bridget and Joseph, who are constant reminders to me that this book is a small matter in the general scheme of things.

WRITING/TEACHING

1

Race, Gender, and (Teaching a) Class

INTRODUCTION TO PART I

To teach is to change. Or at least to try to. Most of us who do this kind of work for a living would assent to that generalization. We want to make a difference. But what kind of difference, what kind of change? And, more specifically, who is supposed to be changed, in what ways, and how much, through our work in the classroom? Oddly enough, we can avoid addressing these questions in any express and systematic way most of the time, content to adapt ourselves to the prerogatives of the various theories and approaches and curricula and course plans that preconstruct our teacherly work for us. And we can be especially inattentive to the ways in which we, as teachers, are being changed, often dramatically, by what goes on in our classrooms. There are certain junctures of circumstance, though, certain courses, that bring these issues to the fore in ways that demand some accounting. The materials that follow here derive from one of those junctures.

In the spring of 1994, Toi Derricotte, a poet in my department, an African American woman, approached me about team-teaching with her a course called Race and Gender in Twentieth Century American

3

Poetry. I agreed immediately. I had worked with Toi the previous summer in the Western Pennsylvania Writing Project's Summer Institute for Teachers, and I looked forward to extending our collaboration. As a middle-aged, white male, though, I was concerned about what sort of knowledge, what sort of capital, I could bring to the table in such a forum. I knew that for me to be an effective partner on our team, I needed to find a way of going about my work that would bring to the fore, address, perhaps even take advantage of, if not defuse, my uniformly majority status. Toi and I met a few times over the summer, laying out ambitions for the course, planning strategies for achieving them. We came to a consensus almost immediately about one matter of consequence: In a course of this sort, unless we could find a way for all of us in the group to bring to the table, and put at stake, our unique personal attitudes and histories in relation to matters of race and gender; unless we could find a way to risk the consequences that fundamental rethinking inevitably entails; our course would be little more than heartily endorsed departmental window dressing.

That goal might seem quite consonant with the ideological imperative of the contemporary critical theory, which tends to valorize, to the point of obsession, matters of race/class/gender—the mantra, for nearly a generation now, of almost all the discourses of critical/cultural studies. It was, in part at least, because of my familiarity with this material that Toi invited me to teach with her. But I knew, or at least deeply felt (after twenty years of trying to effect certain kinds of changes with the critical instruments that the late-twentieth century affords us in this regard) that it was precisely the ideological intensity surrounding matters of race/class/gender that tended, finally, to vaporize them almost beyond the range of comprehension, let alone concern—at the level of change that most interested me—not only for students but for myself as well. Faced with this dilemma, what I wanted in part to do through this course was find a way to reground my political positions in the texture of personal history, to think and write about race and gender not so much as abstractions and imperatives, but in terms of the local and immediate events of my own life,

4

with an eye toward understanding what it was even *possible* for me to know—and teach—about the specific materials we had chosen to read.

The context of twentieth-century American poetry—the primary "content" of this course—which is flush with the adornments of diversity, might seem, as well, to be an ideal vehicle to reach the goal we had in mind. But, again, it is precisely the plethora of alternative positions and voices among the poets of our time that makes it hard to get at the degree to which for us, as readers, the import of these matters is immediate and negotiable, rather than simply arguable or, even worse, settled. One thing Toi wanted to do through this course was to bring forth a conversation among a range of intense, often conflicting, ideological positions, and to bring it forth in terms of the immediate, the personal, the concrete—in part, as a way for her to unsettle, once again, her own attitudes and experiences in relation to race and gender.

So we agreed that firsthand experience would be one significant body of "knowledge" in the course, part of its syllabus, to which all of us would be turning chronically in order to figure out what we already knew and to think about what we didn't. A graduate seminar, though, can be a very *im*personal forum, one in which material of the sort we had in mind is not typically made pivotal to the success of the enterprise, is even sometimes frowned upon, especially in our discipline, as untheorized, naive. We needed some formal mechanisms to "reground" and "unsettle" the work of all the seminar's participants. Toi recommended a device that she had used successfully, toward similar ends, in other courses she had taught: a regular, class-opening read-around, a time set aside for anyone to read aloud any "personal" material they wanted. This material could be couched in any genre— autobiographical sketches, position papers, poems, journal entries, meditations, stories. Such pieces would be read without comment or response, serving then as background to and context for our discussions of the "assigned material" and not as fodder for immediate argument or assent. Out of this format, the following materials emerged.

Every week or two, as my contribution to this process, I wrote and

5

distributed to the class an essay that seemed to me to be germane to the course. Often, but not always, I also read the essay aloud as part of our read-around. Many others in the group did likewise, sometimes distributing copies of text, sometimes just reading aloud, sometimes both. I have arranged those materials here in a "weekly" format—my essay first, followed by excerpts from some of the other texts that were duplicated for distribution (unfortunately, I have no way to recover the many wonderful poems and stories and essays that were simply read aloud), followed then by a retrospective "Postscript" that I wrote specifically for this book. (A more extended accounting of my method of composition in this half of the book comes at the end of the postscript for the first week's entry.)

The role and status of the personal has been a contested topic in our discipline for some time now. That I feel the need at the outset here to account for the legitimacy of these materials—and I do—is indicative, I think, of the problems that confront us anytime we try to merge the writing we do in the classroom into the writing we do for broader publication. One could argue, for example, that what I offer here is either too practical or too local to be legitimately scholarly, that these are, after all, *only* teaching materials or *merely* autobiography or *simply* personal reflections. And they are, of course, all of those things. I present them, though, not specifically for what they *say* about the context out of which they emerged—my personal experience—but for the things that they attempt to *do* with the kinds of change, especially for the teacher, that are part of the stakes, tacitly if not expressly, in any pedagogical enterprise, most especially one that has an overt political component, as this course clearly did.

In this half of the book, I write, among other things, both autobiography and literary criticism. It is important to me, though, and I call attention to the fact, that I am not writing either autobiography (my life is not that interesting) or literary criticism (I am not an established authority on many of the texts I comment on extensively) from the

6

conventional authorial positions that construct those genres. What I want to do is present the ways in which my knowledge about these kinds of texts—my past, the poems—was brought to bear, and was then changed, by the activity of teaching. I believe both of those quite familiar kinds of discourse (autobiography and criticism) are transformed in interesting ways by approaching them from the position of the teacher.

When, for example, I wrote the stories about my life that comprise a good part of the first half of the book, they were written not to render a "life," but to do a certain kind of work in the course I was co-teaching. In that respect my approach is different from that of other recent books using autobiographical material to write about teaching, the most prominent example being Jane Tompkins's *A Life in School: What the Teacher Learned.* Hers is an interesting and useful account of her career as a teacher. Mine is not a book about my career as a teacher. I am not, to begin with, famous enough to warrant such attention simply on the basis of my status in the profession. And I don't in any case see my career as emblematic on a grand scale (as Tompkins may be warranted to see hers) of some trend in the evolution of education in the American university. The texts I wrote from this personal vein were designed not as memoir but as syllabus; their purpose was to model a learning process for others and to engage in a learning process myself. To the degree that my account represents "what the teacher learned," it is on a much more practical and personal scale than Tompkins's. And its general message is a hopeful one: that, like students, teachers can and do learn things of considerable consequence as they teach.

The process the course enacted was never intended to be, or to be taken as, either confessional or forensic. Toi and I had no interest in providing a forum for everyone simply to declare positions, or to tell stories. We weren't even that interested in exploring the mycelial underturf that supports these modes of self-representation. And we were especially averse to the idea of using our missives to allow the class to come to "know us" better. What could be more arrogant, more pointless, for a teacher than that? In the most practical sense, the class-opening read-around provided a space in which a dialogue—couched in familiar genres and discourses—could begin to evolve, simply by the design of the read-around, as one piece reverberated with or against others. Toi and I designed our own contributions so that they might serve in a suasive way to get others to contribute to this part of the work of the course. At least at the outset, for example, we both chose fairly commonplace genres—epistolary and poetic for Toi, narrative for me—rather than more "academic" discourses.

The required texts for the course were:

Women Writing in India—Volume 2: The 20th Century. Edited by Susie Tharu and K. Lalita. New York: The Feminist Press at CUNY, 1993.

The Fact of a Doorframe: Poems Selected and New 1950–1984. Adrienne Rich. New York: W. W. Norton and Co., 1984.

Unsettling America: An Anthology of Contemporary Multicultural Poetry. Edited by Maria Mazziotti Gillan and Jennifer Gillan. New York: Penguin Books, 1994.

No More Masks! An Anthology of Twentieth-Century American Women Poets. Edited by Florence Howe. New York: Harper Perennial, 1993.

The LeRoi Jones/Amiri Baraka Reader. Edited by William J. Harris. New York: Thunder's Mouth Press, 1991.

Complete Poems. Anne Sexton. Boston: Houghton Mifflin, 1981.

Grace Notes: Poems. Rita Dove. New York: W. W. Norton and Co., 1989.

We read the books in the listed order and spent about two 3-hour weekly sessions on each one. During the first two-thirds of the term, Toi and I initiated and moderated the discussions. During the last third, preassigned small groups did that work for most of each class session.

In the context of the apparatus that regulates publication in the contemporary academy, I am by necessity the author of this portion of the book. I want though to qualify that status in what seem to me to be significant ways. Although I use the term *our* to characterize the course numerous times in this text, I want that term to be understood as a very elliptical kind of modification. First of all, the course was fully originated by Toi Derricotte. I simply would not presume to design on my own a course of this sort, a matter of fact that derives in part from very overt matters of race and gender. Such an enterprise might have been plausible, for many of the wrong reasons, a generation ago and may again be, for entirely different and I hope better reasons, a generation from now. It is not plausible right now, at least as I read the ongoing history of race and gender politics in our culture and in the academy. But there is an additional factor that needs to be accounted for, one that derives from temperament and personality, which have such a pronounced bearing on what it is possible to teach and to learn in a course with these ambitions. Toi is a teacher who can animate her vision across an extraordinarily broad range of emotion; who uses language with precision and rigor; who can bring the breadth of her experience immediately to bear on the lives of other people, inviting them to do likewise. She is, therefore, able to create a context for others to render, in the often inhibiting public forum of the classroom, exactly the kind of materials that were to be a significant part of the subject of this course. I have been using the adjective *personal* to describe those materials, and I want that term to be understood from the outset to include the modifying effects of prior reflection, collegial engagement, and public presentation. This mode of the personal is an intellectual and not a therapeutic act. In that respect it strives toward the scholarly.

The other obvious authors of these materials are the registered participants in the course, much of whose work is represented in this text. But I extend their authorship to include more than just the excerpts from their work that I have chosen to use in the "Other Voices" portion of each weekly document. They were not simply the audience in response to which I constructed these essays. They were fully engaged people with whom I found myself conversing, and who answered back in particular ways on such a regular basis that it is impossible to fully divest what should be attributed to whom in the process. I have suggested above the degree to which my use of the pronoun *our* in relation to my work with Toi often masks a specific indebtedness to her. Similarly, in the case of the class participants, my use of the pronoun *my* often masks an indebtedness to what was more appropriately *ours* in the workings-out of these materials.

The contributors to this part of the book are as follows:

Toi Derricotte is a full professor in the English Department at the University of Pittsburgh, where she teaches poetry writing and reading and twentieth-century literature. Her books include *The Black Notebooks* (Norton), *Tender* (University of Pittsburgh Press), *Captivity* (University of Pittsburgh Press), *The Empress of the Death House* (Lotus Press), and *Natural Birth* (Crossing Press).

Liz Ahl received her M.F.A. in creative writing from the University of Pittsburgh in 1995. She is pursuing a Ph.D. in English at the University of Nebraska-Lincoln. Her poems have appeared in such journals as *The Southern Poetry Review*, *The American Voice*, and *Sundog*.

Eve Alexandra received her M.F.A. in creative writing from the University of Pittsburgh in 1997. She currently lives in Vermont, where she is completing her manuscript *Notes on Desire*. In 1998 she was awarded an Artists Development Grant from the Vermont State Council on the Arts. In 1998 she received the *Pittsburgh Quarterly*'s Sara Henderson Hay Prize. Most recently, her work appeared in *Central Park* and *The Harvard Review*.

Robert Casper is finishing his M.F.A. in creative writing at the University of Massachusetts, where he teaches creative writing. He lives in Northampton, Massachusetts.

Paul Hamann earned his Master of Arts in teaching at the University of Washington in March 1999. He currently teaches high school English and history outside Seattle. His poetry has appeared most recently in *The Seattle Review*.

M. E. Kubit received her M.F.A. in creative writing from the University of Pittsburgh in 1997. She currently works as the assistant director of development for the University of Pittsburgh School of Medicine.

Maria McLeod received her M.F.A. in creative writing from the University of Pittsburgh in 1995. She teaches writing in southern Illinois. Her poetry has appeared in *The Cream City Review*, *Critical Quarterly*, *5 AM*, *Pittsburgh Quarterly*, and other journals. She was a 1997 Pushcart Prize nominee for poetry.

Karen Themstrup received her M.F.A. in creative writing from the University of Pittsburgh in 1998 and her Master of Arts in teaching in 1999. Currently she teaches young adults language arts at Falk School in Pittsburgh. In 1999 she won an award for Outstanding Secondary English Education.

Kathleen Veslany received her M.F.A. in creative writing from the University of Pittsburgh in 1996 and is currently at work on a collection of essays. She now lives in Tucson, Arizona, where she is an editor at the Udall Center for Studies in Public Policy and a lecturer in the English Department at the University of Arizona.

There were ten other registered participants in the course. Four of them did not reproduce any of their contributions for the group, though they participated orally in the read-arounds. Two of them reproduced work that I did not use. Two of them preferred not to be represented here via the texts of theirs that I wanted to include. Two of them did not respond to my request to include their material. Many of Toi's contributions were in poetic form, and she preferred, understandably, to retain the rights to that material, which is then, with one exception, not reprinted here.

One of the many problems I have had in preparing these materials for publication in the academic marketplace—and they have been more vexing to me in that respect than any text I have ever worked on—is that my work emerged out of what I experienced, during the process of its composition, as an essentially collective, rather than individual, enterprise. My essays are merely small parts of a very complex, multivocal, and densely textured set of interchanges in which I

11

participated with a large group of smart, vocal, and committed people, and every effort I have made to represent that larger enterprise more accurately has proven to be weak and ineffectual. So I render semblances of our communal classroom experience, hinting here and elsewhere at the ways in which these "other voices"—and I chose that term intentionally to focus on the way in which my colleagues' classroom voices were, by necessity, disembodied, made "other," through the processes of textual representation—came into play in an ongoing way in what has become, for the purposes of this book, "my" work. I take that contradiction now, after much consideration, to be not a disabling flaw in this stage of the project, but an inevitable consequence of the professional apparatus we have (had) created for ourselves to work in.

SEPTEMBER 7

I spoke in class last week about my hope that we could find ways
of approaching race and gender that would allow for accounts, and examinations, of our own personal, even private, attitudes and opinions
—especially as they are embedded, often almost invisibly, in the stories
we tell to and about ourselves to explain the fact that we have ended
up together here to study and talk about this literature. As I was
imagining it, these stories would be subject then to various kinds of
critique—as they collide or mesh with the stories others here among
us are telling, as they are inflected by the poets we will be reading,
who have themselves both challenged and reflected our cultural habits
for marking off race and gender as matters of (in)consequence, and
as they can be interrogated by the range of critical instruments our
discipline offers for systematic inquiry.

Since Toi invited me to teach this course with her, I've been thinking a lot about what I might have to offer here, especially the degree
to which I felt authorized to teach a course like this. I am middle-aged,
white, heterosexual, male. What authority or cachet could someone

13

like me possibly bring to such a course? I have no idea how, if at all, you will allow me to intrude on your thinking here; how, if at all, you will open yourself up to changes by your interactions with me. I believe I will need to persuade you to do that, to begin to imagine that I am worth engaging in a serious way on matters apropos to this course. I intend to use these weekly essays to accomplish some of that persuasion, a persuasion I believe can only be indirect, a process of engagement. As I said above, this course is a place where our personal, even private, stories about ourselves not only have an ancillary propriety, as one kind of discourse through which we can learn; they are, really, as I see it, the most essential materials out of and around which the other kinds of more customary learning—about various authors, periods, movements, critical systems, ideologies, and so on—must circulate.

This notion of learning is problematic. Toi and I both agreed very quickly when we first talked about teaching this course together that what we hoped to accomplish was more than just transmitting a body of information about the poets and critics we already knew a lot about. We were interested, ultimately, in change. Yours *and* ours. Let me be clear, though: Toi and I both agreed that we are not here to proselytize. We are here to put ourselves at risk, and open ourselves to change, in the same way that we are asking you to. For me that means, first of all, finding a way to think specifically about race and gender not as academic or even political concepts but as aspects of my personal history. The way I have chosen to do that is through weekly writings like this one, searching in the process for a way of speaking, a discourse, that will allow me to integrate genres that don't go together so easily—personal narrative, literary criticism, pedagogical theory. I'm tempted to call what I'm after "ideological autobiography." I have no clear idea precisely what that is, but I know where it has to begin: with the stories I tell myself about how and why I've ended up in this classroom with you.

I'll start with some stories about my development as a writer, as a poet, stories that for me tend to revolve around the metaphor of se-

14

crecy. There's the story, for example, of my first memories of poetry as something that could be, or at least seem to be, entirely mine. For reasons that I simply don't remember, I bought the *Mentor Book of Major American Poets*. I was in the seventh grade. It was the first book I had ever bought myself. I started reading Edgar Allen Poe and was just mesmerized: the rhythms were so hypnotic in my ear, the sounds, especially the vowels, so lush, so exotic in their repetitions. I couldn't believe anything made out of words could deliver that much sensuous pleasure—bodily pleasure, the breathing, the tension, the kind of pleasure that simultaneously turns you into someone else and makes you feel entirely yourself. Having been raised in a very rigorous Catholic household, I immediately assumed that it must be sinful and must therefore be hidden—in this case the book went under my mattress, from where I retrieved it nightly to read for a while—and I never spoke a word about it at home, at school, anywhere. That book, and Poe in particular, changed my life around entirely: what I wanted to be, to do, to think about, all of it. I would be a poet. But, to paraphrase the old joke, I couldn't let anyone know it.

This secrecy was amplified by my immediate social surroundings: I grew up in an old mining town in northeastern Pennsylvania. To the extent that a town of 2,000 can be said to have distinct neighborhoods, in ours, for a boy at least, being able to play ball, to spit, to fight, swear, and break windows, were important social skills, and I honed all of them. There were no neighborhood poetry readings. I don't think I could have imagined at that time a greater embarrassment than to have my friends know I read poems. So poetry was something I felt I had to hide from everyone. And I did. I spent the next month or so, maybe ten minutes each night in bed just before I went to sleep, memorizing "The Raven." I knew right then that one of the things I wanted to do in my life was write at least one thing that would have that hypnotic, scary, exhilarating effect on someone; or if not that, at least to find ways to bring this kind of material to bear in a powerful way on other people. I started reading books of poetry in the library at school, although I always hid them inside of books on science or

15

math, the career path that even at that age seemed inevitable for me. I didn't understand why until much later, but this was 1961, a few years after Sputnik, right in the heat of our own hyperbolic national reaction to that apparent humiliation. I was male, I was a good student, "gifted" in mathematics. The pressure to pursue science as a career was overwhelming, from family, from the school, even from the small town I grew up in. None of this, I know, was meant to be destructive, but it weighed on me like an unbearable burden for most of my adolescence. In a context in which I began to feel that nothing of my intellectual life was really "mine," poetry, my secret, played a powerful, compensatory role.

The secrecy in which my early exposure to poetry was steeped has influenced my professional identity in significant ways. For one thing, I have always felt like, and have in fact often cultivated my role as, an outsider in the various academic circles to which I have gained access. Part of that is purely personal, of course: although I knew that the process of professionalization involved getting past the stubborn "mine"-ness of the knowledge I had acquired, I refused to concede this sense of self-possession entirely to institutional forces, quite often, as you might guess, to my disadvantage. Probably the only reason this habit of mind has not ended my career, as it easily could have, is the historical accident of entering the various stages of my professionalization at moments when institutional structures were, basically, coming apart. I went to college during a time (1967–1971) when it was possible to shut down a university. Renegotiating my curricular obligations seemed a minor matter in the context of the other kinds of activities I was engaged in. I did my graduate work in an experimental program (the Doctor of Arts) at a time (1972–1976) when cuts in state funding threatened to dissolve the graduate program entirely. People of consequence in the small world of my department had much more on their minds than whether I did this or that, this way or that way. I began my occupational life in the late seventies when poststructuralism was an "outside" discourse, offering the instruments for a powerful critique of entrenched critical traditions, particularly in our discipline. Reading Derrida's *Of Grammatology* in 1978 was as exciting to me as

16

reading Poe in the seventh grade. It was really in the on-the-fly re-tooling that I and my newly hired colleagues were engaged in at the time that most of my professionalization was accomplished. That I survived the disarray of the profession during those first few years of my employment was more a matter of luck than anything else I can point to.

One of the odd effects of midstream reversals of this sort is a kind of alienation (more, for me, in the ironic than in the disengaging sense) from all of the available discourses: the ones that have been denaturalized by the process of their replacement—which remain very potently "there," even under this mode of erasure—as well as the ones that have been acquired by means of a very obvious and artificial process of reeducation—which never, because of that, have the free and easy feel, nor the solitary comfort, of having been there first. And finally, I came into composition, my primary area of specialization now, almost by accident, at exactly the moment it was beginning to develop into a relatively freestanding "field." Early on, into the mid-1980s even, composition was a very open and negotiable area; it had no long-standing instruments of "discipline" (in either of its senses) by contrast with the much more traditional area of "literature." A compositionist could be all kinds of diverse things that are much more difficult to get away with now. I thought and wrote about textbooks, students, metaphor, modernist poetry, Plato, Heidegger, dream research; whatever seemed useful to me to work through what I wanted to work through. It was also much easier then than it is now for a compositionist to teach and write "in" both literature and creative writing—which I have been lucky enough to continue doing in this department; to avoid, in effect, becoming entrenched in one of the occupational grooves by which work in the academy is channeled.   17

The fact, then, that I was a male of a certain social class who became interested in poetry at a very specific historical moment has had a profound effect on how I have chosen to design and pursue both my work and my career. My personal experience in this regard might not be typical, but its general contours were, I think, common to many young, male writers of my time. The interest and commitment took root outside of any public or institutional arenas, like schools for example. The discourse of the self, of individual identity, took on heroic proportions. And secrecy was, for me, its originator and its keeper. I won math and science awards in high school, got a scholarship to a college known for its programs in the hard sciences, and majored in physics. Since math was always easy to me, what I did, basically, was spend most of my time surreptitiously reading poetry—voraciously, everything from the Greeks to the confessionals—and writing poetry —spare, labored, awful stuff. Language was just the opposite of mathematics. I had to struggle to master everything related to it—eloquence and intelligibility came slowly, painfully; even reading was hard work, and to this day I have a hard time understanding how anyone can both read and relax at the same time. But poetry challenged and excited me in a way that mathematics never did. Late in my junior year I finally decided to complete a major in English, which I was able to do with some overloading. As soon as I graduated, my career as a physicist was over.

In the course of all my subsequent professionalization, whatever secrets I had were pretty much pried loose. At best, I think, what I have been able to do is negotiate the transactions between what seemed to be mine and what was obviously not. And that is what I still spend much of my time trying to do when I teach and when I write: negotiating transactions, bringing incommensurable ways of thinking and talking about reading and writing into contest, and perhaps confluence. That is all part of the legacy—as both a burden and a gift—that comes with the sort of secrecy I am trying here to describe.

18   **Other Voices**

My dear "Race and Gender" Class,

What an exciting and terrifying first meeting. And the old questions haunt me. Will I be a "good" teacher? What is a "good" teacher? What lesson am I to learn here among your hearts and minds? What

lesson do I want to learn? What will I learn in spite of my unwilling-
ness to learn?

Always the fear of being misunderstood and stupid, of being
judged, and the desire to say something that makes me loved, famous, greater than anybody in the room, better, smarter, the greatest
teacher/poet/person ever born in history, Jesus . . . and the face of
Mother Superior before me saying—"Your I.Q. isn't high enough."

The power of the teacher: the teacher who teaches us words also
teaches us how to love ourselves and hate ourselves, how to have
contempt for ourselves and others.

Michelle said, as she was leaving, that sitting at our table she
thought of marriage, how hard it must be.

TOI DERRICOTTE

One fear I have about our class is that comments, and even opinions, will be placed on some sort of scale of importance. I think it's
difficult to discuss such engaging issues as race and gender without
bringing some comments into question and rewarding others. . . .

Also, I have questions as to how democratic such a class can be in
terms of discussion. Last week, the exercise of allowing everyone to
go around the room and state their case was valuable, but will such
an exercise have relevance in later classes? Obviously, some voices
are more eager to be heard (or have less inhibitions about speaking
up, maybe), but I'm afraid that some people will be more quiet than
others, even (or I should say especially) when they have something
important to say. . . .

The emphasis on self-disclosure is also disconcerting—is this synonymous with the goals of a graduate course in literature? I'm going
far into debt to be here as an MFA, and I want to make sure I'm learning what I think I need to learn in order to justify the cost. . . . I think
we cheat the possibilities of our class when we skirt around a discussion of the poem and its implications and engage solely in a discussion
about our perceptions of race and gender.

ROBERT N. CASPER

19

What I'm hoping to express here are the thoughts I found weaving through my head, but which I left unsaid, our first class meeting, all of which pertain to my relationship (emotional and intellectual) to the materials, topics of conversation, and self exploration I expect will occur as a result of my being in this course. I can't recall the exact phrasing of Toi's first question to the class—I remember it as having something to do with our personal connection to the literature assigned—but I clearly remember how uncomfortable I felt even thinking about expressing, or should I say "confessing," that such a relationship exists. Yet, the truth is, writing and reading literature are intensely personal and essential acts for me. Moreover, my uneasiness made me wonder when and why did it become taboo for me to discuss this? This led me to ponder my socialization within the academy and the unwritten (or perhaps it is written) *modus operandi* for approaching literature within the walls of classrooms. . . .

I can't help but compare this course, the direction it seems to be taking, with other graduate courses I've completed here at the University of Pittsburgh. It seems so often that what's real, what's really thought or felt, the individual's emotional and intellectual agenda, is too easily negated or denied by the theoretical discourse to which they defer. It's a rhetorical strategy, and one in which I've participated, that allows for forms of self-regulation and self-censorship in which we all participate in order to avoid exposure.

MARIA MCLEOD

(WITH A NOTE: "DON'T READ THIS ALOUD")

I fear that this class will fall into one of two extremes. First, to say that I think or feel a certain way because of my race, gender and sexual orientation is, in my opinion, to miss what it means to be a human being. There may be tendencies of those in a race or gender to think this way or that way, but there will always be exceptions, and to deny those exceptions is to stereotype. I dislike being stereotyped as much as the traditionally oppressed, and I fight back just as hard. On the other end of the spectrum, I'd hate the class to dissolve into a touchy-feely validation of everybody's feelings. If I wanted validation, I'd be in a support group. I want challenge, so I'm in a university. The middle ground I desire is a razor-thin strip between these two vast extremes. Finding it will prove a difficult job.

PAUL HAMANN

My fear . . . that instead of engaging with the multitude of voices I will shut them out in favor of some false harmony or comfort. That I allow myself to be silenced and don't even realize it. My fear . . . weakness. That I am weak, and that I don't show it, which is also weakness. The language will keep tripping me up like that. Fear . . . that I don't understand the simplest things about myself, which is per- haps that "productive" fear we were puzzling over last week—the fear that I don't understand myself leads me to attempt to understand myself . . . and of course, there is the fear, standing in opposition to this attempt to understand—the fear of what I may find.

And is the lifetime's work of the poet to be chasing after the voice? The voice that leaps out of the throat and runs; the voice that is never quite caught?

LIZ AHL

When you first asked us what we were afraid of, my fear instantly hit me. I had been feeling uncomfortable since the orientation session several weeks ago. I was with a group of M.F.A.'s mingling, when Catherine Gammon introduced herself to the group. The woman next to me introduced me to Ms. Gammon and said, "She's a poet." This phrase really caught me off guard. I have never actually said, "I am a poet," to anyone in my entire life. When I am questioned about what type of [graduate] work I am doing, I have always responded, "I'm studying poetry." I never noticed my avoidance of the phrase, "I am a poet."

M. E. KUBIT

21

Postscript

I think this course could function like a very pleasant sorbet between the "main" courses of my schedule this term.

A STUDENT IN THE CLASS, DURING OUR FIRST CLASS SESSION

Pedagogy is intrinsically ideological. What a teacher chooses to do or not to do promotes change at the most fundamental level. For me, ideological positions develop from two extremes. On the one hand, I begin with principles of the most general and intense sort, beliefs, commitments, ideals if you will, and, on the basis of these, I try to develop a specific agenda and its attendant set of practices. On the other hand, ideology arises from, or coalesces around, specific moments, statements, or actions to which I react viscerally, without quite knowing at the moment why that is so. There is almost always an ultimate connection between the threads emerging from these two extremes, although sometimes it takes me a while to weave them together.

The above quote—from one of the two Ph.D. students in our class during our around-the-table introductions—capsulized for me one of the problems I've seen over and over in trying to teach graduate courses in the way that Toi and I were, here, going to insist on, in a way that accords status to the personal. It is quite often perceived— especially by those who have already been partially disciplined by the accoutrements of theorization—as shallow, superficial, so much fluff. A way to clear the palate to prepare for the next, main, course. I was prepared for the position that this comment indexed. Toi and I anticipated it during our meetings over the summer. I spent time in the first class session trying to suggest the ways in which autobiographical material, as we intended to mine and deploy it in our discussions, was not to be construed simplistically, as either therapeutic confession or mere opinion. It was a place to start the work of critical inquiry, a way to generate the positions and materials that needed to be

22

examined, revised, re-viewed, a reservoir of motives for change. I wanted to use my first missive to reinforce this argument, hoping that I could persuade the more advanced graduate students in the class that it would be worth their while to stay and participate in our discussions.

One chronic tension that afflicts entry-level graduate courses in our department derives from the sometimes fundamentally different ways that "writers" and "theorists" have for thinking and talking about what literature is, where it comes from, and what it is for. I have a lot of experience negotiating that argument—sometimes successfully, sometimes not—in the Seminar in Teaching Composition that first-year teaching assistants take in concert with their teaching assignments. I look forward to such negotiations with an odd combination of hope and dread, knowing full well how much is at stake, not just in terms of how easy or hard it will be to teach the course, but how much we can in fact learn in the process about ourselves and one another as "writers" and "theorists"—when those terms are construed as *positional*, as representatives for habitual ways of thinking and talking about reading and writing. Apparently my comments during the first class failed to persuade the two Ph.D. registrants. They both dropped the course. I was both disappointed and relieved, given what I know is possible, for better or for worse, when the argument I am talking about here takes center stage in a course. But we did retain all of the M.A. and M.F.A. students, eighteen in all, whose variety and enthusiasm were ideally suited for the course Toi and I had in mind.

In my first meeting with Toi the spring before we taught the course, she suggested that we open the reading for the term with a book called *Women Writing in India*, an "anthology" of work—mostly short fiction but a lot of poetry as well—by female Indian writers, many, perhaps most, of whom had no canonical status in their own literary traditions, let alone ours. These works were translated into English from eleven different languages and dialects. Toi's suggestion was so

23

unexpected to me, so out of the realm of possibilities I had myself been considering, that my mind raced to find a way to account for her rationale and for the possibilities that the book might open up. As I remember it now, I thought: What a great opening salvo for a course of the sort we were talking about—a set of texts that alienates every one of us in some fundamental way from its authors, their materials, even the primary genre of the course. I have a very elaborate set of recollections of what we agreed upon in relation to the use of this text. But I'm not sure, in retrospect, if we really talked about it at length or if my mind, so excited by such a wild idea, spun out its own justifications—based on the assumption, or even the *pre*sumption, that I somehow knew what Toi was thinking—for agreeing to use this text. I depict this scene, in a cautionary way, as a sort of metaphor for the acts of interpretation that it became the work of this course to investigate: acts of interpretation in reaction to the unexpected, the alien, the "other." When faced with such a text we sometimes actually do arrive in a mutually negotiated way at a reading of its meaning(s). Sometimes we just think we do by acting as if we already know what we need to know to comprehend the text fully and properly. Most often, we are doing a good bit of both, and it's important to be self-conscious about what is coming from where.

Recollecting this scene of my conversation with Toi is troubling to me now. Perhaps, I find myself thinking, I may never have known exactly why she wanted to open with this book, and still don't know even now. Perhaps I just filled in myself crucial parts of my dialogue with her and operated on the basis of what may in fact have been a fundamental misunderstanding. Then again, perhaps we did talk at length and in detail about these matters. This is the readerly problem I want to posit at the outset here only in an emblematic way, because it is one form of the readerly problem that afflicted our discussions of the book we started the course with, that afflicted so many of our discussions throughout the term: No matter how unusual and surprising is the text we are confronted by, no matter how much it defies our

24

expectations, even resists our entry, we generally proceed in some way to interpret it, and often, on the basis of that work, which is essentially our own, we presume to "understand" something of what it means.

At the beginning of their introduction, the editors of *Women Writing in India* pose a series of questions that might serve as paradigms for the sorts of questions that hovered over the course, especially so when we discussed the several anthologies we had selected to read:

> What was the point, we were sometimes asked . . . , of putting together an anthology such as this? Why did we think women's writing was different or that it called for special attention? Weren't women writers as much victims to social ideologies about the subordinate status of women as men? If we were arguing that women writers had been marginalized and their work misrepresented and misjudged, how did we suggest they should be read? (1)

Tharu and Lalita devote 105 pages in the introduction of this text not so much to the task of answering these questions, which are ultimately unanswerable with any finality, as to the project of laying out their critical method. Their argument became the occasion for translating the above questions to the project of our own course. The discussion we had was both testy and productive. It addressed the larger question of what it means to separate out a particular subset of a culture's literature according to the authors' cultural markers. This was seen as, simultaneously, both a necessary and a destructive move. Toi and I tried to suggest the manner in which the categories of our course were of a different conceptual order than the one of the book. Race and gender are, after all—unlike the category "women"—completely inclusive. We could, theoretically, approach them as well through the writing of white, male writers. Why that was not what we chose to do—for a variety of very compelling institutional, ideological, and cultural reasons—was, we hoped, to become a matter of some ongoing consequence to the work of the course. It was in this vein that, again, I tried to carve out a place for what I hoped to be able

25

to contribute from my own perspective, which is endowed from the outset with both a race and a gender. I'm not sure I was any more successful at this act of persuasion than I was during the first class session.

The other conversation we started that night circulated around the role of, and the potential problem with, contemporary critical theory as an agency for the "recovery" of "marginalized" literatures. Tharu and Lalita deploy a feminist/poststructuralist method that is decidedly European/American to open up the literatures that are their concern. They are aware of the potential contradictions that arise from this choice, and they offer an extensive rationale for it. Our discussion tended to inscribe this choice as a significant "problem" with the project of the book, as well as, potentially, with our course. Most of our class were first-year graduate students and creative writers who had not yet read a lot of theory. But most had read some and were generally skeptical of, if not inimical toward, its apparent intercessory role in pre-reading the texts of these women writing in India. They chafed under the weight of all that Western theorizing, all that politicizing, all that historicizing. The assumption seemed to be that there was a more natural and unmediated way to get at this material. No one, though, was able to come up with it. The initial general sense was, in fact, that we had no capacity, and perhaps no right, to presume that we could ever come to understand anything of consequence about the texts of these Indian women when they are offered to us (1) in translation, (2) in small chunks, (3) through the lens of Western critical theory, and (4) in the distorting format of an anthology. There was some discussion in this framework of how and why Toi and I had chosen the "required" texts for the course, which were in some of their aspects susceptible to parts of the same critique.

26   The first move we made to get beyond this apparent impasse was to ask members of the group to take us to specific pieces in the book, to see what, if anything, it was possible to talk about, to "know" about, one of these "women writing." We looked at three or four specific texts over the next hour or so. One of them was the following poem by Nita Ramaiya:

"Ognisso-Ognyaeshinun Varas"
(The Year 1979)

This is the year
When my mother looked back at us through the water
Submitting the joys and sorrows of sixty-eight years to the
    Machu River

This is the year
Of the last scream of my brother
Assigning to the flood his twenty-three years
Which could not be contained in his piercing eyes and
    shining shoes.

This is the year
That reduced to stammering
Learning literature politics ideology
Understanding intelligence wisdom . . .
How can I explain to my son
Whose each footstep's presence brightens
the courtyard of my parents' home
that each footstep grinds me to dust?
That with each footstep the life is drained out of me

This is the year
Of the invisible scene hanging
Between
My son's ten-year-old's mood
And my face molded by that year

This is the year
Of the shameless thirst
Of the deranged river.
(462–63)

27

This is a recent poem (1985) by a published author who teaches English. It looks and sounds on the surface a lot like a contemporaneous imagistic poem in our own literature, which may have been why it was selected. No one had any difficulty in understanding what the poem was about in either a factual or an emotional way. And we talked about all of that. The poem was, in fact, being read as if there were no barriers at all between us as human readers and its author as a human writer. We had seemingly elided the problem of cultural "difference" simply by presuming to talk. The one part of the poem, though, that kept coming back as somehow baffling, untranslatable, in our evolving reading was the section about the son's footsteps. There was some speculation that this opacity arose from the fundamentally different relative status of male to female in the Indian culture by contrast with our own. And some speculation that it arose from the unrenderable intensity of the initial *maternal* tragedy itself. There was, it turned out, no way for us to resolve this conundrum that arose at the intersection of "self" and "culture." The knot at the center of this discussion would be there throughout the term.

What I remember about each of the discussions we had of specific texts from *Women Writing in India* was that they followed the same sequence. The initial speaker/reader would begin with a disclaimer about not being able to know anything about the text or its author and would then go on to comment, often in detail and with a sense of personal authority, not only on the text in question but also on the "life" that animated it. I remember thinking, "this is, really, one of the paradigmatic acts of reading for a course of this sort: I cannot read this text; therefore I will read it."

This seemingly self-contradictory mode of interpretation is, of course, merely an exaggerated version of the one we use whenever we seek to understand an "other" discourse, whether that otherness is inscribed by differences in language, dialect, culture, race, gender, or historical time. In our seminar, these differences were—through the literatures themselves, through the modes of anthologization by which those literatures were being promulgated, or through the

28

machinations of the course's dialogical method—being quite self-consciously called to the fore. While the exact boundary between insider and outsider was not always easy to locate, the readerly necessity to distinguish between the two was inescapable. If any of us felt that we fell into the latter category—and in the case of the women in India, we all seemed to—our choice was simple: either stop reading, conceding that it was impossible to cross the chasms before / between us, or press on, with what devices and skills we could muster on the way to making sense, and meaning, from the experience.

On a smaller scale, the readerly position of the student is usually analogous to this. Most of the texts we bring into our classes are, in some fundamental way, "outside" their range of familiarity, even if only historically. The readerly position of the teacher is a more vexed question. Quite often we have through long labor made ourselves expert on, and therefore, in professional terms at least, insiders to the texts we teach. But when it comes to a course like ours, one could legitimately argue that this sort of expertise offers no resolution to the problem at hand. The fact that I had previously read and studied many of the authors we were about to read for the course really gave me no advantage whatsoever over those in the group who had not yet read, or even perhaps heard of, them. My otherness was no different from theirs, presenting the same challenges, the same choices, the same opportunities. Which is to say that while authority (a theme I return to throughout the book), at least of the sort that professional expertise accords, has its uses and values, it never elides cultural difference. Nor does it, in and of itself, accomplish change (another theme that recurs in the book) of the sort I'm trying to write about.

29

Now that I've completed one weekly cycle, I'd like to say a little more about my method of composition in this half of the book. My own essays are presented here in pretty much their original form. As I prepare the manuscript for publication, it is now about five years since I wrote them. My thinking has changed—in sometimes consequential ways—about what I have to say in some of these essays. And in some cases I would just say differently what I tried to say back then. But I chose to keep them largely as they were to maintain a semblance of verisimilitude about the experience of producing them in this form and in this sequence for the course. Where I made cuts, it was to eliminate material that was so specific to the course, or repetitious, or, well, boring, that it would have little appeal for a wider audience, or might easily be misconstrued. This included three whole essays and big chunks of two others from my original manuscript, which were removed at various stages of the revision process on the advice of other readers or on my own initiative. Where I made additions, it was to add clarifying or contextual information that was not necessary to the audience for which they were initially composed.

I added the "Other Voices" layer to the text more than a year after the course ended, once I had made the choice to develop these materials into this longer form. I worked from the stack of duplicated pieces that various respondents handed out to accompany their oral presentation during the weekly read-arounds. This was a large stack—everything that had been reproduced for the group—but not a complete index to what got said or read during those intervals. For example, in most of the instances that Toi read, it was from drafts of poems—which she did not duplicate; or, if she did, did not want to publish yet, or in this forum, for obvious authorial reasons. Many others in the group read regularly from texts they did not duplicate for distribution. In the end, I chose to render here about 20 percent of the textual material available to me. I would say that about half of what got said or read during our read-arounds was presented only orally. So in effect, I use here about 10 percent of the actual material that surrounded my texts. (Some weeks the read-arounds took as long as thirty or forty minutes to complete!) And I made all of the initial editorial choices about what to include by myself. I chose excerpts that seemed to me to reverberate with the story I was trying to tell, to present these other voices as interlocutors with my own, which remains dominant. There was another professor teaching with me and there were eighteen students in the class. When I quote them along the way, their "voices" are my take, and a very partial one, on their contributions to the course. Each of them I'm sure would have a different story to tell, and a different way to tell it, if they so chose. If all of these nineteen other texts were to come to fruition, one would have a more complex, although I would argue still partial, representation of this course. What I offer here is my part of that larger story, hoping it will be interesting enough in its own right to be enjoyable, and that it can serve as a sort of object lesson, rendering the ways in which the classroom, any class-room, is always, for every course we teach or take, productive of con-sequential knowledge, knowledge that can and should have standing in the profession. The nineteen other stories that make up the rest of the record of this course are not, in my view, mine to tell.

I decided early on that I wanted to attach a real name to each piece I used. A couple of members of the group felt uncomfortable, for their own good reasons, with having their names attached to the pieces I had selected, so I chose not to use their work. This is not to say that I am opposed to using student work anonymously (with permission) in our public, professional venues. I think that much of the recent work that has begun to restore the figure of the student to our dis-cussions would not have been possible without making that move. But in this case I wanted all parties to the discussion to be enthusiastic— rather than simply willing, or even worse, grudging—participants in the project of the book. In each case, I asked for permission to use the excerpt(s) and for permission to use the name of the writer. I offered each writer the opportunity to revise the piece in question so that it did accurately represent her position in the way she most preferred to see it rendered, and I sent them each a copy of the full text of the pro-ject I was asking them to become a part of. I toyed with the idea of writing myself a brief characterization for each contributor, even per-haps naming the specific positions or interest groups they tended to represent. These were, after all, regular, often dominant, participants to our discussions, and I got to know them very well. I decided quickly against that and in favor of the brief, customary "bios" they composed

31

for the introduction to this section. I felt that the degree to which I brought other parties directly into my story, they should be allowed to speak for themselves. There are after all obvious issues of confidentiality that pertain here, and that I felt needed to be respected scrupulously.

In my retrospective essays, which I began to write about a year and a half after the course was completed, I chose a critical method that is, following that of my weekly essays, considerably more personal than is customary for me. In some cases, I tried to highlight the major trajectory that the weekly discussion followed. In some cases I focused on my own reaction to the social dynamics of the seminar. In some cases I continued, retrospectively, the line of inquiry that my original text initiated. In some cases I do several of these things in sequence. Because I had no initial plan toward publication when I wrote my original pieces, I felt free to write in whatever forms suited my purposes at the moment. The method of the course warranted this freedom for me, and I found it both enjoyable and productive. I decided to retain at least some of that same discretion in my retrospective essays as well. All of this is to say again what I have said in any number of ways thus far: This project is not an aborted effort at ethnography or educational research. My main focus was always on what I learned and how I changed, to foreground that side, the teacher's side, my side, of the transformative equation of pedagogy. Just above, I described this part of the book as both story and object lesson. At least as I understand the term, an *object* becomes *lesson* simply by presenting itself to us and not by offering an explanation of its significance. What I have tried to do in my retrospective essays is to continue to make *my* experience of teaching the course visible. My story becomes thereby an example, whose purpose is not to urge other teachers to do what I do, but to remind them that what they are already doing for their own courses all the time may be worth their writing about.

32

SEPTEMBER 14

I was surprised last class when I heard myself say that the generally negative buzz about white/hetero/male-ness didn't bother me much. While I was sitting here tonight trying to think of something to write about, that kept coming back to me. Mostly because I had no immediate way of accounting for it. So, I decided to do what I did last time: remember some stories about myself. The first one that came to mind happened in 1970 or 1971. I didn't live in Pittsburgh then, but I was dating a Pitt student. On my way to the bus station for one of my weekend trips out here, I picked up a volume of Adrienne Rich's poems, my first contact with her work. The night I arrived my girlfriend asked me to come with her to a feminist event at the David Lawrence auditorium. I took the Rich book with me, expecting us to get a chance to talk about it later. Or maybe because I just thought it was a good thing to be carrying to a feminist forum. I can't remember exactly who all the speakers were. I think it was mostly Pitt faculty and graduate students. Short, fiery talks, a lot of them, in a staccato tempo. There were a couple of hundred people in the audience. About a dozen were men. I think I went into the event with the expectation that I would immediately feel a sense of solidarity with these women, would be insulated from their anger and frustration, would be given some sort of dispensation or "credit" for being there. I knew within two minutes that I was wrong. The speeches, as I said, were short and passionate. In one way or another men were cast in most of them as inimical. I'm sure I was exaggerating it, but I felt as if each of those speakers was looking directly at me. At first I slunk down in my seat and tried to disappear. But women in the general area in the audience kept turning toward me with a look that said, "what the hell are you doing here anyway?" One of the speakers raised the question as to whether the few men there should be asked to leave. Nothing came of that. But I knew, deep down, for the first time, that the fact that I was there could never override the fact that I was a man. That the fact that I was a man, independent of anything or everything I might ever say or do, carried with it a history—or a set of histories—that went way beyond my own, that went way beyond anything I could even begin then to imagine.

That thought was sobering to me. There are probably few things more ridiculous than the presumption that you can participate in everyone's struggle, fathom everyone's pain, join everyone's cause. There are just some fundamental differences that can't, and shouldn't, be overlooked, overridden, overcome. That event went on for a good while, at least a couple of hours. And I knew I had to find a way of grasping and coping with its immediate consequences for me, if only superficially, before it was over—at least if I wanted to spend the rest of the weekend with my girlfriend, whose instinctive allegiances, as far as I could tell by nonverbal cues, were more with the audience in general than they were with me and what I represented there. I won't say I didn't feel anger about being cast the way I was. I probably did. And I won't say I didn't feel shame about being a man and therefore somehow accountable for what men are and have done. I probably

34

did. And I won't say I didn't feel envious of the solidarity that group felt and from which I was precluded. I probably did. But mostly what I remember was feeling chastened. I went in thinking one thing—about feminism and about myself—and came out thinking something entirely different. This event stands in my mind as a starting point not only for my thinking about feminist issues, not only for thinking about things that only much later got to be collected under the heading of terms like *patriarchy*, but more importantly for thinking about whether and how I was going to find ways of listening to critiques of "me," at least the generic me who had such things as a gender, a race, a sexual orientation. My "other"ness, however it might be expressed in a specific situation, was not something I could deny, repress, abdicate, or coerce into oblivion, much as I might like to in situations such as this.

The scene of that evening is one that comes back to me from time to time—and always when I read or teach Adrienne Rich, who is so intertwined with that night I almost always instinctively imagine her at the podium in front of that audience. I've never stopped to pay attention to what other things bring those images and feelings to mind, until tonight, when they came forward for me as I tried to account for the mechanisms I've developed to keep myself from feeling too much or too little in the face of critiques that target the ways in which I partake of the advantages of majority. And maybe also, as I think about it, to keep myself from presuming that I can easily understand, let alone share in, someone else's experience and condition. One of the effects of such assumptions is that, once they are made, there is no more need to listen, to pay attention, to remain open to the intrinsic possibility of alternative, to change.

Part of what all this suggests is that reading, especially when the material is volatile in some ways, as it is in this course, is seldom an impersonal act whereby we simply open up a space inside us to absorb the "content" of something new. My reading of Adrienne Rich is, as I said, always framed in the scene of that auditorium, and it is awash with undertones of my own anger and shame and agitation and

35

courage. While it is too much to say that that is what I have to teach you about Adrienne Rich, it is too little to say that it is irrelevant to this course. We need to know together that my reading of Rich started, and still starts, there. You need to figure out where your reading of Rich started, or is starting right now. And then we have a chance to take each other somewhere else. Part of what I took away from our discussion last time was the paramount importance, to many of you, of Rich's lesbianism, an element of her identity and her project that, because of my framing scene, is subordinated to her feminism. That tendency, for me, has been reinforced by the fact that I have used her essay "When We Dead Awaken: Writing as Re-vision" on several occasions as a reading in my General Writing class, a forum in which the volatility of her lesbianism is magnified and needs to be negotiated very carefully. What last week's discussion offered me was a scene in which Rich's lesbianism was neither dangerous nor threatening to me—either as a teacher trying to navigate a class discussion or as a man trying to navigate my relationships with women.

This is not to say that I now feel suddenly authorized to practice or even fully grasp a feminist position as a reader or critic. The problems for men making claims of that sort are analogous to the problems I had attending that meeting back in 1971. There is often, at the root of things, an other-ness that cannot and should not be overridden or denied. By the same token, to imagine a feminism in which commitment is grounded in, and arises from, to some extent at least, sexual love, and to see the sorts of author-reader identifications that emerge from that nexus, is to complicate in useful ways the more traditional notion of feminism as simplistically contrary to masculinity or patriarchy. And it compels me to see Rich in a much denser and more fully human guise, in which respect she becomes, by definition, more like me. I become, then, a more generous, a calmer and more reflective reader. In our transaction, she is different but so am I. That is a change worth noting.

Other Voices

Dear Workshop participants,

Can a teacher control so much negative capability sitting in the same classroom? BOOM! POW! BAM! or just silence, warm, human silence, and the comfort of it, like a baby curled in its own warm pee.

To live with me and you and the words I write and the words in these books without knowing for a while . . . just for this one minute . . . and see how that feels curled in the breast.

My sense is that there are lots of little dirty secrets and little clean secrets, and longings and fears that no one has mentioned that might blow up the canon, or gently re-make it by touch.

TOI DERRICOTTE

My arguments for men being included are the experiences of the men who went along on the [Take Back the Night] march at Kenyon, my school. . . . After the march ended, women stepped forward one by one to tell of their experiences as victims of sexual abuse. Many of these women—including a close friend of mine—were telling their experiences for the first time. If these stories are told among women only, it doesn't have the same effect as it does being told to both women and men. Many of the men stated their shock at the number of women affected by abuse, and everybody was undoubtedly moved by the emotional intensity. There's not a lot of use in relating the horrors of sexual abuse only to those who know all too well—women. When men come along, not only does education take place, but—if it's done right—a distinct sense of community is created.

PAUL HAMANN

I wanted to be the end of all hunger the first night
I met you. She had told me of your paintings,
so it was your hands I wanted to see. I was surprised
they were so small and simple, these lips of such violet,

gold and the prairie seas. You opened a history inside me,
and I conceived the fear of mortality.

You pull back slowly from my lips like an animal lifting
its head from the drink of dream—
EVE ALEXANDRA

Reading Rich has made me sad again, the unending struggle, the
story of an unending struggle. I think one aim for Rich's work is to
identify the issues of this struggle, not just for women but for men and
women in terms of how gender has been socially constructed. And by
gender construction I mean how we are forced into molds and patterns of behavior dictated by our genitalia, those door-frame-like
perimeters. . . .

Recently I began dating someone new. In his attempt to get to
know me, to learn more about me, this man asked to read some of
my poetry. For various reasons I'm always nervous about the first time
I share my work with a new romantic interest. I wonder, will he understand the politics of my work? Will he read it as autobiographical?
Will he like it/think it's good? Will he still like me after he reads it? In
an attempt to prepare him for my poetry, I wrote a brief introduction
explaining why I return to certain themes and images, especially that
of sexuality. The following is an excerpt from my letter to him:

> I use sex, write of it, because it is symbolically and literally the root
> of women's oppression. Sometimes I write about it as a way of own-
> ing it, as a way of transforming female sexuality that has been tradi-
> tionally represented in response to male sexuality, to subvert the
> paradigm. In other poems, I use sex simply as a metaphor because
> so often it's the strongest, most visceral, sensitive image I can think
> of. . . .

So, you can see, these poems are more than just "my feelings,"
but a very political project. In a way, I see myself as preaching the
word (of feminism) to the masses. Yet each poem begins with the
personal, solitary event.
MARIA L. MCLEOD

38

There's a man from Saudi Arabia who used to get on at the same bus stop as I did, same time three days a week. I hadn't seen him all summer so when I saw him yesterday I asked how he was, how his summer had been. He told me, Wonderful. He had been to Saudi Arabia and Syria. Pittsburgh, he said, there's nothing to do here. This is where I work. But, in Saudi Arabia and Syria, the only thing that keeps me busy is having such a great time.

I have talked to him before, small talk, to make the bus come faster. And it always comes and we board and our conversation stops there. I have never asked him about Islam, about the Middle East, about himself. But today, out of nowhere and at the same time, out of somewhere very specific, I ask him. What is it like for women there? I want to hear it from someone my own age.

For women? he asks back. Well, in Saudi Arabia it's not so good, they cannot do much. That is just tradition and I don't understand why, don't agree with that. It makes me angry.

He assures me, twice, that he says such things not only because he is talking to a woman about women, but because he really believes this. . . .

KATHLEEN A. VESLANY

Postscript

The dominant voices in our group were, to this point in the course, not surprisingly, female—fourteen of the twenty people in the room were women, we had been reading poetry by women, this is a course that attached a positive valence to literatures that run counter to the (male-dominated) canon. Like me, most of the other men in the class had to work hard to find a way of talking, and they tended generally to talk cautiously. Silence is a comfortable and natural state for me when I teach. I use it to resist the traditional authoritarian roles into which the institutional structure of the academy and the expectations of many students seem to compel me. The classroom, in my view, is

39

not a stage designed primarily to host my talk. It is an arena where I hope to initiate and then moderate—in both applicable senses of that term—a discussion in which everyone, ideally, gets to participate. In a venue like this course, for which silence is the safe position from which to operate, in which deference is less an act of humility than a failure of courage, it seemed crucial to me to find a solid point of departure to start talking about both my masculinity and my feminism. I wanted to find an angle into this material, a way of addressing its complexities without apologizing for their consequences or tacitly absenting myself from the more sensitive aspects of our proceedings. This piece, based on a memory that took on archetypal significances, was my first move in that direction, and through it I sought to transform that memory into an emblematic act of reading. This interpretive move allowed me to extend the sense in which the autobiographical was, in this course, obliged to operate ideologically, and to that extent it was an important step for me to take.

One of the productive effects of *Women Writing in India* was to unify us in monolithic "otherness" as readers of its texts, a position out of which, both individually and collectively, we worked persistently to emerge. Adrienne Rich's *The Fact of a Doorframe* had quite the opposite effect, fracturing us into a congeries of often-competing "others" —along the lines, especially, of gender and sexual orientation. Whereas no one seemed to know quite where to stand, at least initially, in relation to the Indian authors, everyone seemed to know exactly where they stood—or were being compelled to stand—in relation to Rich. There was tension. Occasionally it emerged into contention. But this discussion was more an "intelligent conversation" sitting like a hood of rock over a sea of magma. Interest groups began to coalesce—or maybe, having been there all along, just emerge into my sight: subgroups of men with a range of attitudes about a Richian feminism; subgroups of women with various levels of deference to or distance from a Richian feminism; subgroups of women with various degrees

40

of interest in examining and/or critiquing the specific conditions of a Richian lesbianism. I deduced a lot of this not so much from positions that were taken expressly—some were, most weren't—but from the tones, the silences, the body language that defined the mood of the interchanges. It was more like watching a dance than listening to a conversation. I probably did say a lot over the course of this three-hour class. How could a teacher not? But I don't remember participating much beyond reading my essay in the read-around, unless you are willing to concede that extended silence can be, in certain of its aspects, a viable and very expressive mode of participation. I never once felt silenced either by Rich or by the participants in the discussion. I just felt unauthorized to speak. I remember noticing, and feeling companionable with, the other, largely silent, males at the table. I remember wondering what they were thinking and making my various guesses. I remember an awareness dawning of how political lines were being drawn among the various kinds or degrees of feminists at the table. I remember an awareness dawning of who was straight and who was gay and how that mattered in different ways to individual members of the group, and mattered differently in this course than it would in another.

Toi and I used the same method we used with *Women Writing in India* to get us into the day's "material," and down to a level of detail that would allow for a dense discussion of its implications. We asked the members of the group to take us to specific places in the text. We went, I'm sure, to several particular poems and discussed them in detail. But as I look over my copy of the book now, I have only one page turned back—the technique I typically use to mark the focal points of class discussion. In *Women Writing in India,* I have at least twenty pages turned back. I had, in fact, a very hard time trying to select one poem to talk about in my postscript. The one Rich poem I have marked off is, oddly enough, a pretty good one to get at the sort of capped-volcano feeling I had about our discussion, the feeling I generally have when I read Rich, even in her most assertive moments:

41

"A Woman Mourned by Daughters"

Now, not a tear begun,
we sit here in your kitchen,
spent, you see, already.
You are swollen till you strain
this house and the whole sky.
You, whom we so often
succeeded in ignoring!
You are puffed up in death
like a corpse pulled from the sea;
we groan beneath your weight.
And yet you were a leaf,
a straw blown on the bed,
you had long since become
crisp as a dead insect.
What is it, if not you,
that settles on us now
like satin you pulled down
over our bridal heads?
What rises in our throats
like food you prodded in?
Nothing could be enough.
You breathe upon us now
through solid assertions
of yourself: teaspoons, goblets,
seas of carpet, a forest
of old plants to be watered,
an old man in an adjoining
room to be touched and fed.
And all this universe
dares us to lay a finger
anywhere, save exactly
as you would wish it done. (pp. 42–43)

42

This poem was written in 1960, before feminism and lesbianism became defining agendas and motives in Rich's work, or at least defining categories in the way her work was received. But there is menace afoot in this poem, and a few keynotes, that make a discussion of these subsequent "frames" inevitable today. The setting in the kitchen; the figure of the mother as "puffed up," dead "weight," "straw," "insect"; the suffocating effect of the "bridal" satin, the "prodded" food; the gathering of "daughters." What does this poem say about what it means to be a "female" in some of her stereotypical cultural roles? I'm sure we must have talked about that. And then there's the allusion to the "old man," at the end of a long list of domestic objects, seemingly less consequential to this home even than the carpet, there now only to be "touched and fed," like the demanding "old plants," only creepier. Again, what does this poem say about what it means to be "male" in one of his stereotypical cultural roles? I'm sure we must have talked about that, too. There's the passing reference to marriage that inevitably evokes attention to the role of sex and sexuality in the wider frame of Rich's life/life's work. I'm sure we must have talked about that, too. I just don't remember the details, have, perhaps, repressed them into that image of myself sitting silent at the table.

What I do notice now, though, as I read through the rest of the poems from this specific early sixties collection—*Snapshots of a Daughter-in-Law* (1963)—is how haunting and prophetic is its final poem, "Prospective Immigrants Please Note":

> Either you will
> go through this door
> or you will not go through.
>
> If you go through
> there is always the risk
> of remembering your name.
>
> Things look at you doubly

43

and you must look back
and let them happen.

If you do not go through
it is possible
to live worthily

to maintain your attitudes
to hold your position
to die bravely

but much will blind you,
much will evade you,
at what cost who knows?

The door itself
makes no promises.
It is only a door. (51–52)

I read this now as a sort of lesson for negotiating one juncture in the progress of our course. I imagine each of us standing before a door of our own during this discussion. If passage were made, it would be impossible thereafter to "maintain [our] attitudes," to "hold [our] positions." It was a door—I think I knew then, remembering now how apprehensive I was about what I had gotten myself into in this course —that made "no promises." It was "only a door," whose ultimate function would depend on the degree to which I, or anyone else in the class—each of us an "immigrant" of a very specific sort, with our own hope for, and fear of, "remembering [our] name"—could, as Rich does retrospectively in this compilation of her work, provide it with a "frame."

44

SEPTEMBER 21

I've never been much excited about acquiring knowledge in its mode as information, as a transferable commodity to be either given or gotten through classroom display. The kind of knowledge that I've always been motivated—sometimes driven—to gain I think of as almost physiological, akin to perception, comparable in many ways to the sort we accumulate simply by living our lives attentively in the physical universe. Knowledge in this sense becomes for me more a mode of apprehension than of comprehension. An example of this would be how and why I typically read a poet. What I like to do is to have a whole book, or at least a lot of poems, in front of me. My goal as I read them is not to go slower and slower as a means of getting a more and more specific understanding of what the author is writing about. It's to go faster and faster as a means of catching the rhythms of the language, of simulating a view of the "world" that is contingent upon those rhythms, until I feel like I'm actually inside that world, taking on its discursive shapes. When this process works for me, I can see a whole page almost all at once, and I start to feel *as if* I am writing the poems (I accent the *as if* to make clear that this is, really, only a way of reading and not some strange act of transubstantiation). A poem in this sense is to me less an artifact than a tool. I want to get up from that reading not with an array of recollections of the "meanings" of those poems, which I can then reflect on or talk about or appreciate, but to go out and at least for a few minutes reconstruct my experience through new and alien eyes, which give me, reflexively, a new and sometimes useful set of poetic rhythms.

I'm saying all this mostly to set a frame for my first discussion of race in these entries. I'll start, again, with some autobiography. I grew up, as I said earlier, in a small town in a rural area of northeastern Pennsylvania. To give you an idea: Our town of about two thousand people was the biggest in the county. Everyone (and I mean absolutely) was white, working/middle class. Almost everyone (say 95%) was Catholic. There were six Catholic churches in town (four of them within a few hundred yards of one another). There was the Irish church (my mother's background), the Slovenian (my father's), the Slovak, the Polish, the Lithuanian, and the Russian. It was almost unheard of to attend one outside of your country-of-origin background except for, say, weddings and funerals. For most of my youth, this was what I knew of as "diversity." One of the odd effects of this isolation was that I had almost nothing but the most clichéd, naive, almost innocent, attitudes or feelings or opinions about race (among many other things)—more like what you'd learn from a ten-minute cartoon than from a variety of lived experiences—until I was nearing adulthood, and those began to emerge through my political activities in college, via the loose affinity that the war/draft resistance movements had with the civil rights movement.

46

The overriding concept for these various movements, at least as I perceived it then, was "equality." I can remember all of the ways in which I felt driven to live my life according to that imperative. And I specifically remember that it was not satisfactory to me simply to behave properly and "do the right thing." I wanted it to be much more instinctive than that, a matter more of perception than of judgment. I wanted, in the most practical sense, to see other people, and especially people of color (although I extended this imperative also to almost everyone who might somehow be described as "minority") as "equal to" me, to accentuate, perceptually, their likeness to me, what we had in common, and to erase as much as possible my recognition of "superficial" distinctions. I went about this, as was typical for me at that time, with a fierce moral diligence. I used to practice, over and over again, staring at people in public settings, trying to look *through* rather than at the most obvious surface manifestations of their "difference." Once I felt I had gotten beyond or below these surfaces, I would study the expressions on their faces, in their eyes, until I felt I had made the leap past their physical features and into the vast, inner reservoir in which, I presumed, they lived their lives, as I did mine. It was in these inner reservoirs—quite elaborate, personal worlds—that I imagined our differences were grounded; and it was through them than any possibility for concourse would have to be negotiated. In part at least because I was reading Sartre at the time—all that stuff about the "gaze"—I believed that somehow I could initiate such a process simply by studying people at a distance. I know as I write this how bizarre it sounds, even to me, who simply thought of it at the time as a kind of self-imposed (re)socialization. But what I want mainly to get at is the degree to which my racial politics (and I believe this is true of many people of my generation) are driven by the moral (and perceptual) engine of equality, of likeness, of commonality.

When I first encountered the various discourses of diversity that emerged in the 1980s—partly in my work with local teachers through the Western Pennsylvania Writing Project, partly in reading the work of recent poets, partly in the critical discourse of cultural studies—I had a hard time getting comfortable with them, but I couldn't figure out why. Finally I realized I was having a problem at the most rudimentary perceptual level, with the term *diversity* itself, which concep-

47

tualizes race (or more generally *minority*) in terms of difference, distinction, unlikeness. My "natural" instincts, honed through the repetition of the mental disciplines I described above, made me feel as if that were an inappropriate, even morally wrong, way to pursue this political agenda. I had spent all of that energy learning to see commonality. Now I had to relearn how to see difference. I had, of course, already invested a considerable amount of time and energy familiarizing myself with, and comfortably abiding by, an array of critical systems that depended in one way or another on differentiation for their primary strategy. Why was it then so difficult for me to translate this initiative into a racial politics that relied on diversity as its primary concept? Part of this resistance can be accounted for by acknowledging that intellectual, perceptual, and moral positions, and the worlds they generate for us, are not simultaneous. In the scenario I outline above, I began with a moral imperative, and translated it, through a way of seeing, into an intellectual position. I had made a big investment in that position. Undoing it would not be easy. I understood and respected political initiatives that began with differentiation as their primary mechanism for definition, and I began to understand as well the ways in which my adolescent efforts to assert commonality were both simplistic and arrogant—difference is crucial; it needs to be accounted for; and sometimes it is, by necessity, an impermeable barrier to "equality." I was able to come to grips with this reality quite readily in terms of gender politics, as I indicated last week. But in terms of racial politics, the process has taken longer and has been more complicated. Part of what I want to do in this course is to continue to think through and work out this concern of mine: by listening closely to the writers we will be reading, to the conversations we have in class, in the belief, and with the expectation, that I'll be able to translate these readings into some new and more effective habits of mind, of perception.

But what is it that (pre)constitutes what I'm calling "listening to" or "translation" or any of the other key terms I'm using here? This question begins to get at some of the critical implications of the stories

48

I tell about myself, particularly what they suggest about pre(as)sump-
tions I bring to, and therefore take away from, my literary and classroom encounters with "others." In the most practical sense, these
stories might offer me some clues about how I typically listen and
read, about what I can and can't hear and understand. One way in
which I think we all do this is through binaries like identity/difference,
equality/diversity. And that is especially so when we read poetry under
the aegis of rubrics like race and gender. Each author then becomes
a very complex figure who is being framed not just by the designation
of "poet," with all of its own cultural baggage, but by the much more
specific categories of African American (or female, or gay, for example). If we begin with the pre(as)sumption that we are predominantly
like any particular author we sit down to read—or any particular student or colleague we choose to listen to—that we can, in one way of
talking about it, "identify with" that person/writer—we will come
away from that encounter with something quite unlike what we would
if we pre(as)sumed such a relationship was impossible or counter-
productive. This readerly pre-construction has, obviously, a big effect
on what we will count as the knowledge we derive from such encounters, especially as we imagine that knowledge to have an intrinsic political component.

Is there any particular privilege attached to a political/lifestyle/
cultural commonality between author and reader? I began this course
with some genuine and I think legitimate concern about what in fact
I had to offer in a forum of this sort. One of the reasons that Toi suggested starting the course with *Women Writing in India*—which must
have seemed to you a truly bizarre choice in a course on American
poetry—was that it established all of us as outsiders in some fundamental cultural way, forced all of us to find angles into the texts and
worlds of others with whom we could not claim easy or immediate
identification, if for no other reason than the poems were translated
into English from other languages. One of our first discussions started,
you remember, with your questions about whether it was even appropriate to be reading this material, let alone possible to "identify"

49

with the positions of the writers. Within fifteen minutes, we were looking in some detail at the poems and stories themselves, grappling with them in intimate ways that both acknowledged and elided the fundamental differences between "us" and "them." That was an important move for this course, in that it foregrounded for everyone the degree to which author-reader relationships are constructed and negotiated, transactions over which we can assert considerable control, although there are limits and conditions we must recognize and respect. Even through the inevitable fogs of cultural difference and translation, we were able to see some of the mechanisms by which these authors were preconstructing the grounds for our readerly positions and some of the mechanisms by which we were preconstructing the grounds for our response to them.

Other Voices

A brief statement about my philosophy of the class:

In *The Black Notebooks* I say, "We are all wounded by racism, but for some of us those wounds have been anaesthetized." I believe that any class that deals with issues of race, gender, and class must provide opportunities for recovery of some of those anaesthetized parts. External structures—the canon too—always rest on internal ones, sometimes ugly secrets; not until those internal structures are addressed will changes be lasting.

I am not consciously a revolutionary in my poetry. But I think my poems are, in the end, just as much against whatever I have been taught as for it. The tension almost paralyzes me. And at the same time, that is the reason I believe in telling. Just telling. If we can get down all the details, all the lists of things, then we can begin to see clearly.

TOI DERRICOTTE

50

In the past few years, I've come to identify the words "race" and "gender" increasingly with the weight of privilege they carry. I find my identity, in terms of society, measured in terms of political freedoms and the daily ease with which I can live my life—walk down the street, grocery shop, kiss my partner—to be an identity of contradictions. Born a white, middle-class woman I inherited privileges; even if I strive to vigilantly reject white, middle-class privilege, the bulk of an equally vigilant racist, classist power structure is going to hand it over to me, allowing me to browse in stores, unscrutinized for instance, while my partner, with her beautiful, long black hair and dark skin, signals an immediate security threat. . . .

. . . I keep referring to actual skin color, rather than race, because outside of Oklahoma few people recognize [Sylvia] as Indian (she prefers to be called Indian and abhors the term "Native American"), but constantly assume she's Latino, Japanese, South Asian, Filipino—it's obvious that what's important to white society is the level of melanin, not its origin. As I write I'm aware again that my associations with race are all tied up with Sylvia. I grew up in Vermont and being white, being Christian was a given. Loving Sylvia is a powerful exercise in the weight of race in the United States.

EVE ALEXANDRA

In the fifth grade, I made friends with one of the only black girls in my class. Her name was Karla. She was beautiful and bossy and I wanted to be around her all the time. She was the first black friend I had and gave me the first glimpse of my parents' sly racism. I can't remember what they said as much as I remember my anger, my outrage. I was in the fifth grade and already felt that I knew more about race than they did. . . .

In my sophomore year of college, I saw Gwendolyn Brooks. It was the first poetry reading I have ever been to and when she stood up, with her glasses on, the room closed and became still. I watched closely and recognized my father in her. They were both writers (al-

51

though my father stopped writing after college), powerful speakers, but the most intriguing similarity was in their mouths. Both Brooks and my father had inverted bites. . . .

I don't know exactly how these anecdotes relate to the framework through which I enter this course. I only know that during the first meeting I jotted down "Karla" and "G. Brooks reminding me of my father" in my notes. I had not thought of these things in a long time, and never, to my recollection, in tandem. But the conversation triggered not only the memory, but the act of writing words to trigger the memories again later. I wanted to preserve those flashes.

I am not sure how I "enter" the literature based on being female and white. As I mentioned briefly during our first meeting—my perspective contains an inherently useful duality. I can love and study Black Literature, but fear speaking about it. My lack of authority paralyzes me—I will say the wrong thing, I will not understand the meat of it, I will offend. And I can hear that a male colleague is teaching Women's Studies. He is bright, he is well-versed in feminist studies. Still, I come to expect that the silence I have applied to myself in Black Studies should be reciprocated by a man regarding Women's Studies. I distrust an "other" authority—he will say the wrong things, he will not understand the meat of it, he will offend. He will offend me.

KATHLEEN A. VESLANY

When I began graduate school here at Pitt there were very few poetry students who were male. Although I walked into workshops extremely intimidated, I soon found I had landed in a place where it would be safe to write about what I considered sensitive "female" issues. (Now I see the split in claiming these issues only for women as detrimental in my hope for resolve and edification.) When I think about how many female poets I know who have been molested, raped, or survived some other horrific event in their lives at the hands of a man they trusted and/or love(d), I am reminded how it feels to bring these issues to the table as they appear in a poem to be work-

52

shopped. It's frightening because in some way, in a way I hate to think about, every man in our lives is the potential enemy. Whether that man be our father or our brother or our lover or our peer. It's ugly and I want to take it back the moment the words leave my mouth, but it's our lives.

> I think of my brother Michael, the most gentle,
> and the woman seeing him on the street; he, a stranger,
> a frame of 6 foot 3, long hair, beard. I think of Michael
> who is soft spoken and kind. I think of the woman
> who, in fear, changes direction,
> avoiding the potential attack.
> I think of the woman as me.

MARIA MCLEOD

Postscript

During the month or so preceding my first term as a teaching fellow at SUNY Albany, I spent countless hours trying to "plan" my first class, day after day, trying to think about what it was I wanted to do. In all that time—and I mean maybe fifty hours of thinking hard enough to give myself a headache—I was not only unable to plan even the first minute of the class, I was unable to formulate any coherent thought or image at all of what that experience would be like. It was, as far as I can remember, the only time in my life I actually "thought" with all my energy with an entirely empty mind. The effect was like revving a car as fast as you can to get out of the mud and have it go nowhere. You know it's bad for the car, and you know the hole is just getting deeper and deeper, but you persuade yourself that any second the wheel is going to grab and you'll be on your way. One lesson, among many, that I learned from this is that I have to have some actual experience of my own to begin with if my thinking is to advance, something I've seen or heard or felt or read. I knew nothing (or maybe it's

53

more accurate to say that I had no experiential fulcrum to lever out all the pertinent things I did know) about college-level teaching, and even less about "composition," so I had nothing to begin my thinking with.

Until I was nearly an adult, race was a concept in that category for me. I knew—at least in a conscious way—nothing whatsoever about race as a mode of economic and cultural differentiation. The people I grew up around used no epithets for Blacks or Asians or Native Americans (although there were a plethora of slurs for the multitude of Caucasian ethnic groups that our community comprised). Such "others" didn't even exist in our world, let alone merit derogation. And that's the place I knew I had to begin writing, and thinking, about matters of race in the framework of these essays, of this course, a process, to be honest, I dreaded initiating, not simply because of the inherent volatility of the subject, and the prospect for conflict or embarrassment that addressing it courts, but because I wasn't sure what, if anything, I could *teach* others about it, outside of the predictable canon of texts, the acceptable clichés girded up in the armature of contemporary critical theory, which is exactly what I wanted to avoid.

This trying-to-teach-something-I-don't-know is as unpleasant to me as trying-to-think-about-something-I-have-no-experience-with. The wheels spin on and on in the vacuum. A lot of useless noise. No knowledge either proffered or received. The teacher-as-fraud. Revealed and exposed. Forgotten clothes. The nightmare of all teachers. I have no such insecurity about gender-related matters. I know a lot about being a man. I've spent a lifetime obsessing about it. And I know a lot about women. I grew up with them, lived and worked with and loved them. Mother, sister, wives, daughter, friends. I've spent a lifetime obsessing about them. As for race-related matters, I had, for most of my life, as little *conscious* knowledge—the kind that comes from day-to-day obsessions about what's right in front of you—of what it meant to be white in this society as I did of what it meant to be of color. And this suggested to me a fundamental incommensurability, at the epistemic level, between the race and the gender aspects of our course, one I

54

hadn't thought much about, for example, when we were choosing our texts or designing our syllabus, one that our disciplinary discourses tend to erase or elide for us by joining these concepts—along with class—so chronically and so casually, as if they are all of a piece. It was therefore with the epistemic, rather than the literary-critical, that I decided to start.

Our discussion of *Unsettling America: An Anthology of Contemporary Multicultural Poetry* was "unsettling" in quite a different way from the one we had of Adrienne Rich's book. This was our first move directly into literature(s) that foreground the concept of race from our course's title, although this is not, to be sure, a collection that can be easily pigeonholed according to the binary structure that was tacit to our previous discussions of gender. It is in this respect that I use the term *unsettle* in relation to the effects of this book. In some ways, its mode of anthologizing the material—by a thematic progression from "uprooting," to "performing," through "negotiating," to "re-envisioning" —preconstitutes the manner in which racial otherness will be construed. Instead of seeing distinct groups of minority or marginalized writers struggling *differently* in the face of a monumental majority canon, we see collages of diverse individuals striving to negotiate broad imperatives of which, as individuals, they would have to remain largely unaware. Instead of having a connected body of work by a single author by which to measure her authorial and human project, we have what the back cover of the book accurately characterizes as an "array of poets" who "explore what it means to be American." Instead of having obvious ideological positions around which authors are collected, or are collecting themselves, we have a general effort to "highlight the constant erecting, blurring, breaking, clarifying and crossing of boundaries . . . among peoples, cultures, and languages within national borders" (xix–xx). The effect of all of this is to make it very difficult to differentiate, for the purposes of discussion and potential

55

affiliation, a set of specific racial/ethnic/minority literatures. There are, of course, certain advantages to making race an amorphous category, with African American, Native American, Chicano, Asian, and so on foregrounded as a whole against a dominant white background. But as the discussion went on, it seemed to me that those advantages emerge in their best form only after a process of differentiation is allowed to take place. In other words, pronounced cultural conflicts must be provoked before they can be ameliorated. And, in the dialectical movement of our particular course, the "first" stage of its movement took place in our subsequent discussion of, particularly, Amiri Baraka, several weeks after this "second" stage has already been effected.

Like the broader educational debates and initiatives concerning multiculturalism as a social agenda, the narrative momentum of this collection is generally affirmative in its tone, prescribing a liberal teleology to the recognition of difference. While the anger, the conflict, that inhere to many kinds of cultural differentiation are present in good doses, their edge is dulled, their threat diminished, by the manner in which the works are juxtaposed. In effect, by the mode of anthologization, the works have already been "read" for us in politically significant ways that were extremely difficult for us, at the point of discussion, to read our way(s) back out of. I thought that was a problem. Not so much with this book, which is quite forthright about its method and its agenda, as with its placement in our syllabus. We would have done better, I think, to use Baraka, in much the same way that we used Rich, to fracture us positionally in relation to matters of race. That we were unable to do that here meant, as I look back on it, that gender remained the dominant conceptual frame for our discussions until past the midpoint of the semester.

SEPTEMBER 28

Last week's discussion got me thinking again about father-hood, a theme that has been oddly and vaguely distant during this course when it seems like it shouldn't be. After I left class I spent a few funny and puzzling minutes trying to imagine myself as "patriarchal." Not so much in its current pejorative sense, as it applies broadly and structurally to cultural or social systems. All of that is pretty easy to hold onto from (and off at) a distance, as if it applies, say, to averages or percentages of which I may or may not be a part, or to institutions and economies far too large for one person to make a dent in. I was more interested in its personal, extended-family sense: the chief, the head of household, the breadwinner, dad, the old man. I just couldn't make a connection between any of that and my real life. And I'm not sure why.

Part of it I suppose is the accident of my upbringing. Where I grew up, everyone's grandfathers, including both of my own, had been coal miners. And almost all of those men died young—of black lung or some other work-related malady or accident. There were therefore no old men in our town. It was eerie. I didn't know either of my grandfathers, and I can't remember anyone else's either. These immigrant men—Slavic and Irish mostly—had been hard workers by day and hard drinkers by night. I mentioned in an earlier piece that there were six Catholic churches in this town of two thousand. There were also, when I was growing up, twenty-two bars, or in the local parlance, "beer gardens," and that was down quite a bit, we were told, from the peak during the heyday of the coal mines. There were several of these beer gardens within a hundred yards of our house. These were not places where you sipped a gin and tonic and listened to a band. They were dim-lit, even dingy, inside: just a well-worn wooden bar, some red-plastic-covered bar stools, maybe a bowling machine, an overpowering smell of alcohol and smoke, three or four middle-aged men sitting silent, drinking shots and beers—the kind of places you hated to have to go into as a kid, to deliver a paper, pick something up, track somebody down. My grandfathers, who under more favorable circumstances may have developed into extended-family "patriarchs" in some traditional sense of that word, never got old enough to qualify. As a consequence, most of my parents' generation grew up in households that were run, sooner or later, by widows of coal miners. I have no idea if as young women they bent to the wills of their husbands. All I know is that when I knew them—my own grandmothers, other peoples' grandmothers—they were strong, stern, stubborn, powerful people who seemed unshakable, incontrovertible, unconquerable. Perhaps this strength was born of the urgency to raise large families alone and unsupported. Perhaps they would have turned out this way under any circumstances. I don't know. What I do know is that the unutterably destructive patriarchy of the (coal) company town spawned on this smaller scale a plethora of families headed by women.

I was in my late thirties when I had my first child, about the same age my father was when I was born. My daughter is eight, my son is three. When I go to open house at school or pick one of them up at some party or function, the other parents don't look like me. They're ten or twenty years younger and don't have a lot of gray hair. I'm not quite far enough along to be mistaken for the grandfather, but the prospect of that always makes me a little nervous. I had never planned to have kids. Why that's so and how it got turned around is a long story. But I never had the sense—and I know many men who do—that having a child was something I needed in my life, to feel complete or fulfilled or the other things people feel about having children of their own. My wife has that feeling about her life. I try to understand it by comparing it to things I do feel I need. But I just know by the way she talks about it, and by the way men I've known have talked about it, that I really don't have the gear that turns that wheel. I think my father felt like that, too. He's a wonderful man whom I love and respect, but he didn't have much of a clue around us as kids. He worked hard six days a week and played golf on Sunday. My brothers and I spent our time by ourselves or with our friends. Very happily, I might add; in the same way that I have no sentimentality about having children, I have no regrets about my relationship with my father. It was in fact ideal. My brothers and I and our friends played baseball endlessly in a vacant lot over the street. We fished and swam and rode bikes and occasionally wreaked havoc in the neighborhood. As we got older, we spent our time at the local hangout playing pool, smoking cigarettes, drinking coffee, and talking. We had a great time. And we wouldn't have if my father had been tagging along with us, or even asking us much about it afterward.

My mother worked during the Depression and the war. I could always tell by how she talked about those years that she loved working. She was, and still is, happiest when she is busy and with other people. In her midthirties she had four kids in five years. This took her out of the work force and stuck her alone in the house with just us. My memories of her during the ten or so years that she didn't work were, well, of someone struggling mightily to run the house, to keep us in line, to get through the day's chores. She disliked housework and, she said, she wanted us all to grow up independent, able to take care of ourselves (unlike my father, for example, who was in his seventies before he learned how to make a can of soup: My mother was in the hospital and he called my sister to ask if you opened the can before or after you heated it). So we were assigned many of the household duties: laundry, ironing, dishes, cleaning, vacuuming, dusting, and when we were old enough, cooking. She went back to work when I was about ten and was instantly much happier. And we were happier, too, especially to have the house and time to ourselves after school. We usually told our parents only the most general and innocuous things about our lives. In the beginning this strategy was a way of protecting ourselves from them; as we got older it became a way of protecting them from us.

I think part of my point in all this is to suggest that I never had—nor did I ever want, nor do I now miss—an intimate, friendly relationship with my father or my grandfathers. So as I try now to be a "good" father to my own children, in a world where you can't as easily, or at all really, just let your kids go off somewhere and safely have totally private lives of their own, I feel most of the time as if I'm starting from zero, over and over, every time something new comes up or something changes. I think: What kind of father would I like to be? How do I translate that into some action I can take? How do I translate that action into something my kids will understand? And then afterward, I reflect on it, evaluating it, wondering if I did what was best, if I did enough. I have no reservoir of memories to gauge my behavior against.

My lack of models is complicated also by the fact that as far as I 60 can tell, I have no "natural" fatherly instincts or intuitions, which I believe other men do because I see how much more easily and smoothly they appear to function around children, how they just seem to know what to do and how to do it. For me, it's more like going to school without any teachers. I work very hard at it. I think about it. I believe

that I'm a good father. But sometimes I wish it were all easier or simpler, that the culture or society we live in were easier or simpler, that
I knew more clearly what my role was and wasn't, when I was doing
better or worse, right or wrong, or just plain enough.

In my view, that's one of the biggest problems that has arisen for
all parties from the breakdown of traditional family roles: no one has
a clear sense of just what or how much of this or that is enough.
Women have for a generation now been coping with and renegotiating the terms of the social contract that governs the balance between
home and work. The metaphor of "having it all" is one of the key-
stones around which that renegotiation continually revolves, and
women have become much more realistic about what is possible and
what is not. In my view, men need to start figuring this out for themselves, to find ways of thinking and talking about what, and how
much, is enough, about what, and how much, is not. It's just no longer
a viable option for fathers to do what my father did in the fifties. Even
if we earned enough so that our wives could stay home—and most
men don't these days—they wouldn't want to. Which means that matters related to child care and running a household become pressing
problems. My wife and I used day care on and off for our daughter,
but decided, for a variety of reasons, to care for our son on our own.
As a consequence, our schedules have become intricately complicated,
and who does more or less of that care varies widely from day to day,
week to week, month to month.

I have no idea how much time I spend a week on family care matters. I do know that I often feel guilty about how much or how well I
do it. Sometimes I feel guilty because I'm taking time away from
"work," that I'm shirking my responsibility to my employer or my career, one of the unpleasant consequences of the otherwise wonderful
advantage of managing your own professional time. Again: When is
enough enough when no one is there to blow the five o'clock whistle?
When I do my work at home I feel guilty that I'm shirking my responsibility as a caregiver, a householder, a father. Right now, for example,

61

I am typing this up while my son is in the other room watching a video he's seen a dozen times. It's what he asked for, and I was happy to oblige, hoping to get time to write this afternoon. But it's also a nice day out. We could be out in the yard playing. Or I could be at the grocery store. The consequence of all this is that I never feel as if I'm doing a satisfactory job at anything. And the stress of having to balance and compromise so many competing—even mutually exclusive—obligations, of having to accept the diminished view of myself that comes with all of those compromises, is a significant factor in my life. This stress has always been there in the lives of women whose work outside the home often comes not wholly as an opportunity for self-fulfillment but as an unpleasant economic necessity (as working a job has always been for many men) and, beyond that, as an add-on to their obligations as housewives and mothers. What men need is less Iron-John-around-the-fire and more discussions about what, and how much, is enough, about what, and how much, is not.

❧

Okay, just so you know: I went outside and played baseball with my son. We walked down to pick up my daughter at the bus stop. My wife came home from work and made dinner. Then I went to the grocery store. Now I'm back to this. I'm not sure what more I have to say. I'm afraid I'm sounding whiny about what are in the final analysis very small things.

Two weeks ago one of our friends brought her kids over at about six o'clock (I was in class here) and asked my wife to watch them while she took her husband to the emergency room. He had been throwing up every day before work and was becoming more and more distraught. She came back about four or five hours later. There wasn't much they could do for him right then because he had no evident physical problem, and he wasn't willing to wait around all night to take a battery of tests to determine how he should be handled. So they came home. I talked with her about him. She said he felt guilty because he had to work overtime every day and on most weekends, and he felt he wasn't being a good enough father to his children. But she had been laid off last spring and for him not to work the overtime would reduce the size of his paycheck (thereby making him, I fully understood although I'm not sure she did, not a good enough father). He saw no way out. I found myself in a similar place a few years ago. It took me months first to seek, and then to find useful help. I struggle, more successfully now, with those problems every hour of every day. I knew exactly what he was feeling. I told her to tell him to call me, that I'd be happy to talk with him. He never called. When I was where he is, I wouldn't have either. And I wouldn't have wanted him to call me. So I do nothing, except hope he finds his way out. I know of at least two other men who have had equivalent experiences. Neither one of them ever talked to me about it. I found out through my wife who talks to their wives. Maybe they know about me that way, too. I know I never told them. What we have in common is a sense of inadequacy at meeting what we feel are our various obligations, at living up to our own internal set of self-expectations, which are deeply ingrained by a wide array of cultural and social forces, and the expectations we presume others have for us. I think men need to find a way of talking about this, of helping themselves to know what, and how much, is enough, and what, and how much, is not.

My daughter is standing over my shoulder right now asking me when I'll be done. She knows how to read, but I'm hoping not fast enough yet to read this. I'd rather not explain it all to her. She wants me to help her with her math so she can get a candy bar before she goes to bed. Hey, I'm a whiz at math. And I'm still not sure that the help I'm about to give her will be enough.

63

Other Voices

Ten years but I could find my way,
to the Kittyhawk fishing pier;
each road, turn, sign was memory.

My father is here
teaching us to fish
in faded green pants, hat with lures.
Leaning against this bait, gut, covered rail
wind at his back, casting out his line,
he is not a tourist.
His heart is a fish, shiny, slippery
glistening beneath the water.

On the way home from the funeral,
even at twelve, I knew that he had gone
to the sweat silver August heat,
a fish under these waves, the salt in the air.
· · · · · · · · ·
I stretch, expand from these outer banks,
lean against the end railing,
just ocean before me.
He is in this wood
the rough grooves, weathered cracks,
the endless spiraling water beneath me.

I can smell his salt in the air—
I open my mouth
to taste him.

M. E. KUBIT

We belonged to our mothers, to women, to our mothers' sisters and aunts. When my mother's mother died and she had to leave the South, she went to live with her sister in Detroit. And when she married my father, in spite of my uncle's protests, we lived with them until I was seven. My uncle was furious. People in the North didn't do it that way. He was a WASP in spite of his blackness. He expected his wife to choose her husband. But my family was *women*. Really *only*

64

women. Not just because men were often missing—my mother's
mother had left her father in an alley in a house with no address in
Beaumont, Texas, when my mother was three, to go off and be a cook
for the wealthy Kaplans—and not just because those who stayed,
stayed through the earthquake of her reaching her limit and putting
down her foot—(those who didn't desert with "the whore"; or emo-
tionally desert when they knew their word didn't stand a chance, who
found a place on the couch and chewed Beeman's, rolling, uncon-
sciously, the silver wrapper, as if it were a petite woman's head; or
who blew up and blew up until there was nothing to be gained)—but
because we didn't really believe in them. Never. We were always
prepared for their infidelity, their insufficient love. It was women who
almost died giving birth to you. It was women there to wipe your shit.
It was women who, in rage, tried to strangle you for coming in too
late, who cared that much to make you, by guilt, by coercion, by
screaming, by even dying if they must—it was women who would
never give you up.

Daddy was a do-dad. An excuse for bad luck. A habit. A sometimes good good day. He might as well hit the street where he was
King and wanted. "Can't I put a god-damned cigarette down for a
minute before you come and wash the ash tray? Your mother is a
clean freak," my father would shake his head and say. My father
could bash me around. That was all right. Sometimes I thought my
mother even liked it, as if he were her right hand man. "I bet you
won't act like that when your father comes home!" In spite of my
father's rages and depressions, things continued pretty much the
same. "Why did your mother stop liking sex," my father once asked
me, "she use to like to walk around naked." Once I found fifty
kotexes wrapped in tissue as neatly as gifts, in a hatbox in my aunt's
closet. The blood and pain of it. That was what we were entitled to.
We had to be perfect for our daughters.

TOI DERRICOTTE

65

I've been thinking of Confession
how the Catholics make you enter
their wooden closets
in the second grade.
How at seven, you've done
so little but begin
to learn
that if you can only say
that you lie
about your mother's broken pearls
if you can just whisper
through a wire window
that you don't always like
your brother, that your body beats
against him in mysterious defense
if you can know the wrong
in you
and find words for what you've done
you'll get forgiveness.

KATHLEEN VESLANY
FROM "OFFERING (OUT LOUD)"

Postscript

The piece that opens this chapter took me by surprise. I think I began the course with the assumption that while my past—the "accident[s] of my upbringing" I refer to in the second paragraph—had some necessary bearing on my work in the course, what was going on in my life right now was still safely off limits, a little preserve of privacy I could continue to maintain as a refuge from the demands of our agenda. I'm like most people: I resist change, even while I'm calling for it. I am stubborn, I will resort to subterfuge, dissimulation, even self-delusion, to convince myself I have already gotten where I say I want to get, even though I know on some level I haven't done the work or endured the hardship that is necessary to get there.

I started this off as a generic "ethnographic" reminiscence, the sort that is common, almost ubiquitous, these days, especially among poets. Some people refer to this as the "Pittsburgh style"—because so many Western Pennsylvania poets have taken a writerly interest in their working-class, extended-family backgrounds and written about that material so passionately and eloquently. I write no poems in that vein, for reasons I have difficulty fathoming, given their obvious marketability and the ease with which I could access the appropriate material. I think it has something to do with my attitude toward the past. I remember about ten years ago showing my mother a small magazine in which a poem of mine appeared, a magazine dominated by poems in the Pittsburgh style. My mother, whose father was a coal miner and who knew firsthand the working-class world that these poems purported to both capture and eulogize, was not impressed. She said: "They make it all sound so depressing, like all we had was grief and struggle and death. We just lived normal lives. We were happy a lot of the time; we had a good time. It wasn't like this." It wasn't like this. Which is to say, of course, that it wasn't like that for her, for the people she knew, maybe even for all the people who were being represented, both individually and generically, in the poems I showed her. Then who was it like that for? If I took her implication correctly, she was saying it was like that for the poets, that they were really just writing about themselves—not their subjects—their own feelings—not their subjects' feelings—and needed to become aware of the duplicity that arose from the failure to acknowledge that. Since then I've tried to be a lot more attentive to the inevitable presence of that duplicity when I write about someone "other" than myself. What I'm calling duplicity here is not, obviously, an entirely negative thing. I think of it more as the inescapable doubleness that arises from the

67

desire to tell someone else's story, of seeking to cross, or at least blur, the line that divides autobiography from biography, which is what the Pittsburgh style often does. It is this very move that brings in simultaneously both what is "true" and what is "false" about such a text. I find that kind of dilemma, for which the term *duplicity* is the best one I can think of at the moment, extremely attractive, powerful. That I have not been able to tap its potential to render my own family/ethnic history poetically is less a matter of my suspicion of the method—which, after all, I am using extensively in these pieces— than of my inability to feel a sharp distinction between myself and my ancestors. In poetic terms, they just still feel, to me, to be just like me, not monumental enough, not distant enough, not, well, "other" enough, to serve as poetic alternatives.

Autobiography, as I've been using it so far in these essays, obviously begins with the generic, with the familiar ways for telling stories that we share commonly across the culture. The Pittsburgh style is one of them: it has a hard veneer, comprising sharp detail, and a soft core, elegiac in its tone and mood. I thought it was a good vehicle in this context to speak about my past, my family, the habits and values that shaped them. And it was. Then it took an unexpected turn: to me, right now, to how I live and feel, in ways I'm embarrassed to admit, if only because the genre, the Pittsburgh style, whether it's applied to a writer or a teacher, generally works through a more reserved narrator.

The urge for perfection—like many academics, I am driven by it in ways I find by turns admirable and intolerable—is I think endemic to certain kinds of teaching, as it is to certain kinds of writing. The classroom, to me, demands that I rise above the mediocrity, the tedium of my most immediate physical and psychological needs. When I close the door behind me, I symbolically think about leaving outside it all the "extraneous" things that might at the moment be bothering me, about becoming not simply professional in my behaviors, but becoming a perfect version of myself, about saying and doing exactly the right things at the right moment to invigorate and transform the lives of everyone in the room. The "class" as a timeless space, or spaceless time. This doesn't always happen, of course. I work and work and some students still sit puzzled or bored, unmetamorphosized. I have learned to carry the weight of that inevitable failure. Like the story of my family background. So seamless, so perfect. And then some other reality intruded, one that governs life outside of the stories, outside of poems, outside of classrooms. The genre ruptured at that moment— which is exactly what happens with any genre when we stretch it beyond its means. The Pittsburgh style begins to break down when the narrator-of-the-past begins to question his motives, his intentions, to sense his duplicity—which I did when I started to sound "whiny" to myself. What came after that was a form of self-disclosure I hadn't intended. Which is why I chose that genre in the first place. Ironic.

This course was the first time I did a notable part of my teaching in the form of finished, written texts. In many respects, what that allowed me to do was to transgress the unwritten conventions of classroom discourse as I had constructed it for myself—in keeping with my discipline and my ambitions—over a period of many years. In that classroom, whose practices were geared to the production of "discussion," there was no place for any sustained discourse, especially if it was mine. So these essays became to some extent the "lectures" I never allowed myself to deliver. In that classroom, whose practices were geared to the maintenance of an "intellectual" dialogue, there was no place for any sustained attention to "me" as a real, historical person, with an immediate life. So these essays allowed me to disclose, appropriately I thought, a side of my identity that would otherwise remain invisible, not so much repressed as precluded. In that classroom, whose practices were geared to the regimentation of argument around and toward someone else's "point" besides mine, there was no place for this sort of meandering, for just thinking about what happened to be on my mind. These essays, focused as they might seem to be by comparison to other kinds of extemporaneous writing, allowed me to explore a broader territory, and one controlled more by *my* whims and wishes than those of the other members of the group.

Oddly, the voice of these essays becomes more and more paternal as they proceed through the semester, at least to my way of hearing them. Yet they made it possible for me, by some mechanism I don't yet understand, to function less and less paternalistically as the term went on. That was especially enjoyable to me in a graduate seminar, where I feel much more compelled than I do in undergraduate class-rooms to demonstrate expertise, mastery of the material; to satisfy through performance what I imagine to be the demand for a certified commodity. By this point in the term I hadn't done much of that at all. And to the extent that I did it later in the term it was largely via these class-opening monologues rather than in the actual exchanges in our discussions. I found that to be a welcome form of relaxation in my obsession-with/aversion-to the fatherly.

OCTOBER 5

About halfway through reading my piece in class last week I found myself thinking: What am I doing this for? Why would anyone want to know this much about me? Even I don't want to know this much about me. Part of my aversion to this kind of writing is purely temperamental: a discomfort at being in the center of attention, even if it's only my attention. But part of it is rooted in a much broader set of attitudes about what the past is and is for. Whether it's on the level of my personal history or in terms of literary/cultural history, the past has never been something I've been inclined to revisit, recover, recapture, reconstitute, whatever. I can't really think of any period of my life, or of history in general for that matter, that I would return to if given the opportunity. Whatever is happening at the moment seems much more attractive to me than anything that's already happened.

This brings up from a different perspective the issue of readerly/ pedagogical authority I've touched on before. The question(s) might

be posed this way: In the reading you do for this course, whose project predominates? That of the author(s) we happen to be reading?
The many critics and scholars who have written on or about these authors? Mine and Toi's? Yours? I don't see any easy answer to that. All
of these figures have certain kinds of intrinsic authority and each is
obliged—and usually desires—to stake a claim for centrality. All I can
suggest to you is the advice I give to myself, both when I do my scholarly work and as I try to navigate my way through the "texts" of our
course: Don't give up your own claim too easily in the face of the
others that seem so much more powerful than your own. And I don't
say that to suggest that what most matters is simply what you think
or feel about an issue or a text. Mostly I think quite the opposite: What
I already think or feel, or what I happen to think or feel in the immediacy of reading, is merely a place to start, the place I don't want to
end up, or, if I do, the place I want to see in a new light when I return
to it. What really matters is using what I read to renegotiate, to re-vise,
to re-new, my broader sense of what I have taken here to calling my
"project." That term for me carries a lot of baggage. My project is, I
guess, a kind of amalgam of my personal and professional ambitions,
the context in which I feel authorized to sit down and, in some real
sense, converse on relatively equal terms with, say, a Rich, or a Baraka.
Of course I know how much smarter, more accomplished, and more
important in a cultural sense these people are than I am. That's not
the point. What is the point is that I still have something of consequence to think and to say, and it originates in my position, my place,
my experience, not in theirs. If all I have to gain from reading them is
to learn what they said, to extend their project into my consciousness,
I'm just not very interested.

72

I can recall only one occasion at which my work has been characterized as "nostalgic," in the sense that contemporary critics have been
using that term over the last generation to impugn work they feel is

hopelessly enmeshed in a philosophy of presence. I was reading a paper on metaphor, about fifteen years ago. It's funny how little things stick with you. So I've been thinking about nostalgia occasionally since then. As I said, I am not by temperament nostalgic for the past in the traditional sense of that word: as a desire, say, to preserve or recuperate or restore something that is clearly lost in temporal terms. By the same token, I have a very strong sense of loss in my perception of the present. The kind of nostalgia I feel is for what I think should be there but is not, what was promised or hoped for but was not delivered. I feel that sort of nostalgia more and more about contemporary critical theory. I can still recall what great excitement I had, almost twenty years ago now, about its prospects for revamping the university, especially English departments, which seemed to me then like great dinosaurs hopelessly fractured into illogical areas and subdisciplines providing for no concourse among themselves, relying on bizarrely constructed distinctions between research and teaching, derogating certain kinds of important work—teaching writing and reading at the entry level, for example—in favor of others—teaching graduate courses and producing tons of mediocre articles about seemingly irrelevant arcana.

And I look around now, a generation later, and I feel a sense of loss —again, not for what was there and is gone (good riddance to it), but for what could/should be there in its place and is not. I am happy to laud the work that we have done in English to deemphasize the literature of the dead-white-male, to recontextualize all of the other literatures that were obscured in his shadow and have now been recovered, at least in the limited ways that it's possible for such recovery to take place in the insular framework of the academy. But it's one thing (and a fairly easy one) to deemphasize the DWM's products. It's another and altogether more difficult thing to overcome or change his institutional habits. When I look at the university (or English studies for that matter) as a structural system today, it's really not that much different from the one I reacted so strongly against twenty years ago. It's still

73

divided into its various parts, with not much concourse among them. The teaching/research binary is still driving/dividing our workplace priorities—if anything, even more so than a generation ago. Status is accorded or withheld for essentially the same reasons and by essentially the same mechanisms.

When I was growing up in the fifties and sixties there was a tremendous emphasis on "science and the future" sort of things—World Fairs, TV programs, and so on. I remember thinking (maybe I was ten or twelve at the time): "By the time I'm old enough to drive, there won't be cars anymore. We'll be flying helicopters or jet-packs or levitation vehicles." I truly believed that cars were the horse-drawn buggies of my parents' generation. I've been driving now for thirty years, and the car I drove in with today is not really much different from the ones my father drove to work in when I was a kid. And why is that the case? I think it's at least as much because of the self-conserving tendencies of powerful institutional/economic systems as it is because of problems with technology. The university (and English studies) is pretty much the same today as it was when I came to it—and for the same reasons, in my view. It looks more stylish in terms of appearance and design (and I don't want to underestimate the importance of those changes and the difficulty with which they were achieved) but in certain fundamental respects, hey, it's still basically a 1955 Dodge. And I was so sure twenty years ago that it wouldn't be by now, that we'd be flying around in conceptual helicopters or jet packs or levitation devices. When I feel nostalgic it is because I miss those things.

Other Voices

74

This is not a body I can believe in. It is the body I made up. Called from the sky. Skin. Hair. Bones. It is a body I brought to myself. A gift. I called to it. Said, *muscle, mouth, cock*. The wrist. The inside of his arm. Soft. It came to me, a boy. Not a boy. A man. Yet, not whole—

ephemeral, fragmentary. The skin I touch now is lost to me, to him. He will lose it: it comes off. But there is replication, regeneration. Come. It comes back, returns. Dust: a partition between what is permanent and what is temporary. . . . Open, an opening. The eyes. The blue-grey color of the iris. A door we leave through, have left from, while there are words, last rites, still to speak. But he is see-through, an apparition, illusion. His body thin, delicate. Womanly. His arms spread apart; I grasp his wrists, hold them at his sides to the bed. A crucifixion. *My own sweet Jesus.* My words travel into the air, decompose, defuse, break apart, collapse. Beneath me see how he turns and turns.

MARIA L. MCLEOD
PUBLISHED LATER IN *CRITICAL QUARTERLY*
(VOL. 37, NO. 2, 1995) AS "SKIN.HAIR.BONES."

Baby, we ain't no flowers.
We may open up and be petal-soft
but we ain't fresh, we're scary
and thick, you might have to
put on your thinking cap
when you go exploring in us.
You may have to squint and pull
and prod a bit till you hit the spot,
and even then sometimes we don't like that.
We don't have dew like a flower, and we don't
secrete sweet nectar like a flower.
In the mornings we need a wash,
just like your fingernails
or behind your ears, and sometimes
we need a trim, like your favorite hedge
needs trimming. Flowers don't
shed but we do, sometimes, so forgive us
if you got something you weren't hankerin' for,
and turn your cheek and look the other way

and don't embarrass us by poking around
your mouth with your finger.
'Cause we get embarrassed easily,
and then we may fold up
and you might only see our outer petals,
which you don't want to happen,
honey, 'cause then you'll miss the best part—
the big smile on our lips
when you do the job good.

KAREN THEMSTRUP
"VAGINAS OF WOMEN," A REACTION TO
ELLEN BASS'S POEM OF THE SAME NAME

. . . I talk about fear, how few
things come right in the classroom, how knowledge
comes from what you know, not from a night
at the movies. I rail against
cliché, against abstraction. I praise
reading, rereading, closely, critically. I
praise the free write, how writing fast
and furious yields so much without
the pressure of polish. I want to be
my own best student, I pretend to know
everything because I do not.
I will sit in this chair and face
myself at the front of the room and hope
I can learn without lying.

KATHLEEN A. VESLANY
FROM "TAKING MY CLASS"

I'm awake when I'm sleeping & I'm
sleeping when I'm awake, and no one

knows, not even me, for my eyes
are closed to myself.

> I think I am thinking I see
> a man beside me, and he thinks
>
> in his sleep that I'm awake
> writing. I hear a pen scratch
>
> a paper. There is some idea
> I think is clever: I want to
>
> capture myself in a book.

TOI DERRICOTTE
FROM "INVISIBLE DREAMS"

Postscript

There is something stressful and tedious to me about the middle third of most semesters. The rush of adrenaline that fuels the first moves toward relationship between teacher and class, our mutual grappling for a handle on the "material" of the course, has abated. The elation that comes from anticipating the end of long labor has yet to find its incentive. Just the bland plateau of "midterms," like the Piedmont Belt somewhere between mountains and the sea that I could never quite get a fix on in any of the maps in my third-grade geography book. I still don't know where it is or what it's for. That's how the middle third of the semester used to seem to me. I've been teaching long enough now, though, to know those weeks serve a purpose. The tension of having started so much and "done" so little creates its own sense of urgency, allows the digestive processes of rumination, boring and repetitive as they might be, to begin in earnest. It is during this time of the term that I really begin to focus on what it's possible to do in the particular course I'm teaching, with these particular people in this particular room in this particular weather, to pry myself loose from the obligation to try to do everything I imagined I wanted to do,

77

or felt I should do, when the course started. It is a time to get goals formulated, to focus on performance rather than potential, to ante up. In the case of these essays, it meant shifting the focus away from my own private experiences, my own past-as-emblem, and toward something more academic. It meant "getting down to business."

Here I am, then, at the beginning of this piece, in the self-contradictory position of apologizing for doing exactly what Toi and I had stated from the outset was a major part of the work of this course. I think now that that apology is rooted in more than just my temperament. It's rooted as well in some of my basic assumptions about the classroom. To wit: It is a public, professionally regulated arena in which certain kinds of "work" need to go on and get done, whether I am happy or not to be there, perplexed or distracted by family or personal problems, worn down or worn out, worried, even ill. The work supersedes all of that. This imperative—which, as Gwen Gorzelsky has so aptly pointed out to me, is endemic to the modes of cultural patriarchy I am trying to get a more personal grip on in that last piece—is compelling to me when I teach. And the way I usually accomplish it is by keeping the focus on something other than my personal self. This course, though, made that aspect of my identity an express part of the pedagogical transaction, and properly so. Despite my resistances to such a role, I did make a strenuous effort to do what Toi and I were expecting of everyone else. Still, I wanted to move on to some other more customary academic genres. This entry became my transition to those genres, primarily by allowing me to disavow my preoccupation with the past as a temporary, if necessary, aberration rather than a permanent condition.

78

The discussion concerning the preconstitutive "reading" intrinsic to the process of anthologization that had begun in tentative and rudimentary ways when we discussed *Women Writing in India*, and, more so, *Unsettling America*, dominated our opening discussion of *No More*

Masks! An Anthology of Twentieth-Century American Women Poets. In its most material form, this discussion began with reactions to the prefaces of these books. Many, for example, seemed to feel that the extensive and highly theorized introduction to *Women Writing in India* was itself an act of appropriation, even colonization, of the materials presented. The preface to *Unsettling America* was, by contrast, deemed to be far too brief and untheorized to explain, let alone justify, the editors' method of compilation.

The thread of this ongoing examination of anthologization—one of the principal means by which poetry, especially, is marketed in America—was picked up in our discussion of the genealogy of *No More Masks!* this aged stalwart of our literary landscape, one of the original anthologies of poetry "by and about" women, published first in 1973 and reincarnated in its present, updated form two decades later. A consequence of this extended shelf life is that its editorial method is dated, becoming thereby a reverse index for the dramatic changes that have taken place in the interim with how we delimit "feminist" poetry and how we choose to locate that poetry in cultural/critical ideologies. There was discussion, for example, about the impropriety of originating a work of this sort with a "lark, a game, entertainment to while away a summer at the Cape" (xxiii) which is how Florence Howe characterizes the first edition in her preface. Why should we— the drift seemed to be—take seriously an undertaking that is obviously rooted in such a "personal," and perhaps idiosyncratic, position? The fact that this anthology was not explicitly politicized in some way—as for example, *Women Writing In India* obviously was—became a serious problem for the group.

The categories of "race" and "gender" that carved out/up the domain of our course are, admittedly, both vague and spacious, subject to a wide variety of constructions. To the degree that Toi and I had conceptualized them beforehand, it was largely through the process of text selection. An analysis of those categories had been simmering in our discussions since the first class. With this book, that analysis boiled up into a full-blown critique. The process started innocently enough, with a mention of the fact that Elizabeth Bishop declined an invitation to contribute to this anthology, a fact that is acknowledged in a footnote on page xxvi. There was some discussion about why this was the case. It was via this point of entry that what I'll call a diversification of the category of gender—which is most often intuitively construed as a simple binary system, each half of which is relatively monolithic and relatively homogeneous—began to take place. Questions were raised about what it meant, or didn't mean, politically, to participate in such an enterprise of anthologization, particularly one that seems to originate in the "personal" lives of the editors. This, of course, reagitated the ongoing debate concerning the relationship between autobiography and cultural/critical ideology. There were opinions so various and mixed on this matter of inclusion/exclusion that it was clear we needed a way to interrogate them. The impetus for that interrogation became the expression that Howe uses in the first sentence of her preface to define the criteria by which she and Ellen Bass "collected" the poems for the original edition: They were, she says, "poems by women, 'about' women" (xxiii). This is an interesting formulation. What is, in fact, the connection, or hierarchy, between this "by" and this "about"? And, further, what is it that defines this quality of being "about" women, especially when that term is rendered in quotation marks? One way at this is to look at the anthology itself. All of its poems are written "by" women, so clearly that is the dominant criterion, suggesting of course that gender is being construed from the outset in a binary way. There are, that is, no men in the "inchoate" feminism that motivated the project (xxiii). Part of our discussion became then one of the degree to which feminism(s) were or were not entirely circumscribed by this binary. There was, for example, serious disagreement among the women in the group about what feminism meant and who really qualified for it. The degree to which men were or were not precluded was only the point of entry. It soon became more a matter of what groups or classes of *women* had the stronger claim for defining the issues most pertinent to gender politics. Some of this was driven by differences in sexual preference, but it didn't at all divide neatly into the straight/lesbian binary either. There were, by the end, maybe four or five subgroups representing politically divergent positions. Some of them allowed, and contained, men. Others didn't. It was here and in this way that one of the major categories for the course began its progress toward diversification.

Then we tried to address the "about." What exactly, at the level of practice, does it mean for a woman to write a poem "about" women? How is this different from a man writing a poem "about" women, or a woman writing a poem "about" men, or more vexingly a man writing a poem "about" men? Again, we turned to the anthology for some guidance. Some of its poems clearly mark off the voice of their narrators as female, some of them clearly prescribe by gender the roles their readers can assume—in terms of identification or allegiance, for example. Some of them differentiate audience even more narrowly, along lesbian/straight lines for example. Some of them open up thematic or material territory that had/has not yet been completely dominated by male intervention: marriage, family, children, female sexuality, the female body. These are all quite different ways to write poems "about" women.

And what, then, might a poem by a woman that is not "about" women look like? What kind of poems by women would not make the cut for this anthology? And are there any women writers *none* of whose work would make the cut? This brought us back to Elizabeth Bishop. We did not have her work before us, so it was impossible to specify in any exact case whether a particular poem, or her poetry in general, was not "about" women because of historical context, narrative positioning, readerly positioning, theme, or subject; whether certain women writers strove, or happened, to write like men or to write in a way that somehow "transcends" gender. There was on all of these matters a wide range of opinion and some serious disagreement, which further accentuated the ways in which the group was fracturing along gender-related lines.

Once we got to a detailed discussion of some of the single poems selected for the anthology these problems seemed to recede from the forefront, and we began to do less controversial kinds of work with the material the book offered. This was, after all, the only text of American poetry we used for the course that "covered" the whole century to which we had staked our claim. In our initial planning for the course, I had imagined a much more comprehensive approach to our chosen subject. Toi felt, and wisely I think, that we should concentrate on more recent writers and work the prior history in along the way. This became one of those places. I got to talk for a while about the Imagists, especially H. D., whose work has over the years come more and more to impress, even amaze, me with its range and depth. I got to talk as well about my own sense of the democratizing effect, at the level of technique, of this turn away from form and toward the image at the beginning of the century.

Another major element of our discussion of this book involved its use of the metaphor of the mask, which the editors derived from Muriel Rukeyser's "The Poem as Mask: Orpheus" (xxvii). We had been talking a lot in the first half of the course about the difficulties inherent in trying to write one's experience directly, on the assumption that life could somehow be transubstantiated into words. And about the difficulties inherent in the process of understanding an "other's" text, particularly one that positions its reader from the outset *as* other. This conversation tended to coalesce around the terms *self* and *voice* and their modes of interrelationship.

82 Rukeyser's poem introduced the concept of the mask to add another dimension to this arrangement. "No more masks! No more mythologies!" she declares near the end of this poem about identity, gender, and childbirth. The equivalence she establishes between mask and mythology allows for one way of examining the purportedly

genderless qualities of Modernist poetry, against which so much of the more recent "gender" poetry seems to be a counter. Most of the major male Modernist poets, starting with Yeats and running through Williams, created, or assembled, mythologies to support their poetics. Because the raw materials for these mythologies are drawn from a patriarchal cultural reservoir, the possibility for consonance between the individual male poet and his mythic mask is dramatically enhanced. But is it, we began to ask, possible for a woman to accomplish something comparable through such a process? H. D. is, of course, a good case to study in this regard. She seemed to be struggling throughout her career to find a way of renegotiating the great Western myths through a female lens. In "Eurydice" for example, excerpts of which are included in the anthology (29–31), the poet works with the same myth—and much the same mask, that of Eurydice herself—as Rukeyser does. In H. D.'s poem the woman is lost to the underworld as a consequence of the "arrogance" and "ruthlessness" of her husband's selfish backward glance. She is thereby cut off from both "earth" and "above the earth." Orpheus and she are fundamentally different in their respective "presences." He has his "own light," is to "[him]self a presence." She has "the fervour of myself for a presence/ and my own spirit for light." These are not the same things, obviously. Eurydice is not and cannot be self-identical nor can the female poet, through her, achieve identity between mask and mythology. What each stakes a claim to are "flowers of myself,/ and my thoughts" that "no god can take." By which at least some of the group also took her to mean "no man." The mask of Eurydice remains fully intact throughout this poem. But about halfway through the Rukeyser poem—at the moment of childbirth, that preeminent expression of the impossibility of self-identity—it breaks down completely. "There is no mountain, there is no god," at least for this woman and "the rescued child," until the patriarchal "masks" and "mythologies" are thrown over. Then, "the fragments join in me with their own music."

These two poems in concert—and especially the metaphor of the

83

mask—allowed us to lay open, and lay to rest, the overly simplistic and misleading self/voice conundrum that tends so much to baffle serious discussion about poetic expression (and about autobiography more generally.) The mask in its most literal sense is neither transparent or opaque. But it must, we concluded, be gendered. The masks, and the mythologies, behind which the first two generations of women represented in this anthology learned how, and were compelled, to speak could be construed as (false, overlaid) male shrouds that prevented the (true, underlying) female from breaking through until the crisis of "birth" had been passed. Muriel Rukeyser wrote her poem in 1968, which is as good a year as any to announce that only when women break through patriarchal masks and mythologies and begin to develop those vested in their own bodies and bodies of material will a true poetry "by and about" women begin to emerge.

OCTOBER 19

There's a certain slant of light
On winter afternoons
That oppresses, like the weight
Of cathedral tunes.

Despair is a common theme for poets, as it's a common
human experience. The Emily Dickinson poem that these lines open
is one of my favorites on this theme, a depiction of the sort of sudden,
seemingly unwarranted, anguish that afflicts us, almost predictably,
under certain arbitrary circumstances. Thomas Hardy's "Neutral
Tones" is another, using a similar winter scene to render the equally
disturbing, and oddly blank, moment of resignation that accompanies
the realization that an intimate relationship is, in fact, not simply lifeless now, but has been, unawares to us, lifeless for years.

We stood by a pond that winter day
And the sun was white, as though chidden of God,

And a few leaves lay on the starving sod;
　　—They had fallen from an ash, and were gray.

And there's John Berryman's "Dream Song # 28" which captures the fear and perplexity that arises when we look inward and, almost unsurprisingly, find next to nothing there:

　　It was wet & white & swift and where I am
we don't know. It was dark and then
　　it isn't.

Among these and other great poems about private pain, I include LeRoi Jones's "Preface to a Twenty Volume Suicide Note," which I'm going to use here to try and work out what I said during the last class about my personal, readerly relationship—from my point of view a rich and complex and rewarding one—with Amiri Baraka's work. If I remember correctly, the discussion at the time was asking: "What is a white reader to do in the face of what seem to be express writerly moves to preclude him from the poems?" I said something to the effect that it might take me a while to work out the details of a position that would override that obstacle, but I had no doubt that I could. Let me try to do the first bit of that work by offering a reading of Jones's "Preface," a poem I first read back in the late sixties and have come back to from time to time—maybe half a dozen times, total—since then. I know this is precisely the kind of poem—perhaps exactly *the* poem—that most white readers would turn to as a way of assuming some fraternal relationship with Baraka. And I know it makes no overt effort to mark off segments of its audience in terms of race, as much of his later work does. But none of this, as I see it, is enough to preclude it as a place to start a readerly relationship with his later work. So this poem, the first Baraka poem I read, is where I start.

Most of the stereotypical, pop-cultural images of the 1960s—hippies, free love, drugs, demonstrations—while they are clearly based on realities of the times, tend, from my point of view, to obscure, to underestimate, the anguish, the sadness that I remember underlying, rising up from, many of the more volatile activities I found myself engaging in at the time. While Jones's poem is clearly from an earlier, quieter period, it offers a certain kind of window into the very particular kind of despair that concerns me here:

> Lately, I've become accustomed to the way
> The ground opens up and envelopes me
> Each time I go out to walk the dog.
> Or the broad edged silly music the wind
> Makes when I run for the bus . . .
>
> Things have come to that.
>
> And now, each night I count the stars.
> And each night I get the same number.
> And when they will not come to be counted,
> I count the holes they leave.
>
> Nobody sings anymore.
>
> And then last night, I tiptoed up
> To my daughter's room and heard her
> Talking to someone, and when I opened
> The door, there was no one there . . .
> Only she on her knees, peeking into
>
> Her own clasped hands. (3)

This poem depicts a world in which there is absence and loss at every turn: "The ground opens up and envelopes me" . . . "I count the holes they leave" . . . "Nobody sings anymore" . . . "Her own clasped hands." These are very specific kinds of absences. Absences I felt I could identify with and understand when I first read this poem, the sort of absences that arise astonishingly, almost beyond immediate

87

comprehension, when something that one is so accustomed to, that one could never imagine being missing, is, in fact, suddenly gone— the ground, the stars, the music, somebody to hear our prayers—and gone in such a way that one can hardly remember it ever having been there. The Beat poets, among whom Jones was generally classified in this period of his career, and upon whose disaffected personae the hippie generation, to some extent at least, built its agenda, offered a variety of responses to these kinds of losses: anger, as in Ginsberg's "Howl," serendipity, as in Kerouac's *On The Road*, and, in poems like this, a very specific and poignant kind of despair, which is captured here by the image of the poet's daughter in the last stanza. Think for example about what weight this poem would carry if it ended with an image of the poet praying pointlessly into his own empty hands. Not as much. What we get in that final scene is not a figure, a father, who has lost his faith, or is confronted by the Death-of-God problem that philosophy was rife with at the time. We are led into the scene of a bedroom, that most private and secure enclave in the home, in which his daughter becomes almost an afterthought to the observation that "there was no one there." We get a man who seemingly cannot re- member ever having possessed, or even heard about, a reason to ex- plain his daughter's "peeking into/ Her own clasped hands." In one respect, the disjunction between father and daughter in that scene could not be more profound: her innocence and apparent faith making his lack of either, his mystification at the very ritual she is performing —one that he may at one time have taught, and perhaps shared with, her—seem even more pronounced, more depressing.

When I first read this poem it was that sense of utter loss that most moved me: You go to all the places once so alive—the earth, the stars, the music, home—and you draw a blank. That is a very specific kind of anguish, one that I'm sure no one would argue is entirely race- or gender-specific. By the time, though, that I was reading this poem, Jones had already entered his Black Nationalist period, had in fact turned his back on the poet who composed these lines, precisely, one might be tempted to argue (though I'm not sure I would) because someone like me might presume to understand the despair that is at their core. How must all of this inflect any reading, including mine, of this poem? From my point of view, Jones's disavowal of his earliest work during the sixties and seventies ended up complicating, enriching, rather than invalidating my first pass at reading this poem.

Let me explain how. In the simplest terms, if suicide does not follow immediately upon despair—and it was clear right from the start that it wouldn't in this instance, not, at least, until the remaining twenty volumes were completed, which one could, perhaps, say Baraka is still in the process of writing—then something else must. Emily Dickinson sees what underlies her despair and moves into it, moves through it; as does Thomas Hardy; and for a while at least, John Berryman. Likewise for LeRoi Jones. By the late sixties, gone is the man poignantly afflicted by the absences that haunt him in this poem. Enter Amiri Baraka, who knows who and what the problem is, who knows who and what is at the center of his loss, his daughter's inevitable loss, who feels not confusion but anger about it, who actually sees what is taking the ground from under his feet, the stars from his sky, disabling song and prayer.

When I went back to this poem after reading Baraka's *Black Magic,* for example, my original feelings of sadness, of poignancy, did not suddenly go away. They were, though, reoriented, turned over a bit. In *Black Magic,* he made me think about why this man and his daughter ended up in such a vignette, about how we all end up in such vignettes at one time or another simply because we cannot or will not or are not allowed to see just what is at the heart of our darkness; that culture, society, institutions, discourses, have a stake in keeping us blind in those ways, at making us believe that the anguishes that afflict us are our fault and our problem, that tempt us to solve that problem not by attacking those cultural or social systems but by turning on ourselves. The dialectic of rebellion is based on the conversion of despair into anger; disaffection into action. It depends on our being able to

89

look where there is seemingly nothing and see not only the something that is there, but also exactly what is keeping us from seeing it.
"Preface" remains in this reading a poem about anguish—one no
longer rooted simply in a personal story about a man and his daughter but in the context that makes that relationship inevitably what it
is; that will, if unchecked, take this daughter, who has her own reasons to have faith in the apparently one-sided conversation she is engaged in, and turn her ultimately into her father, who can't himself
recall a set of terms upon which a legitimate faith might be premised.
The incapacity to even remember, let alone pray to, a transcendent
figure, which seems in my first reading to be a failure of the father,
the man, the poet-narrator, becomes now the inevitable consequence
of pernicious cultural habits and systems. The psychological dynamics
of depression become complicated by the societal dynamics of oppression.

Baraka's Marxist period adds yet another layer to this palimpsest of
readings, bringing into play the much larger dynamics of economic
ideology. The figure of the father is no longer either a solitary failure
or a victim of destructive societal conditions. He is a production of
historical forces that span epochs rather than decades. The scene of
the bedroom becomes emblematic of a much vaster and more un-
nerving paternalistic conspiracy. And the disappearance of God is no
longer a mournful symptom of personal neurosis, nor the insidious
product of social deprivation, but an important and inevitable step
along a much different road to salvation, one that both begins with
and inevitably transgresses the private father-daughter relationship of
"Preface."

While the Amiri Baraka of 1970 or 1980 or 1990 may disavow this
earlier incarnation of himself, this LeRoi Jones, he cannot erase him.
That he allows these early poems to be included in this volume is
evidence enough that he is willing to defer to that fact of personal
history. He can, of course, put a good bit of distance between these
various figures of himself, put them in play with and against one an-

90

other, complicate our reading, our way of feeling about all of them. Or maybe it's more accurate to say that it is we, as readers, who initiate and, to some extent, control that interplay. The degree to which any writer, by means of external pronouncements or internal machinations, can preclude anyone as a viable reader of his work—or even force a specific kind of readerly response—is really quite limited. That writers can position themselves in different ways with various parts of their audience, that they can make it easier or harder for their various kinds of readers to enter the provinces of their work, all that goes without saying. But writers simply can't presume to control everything about the reception of their work.

When I sat down to read Baraka again for this course, I started at the start, with "Preface." I don't think I had read that poem for at least ten years, since before my own children were born. I was taken aback by the immediate emotional extremity of my response to the poem. It was as if another new and unexpected layer of feeling were being added to my reading, this one arising out of my autobiography rather than his. Or perhaps, again, that simplifies it too much. All of the other layers are products of my autobiography as well as his, of having lived through, and been formed by, the same epoch as he was, of having followed, or forsaken, some of the available paths, arrived at, or avoided, some of the same places, of having read and reacted to his work at very specific moments in my life, my culture's life. Amiri Baraka's poems may be purposely resistant to direct or intimate access by certain kinds of readers. Perhaps I'm one of them, though it never really seemed that way to me until we started talking about it in this class. A lot of writing is like that. In the face of such barriers, we as readers can choose to do what is necessary to get in, or simply move along, which is itself a legitimate choice: After all, we can't do everything and shouldn't be expected to. I am very grateful to have read "Preface" first among Baraka's work and to have read it when I did. It became a kind of key that gave me a very specific point of access into all the rest of his work—one I might not have found so easily if I had to start

91

with *Hard Facts,* for example—and one I could keep going back to in a series of retrospective revisionary moves. I make no claims that my life and Baraka's are in any way equivalent or even remotely comparable, that our relationship through his work is even very comfortable, let alone fraternal. I do lay a claim to certain points of contact, of intersection, where my interpretive work meets or collides with his in interesting and productive ways. At one of those intersections are the various kinds of despair that organize my rereadings of "Preface to a Twenty Volume Suicide Note."

Other Voices

What does it mean to read? Is reading a relationship between an author and an audience? A relationship between a text and an audience? Should I say an "imagined" audience? Does text mediate between people, or is the only relationship in reading a relationship with oneself? As I type that, I like the sound of it—reading as a way of talking with yourself about something.

. . . .

How do I read Amiri Baraka: I open the book to "SOS." I read the poem to myself, first and foremost, to get the gist of its language on a very basic, very literal level. With Baraka, I make it quickly and successfully through this part of reading. Then what happens? What does it mean when I find things to admire, like the fact that I think this particular poem is not a "representation," but is an actual "SOS?" (As I said in class; analogous to Mondrian's squares as being "the thing itself.") Is that the writerly part of reading? Does finding things I stylistically admire equal saying "I would do that as a writer" or "I would make that linguistic choice given the circumstances" or something like that? As a writer reading am I attempting to put myself in the place of the author? If so, let's toss in the fact that I'm a white woman reading. Does my way of reading my own aggression into the text become something false? When I read Baraka, then, am I Baraka?

92

Of course, I cannot be Baraka. I can only be myself. I know this. And if Baraka imagined or determined an audience, I may not be a part of it. Regardless, I am a reader of something he has written. But I may not be a reader of Baraka; I still may be a reader of myself, because after I consider, as a poet, I guess, what I "admire" stylistically, I move on to another space in reading—the space where I have a conversation with myself about what I think about not being Baraka. What I think about being a poet. What I think about being a reader, being in this class, being a woman, being white. This is not a conversation, I repeat, with Baraka. Spurred by his words, it may not even be a conversation with his words. No, a conversation with myself or myselves.

    LIZ AHL

Other things happened at that reading that have my mind cooking about race, gender, and writing. Most interesting, I think, is Gardinier singing her own blues poems. She said that she wrote blues to fulfill her desire to write in a truly American form. That's fair enough. Was it good blues? I have no clue. Her whiteness got in the way like so much static on a TV screen. But then it occurred to me—if a black woman were singing the same words, I'd probably think it was fine blues.

    PAUL HAMANN

"Dinner for Two at the Manifest Destiny Restaurant"

Sylvia says being vegetarian is for white people.
Three years ago, she moved
to Vermont from Oklahoma,
and I tried to convert her with marinated tofu,
curried chick peas, my famous hummus.
Failing, I posted a memo
on the refrigerator, *Rules:*
No kissing after mouthfuls of flesh,

93

no meat in the house.
Cornered by the slaughterhouse
echo at twelve,
I buried my little brother
into my breasts, as my father
and two other men wrestled the pig.
I refused hot dogs, pork chops, and bacon.
Two years later, I eliminated all meat, poultry
and fish. By twenty, I was a vegan.
My resistance crumbled

in the force of her desire. New rules
posted: *I won't touch it!*
Don't use my pans!
I'd sworn you could smell carnage
in a meat-eater's sweat,
detect blood on the tongue after sex,
but I was head-over-heels in love,
so Sylvia's carnivorous body tasted
like pure ambrosia.

On her first birthday up North,
I bring freesia and roses, promise
her anything she wants to eat. Of course
she wants filet mignon and I remember a place
voted *#1 Steaks in Town*, the Sirloin Saloon.
We get a candle-lit table for two in non-smoking,
right this way ladies,
but somehow we've taken a wrong turn,
they're serving dinner 'til ten in the Holocaust Museum.
We are drowning in a sea of feathers.

There's breast plates, buckskin dresses, beadwork,
cradleboards, and fringe. Santee,

94

Choctaw, Kiowa, and Crow—
how did they get to Vermont?
Where do they keep the bodies? In the kitchen?
Starved to death or simply shot? Whole families
line the wall, their heaven a glass case
above the famous salad bar.

A waiter tells us, *The specials are ribs tonight*
or veal, for only $10.95.
Would we like some wine?
There isn't room to toast *Happy Birthday*
without hitting the baby's shoes,
dangling over our heads.

Tonight we sit on opposite sides of the table.
Good students, we know our history.
My lover's Comanche skin complements the menu.
I am the spawn of the white man.
My people omnivores, still hungry
for the taste of her.

EVE ALEXANDRA

Postscript

The issues that came to the foreground for me as reader of Baraka were, at least in their basic form, the ones that dominated our discussions of his work, which were as heated as any we had all term. As I said earlier, it seemed, in retrospect, like it would have been better to introduce the "race" aspect of our course's title through Baraka's work, earlier in the term. His effect was much more "unsettling," and in very productive ways, than the *Unsettling America* anthology, which would have been a more useful book at this later point. Baraka is the only male writer we included in the syllabus. He would have been a

95

strong counterpart, and offered a strong counterpoint, to Adrienne
Rich, his contemporary and peer. And we could have fed directly off
the general fervor that her work excited. I don't know why we didn't
see the potential of that juxtaposition going in, but we didn't. As a
consequence, the category of race remained fuzzy, undifferentiated,
and the figure of the male was largely marginalized in our proceedings,
until past midterm. All of that came dramatically to a halt, though, as
we talked about, contended with, argued over Baraka. Although we
moved around in the book, the group tended always to gravitate back
to the Black Nationalist period of Baraka's life, especially the poems
from *Black Magic*. The class was 90 percent white. There was a lot of
talk about who gets to be "included in," and who is being "excluded
from" the "audience" Baraka is writing to. The terms of this discussion, at least at the outset, echoed in many respects the readerly problems we considered in relation to *Women Writing in India* early in the
term. Baraka's work seemed in some respects to be as "foreign" to
many of us as theirs was. There was one major difference, though: As
I explained earlier, in almost every case with the Indian women, com-
mentators on the texts were able, despite their initial disclaimers, to
just go on and offer extensive and detailed "readings" quite unproblematically; that was not the case with Baraka. This was not, obviously, a consequence of any literal difficulty in the poems. The poems
are very accessible, quite straightforward, in every respect. It was a consequence of the fact that unlike the Indian women, who "excluded"
us from their audience unintentionally, as a geographical accident of
cultural difference, Baraka made his exclusionary moves intentionally,
as a political act of cultural differentiation. This was a "difficulty" of
another order entirely. Many readers had a hard time trying to figure
out how to overcome the sense that they didn't belong to the poem's
audience, or did in a way they found offensive. We had for several
weeks been talking through the issue of who gets to speak *for* whom
in the politicized poem. This was more an issue of who gets to speak
with whom in such a poem. My impression was that we made a lot of

96

progress in working into this set of conundrums. I classify it as an impression because I could very well have been misreading the gradual reduction in rancor in the mood of the discussion as an index of understanding and resolution rather than, say, of exhaustion and futility. In other words, I'm not sure how many in the group actually found a way to read Baraka and how many just purported to as a way to stop arguing about it. These were very exciting and troubling classes to me. When I moderate (in the sense of orchestrate) a discussion as a teacher, one of the things I think I sometimes do is moderate (in the sense of trying to reconcile) competing positions. In the poems that became the centerpieces of our discussion, Baraka is not interested in engaging in, or being subjected to, that latter sort of moderation. So I tried not to do much of it. What that meant was, given who I am and how I teach, I wasn't able to do the other sort of moderation very well either, which left me less confident in my assessment of where we all ended up. What I do know is that these discussions were extremely generative for *me;* they got me thinking about a lot of things myself that I would not otherwise have gotten thinking about; and they helped me to continue exploring the issues I addressed in my essay to the class. I attach here two of the "fragments" I ended up writing—for myself (I never got them well-enough developed to share them with the class)—on the basis of that thinking.

I was attracted to poetry initially by how it made me feel: in the same physical way that actual experiences are flush with the richness of our feelings. I could have cared less about the poet's biography or why he wrote the poem; I had no interest in the formalistic machinations of the poem-as-text, from the names of rhythmic patterns to the more elaborate examinations of things like ambiguity that characterized the work of the New Criticism. All of that was "school" work. I did it extremely well when I had to—for a whole other set of reasons—but I thought, basically, that it was silly, that it missed the point of reading

97

poems. Or maybe that you had to *get* the point *before* these modes of criticism were to be useful. And, when I read poems in school, no one seemed to be getting the point. I remember in the tenth grade buying a book of poems by the English Romantics, and reading Wordsworth at night, just before I went to bed, with great pleasure. Coincidentally, we happened that week to be studying Wordsworth in school. I can't remember the exact poem, but it was one of the same long poems I was reading at night on my own. We were into our second day of discussion in English class when it finally dawned on me: "This is the same poem I'm reading at home." I had been operating on two tracks of reading so distinct from one another that it took me two days to recognize that, in this instance, they were traversing the same ground. I try to remember this event periodically, not so much for what it says about reading poetry, but for what it says about school, about teaching, about learning. It's hard to get something to happen in a classroom that feels "real." Maybe that's why we have those jokes about the difference between teaching and doing. If you rely on the magnitude of the material or the most routinized methods for approaching it, whether they be critical or pedagogical, chances are not much is going to get "done." One of the fundamental conditions of the classroom experience is alienation. It's built into the furniture.

I had the sense in class tonight that we were in fact doing something other than school work with Baraka's poems. But I'm not sure how much we got "done," in that practical sense of actual-change-in-the-world. I found myself wondering how, if at all, Baraka would respond to our conversation. Would he take an interest, listen? Would he ask questions, probe? Would he get angry, berate? Would he just laugh out loud and walk out? Does the classroom—whether it's high school English or a graduate seminar—inevitably domesticate, even eviscerate, political writing? I look again at the *LeRoi Jones / Amiri Baraka Reader*, this huge book that we only touched into here and there in our discussion. How much time would it take for us to *really* read this book? Is that even possible for *us* in a setting of this sort, built into our

98

furniture? And what would I, a middle-aged white man, have to be able to claim or demonstrate in order to prove—to Baraka, say—that my work with it—or his work with me—was "done?" There isn't a way I can think of to start to answer that question that doesn't in some way scare me.

I spent an inordinate amount of time as a teenager thinking about poetic epistemology. That was because, while I knew that poetry was akin to pornography in its effects, I expected it to have some redeeming value to be worthy of the attention I was devoting to it. The answer I came up with was a simple one: It increased my capacity to experience. I knew I wasn't simply accumulating other people's experiences, making them my own somehow, as if I could add their lives to mine like fresh cord-wood on the pile. But I knew also that this work made me reflect on, and change my understanding of, my own experiences; and it enlarged my capacity to entertain new ones. This made me a "better" person—not so much in the ethical sense, though that was a part of it, as in the sense of just knowing more, of understanding more, of being capable of more, of becoming "educated," in the largely writ version of that word I inherited from my parents.

I've long known of course that I can't rely on an epistemology I developed as an adolescent to justify to myself a desire to continue reading and writing poetry. But I think it's not a bad basic position to start with. It allows me still to argue that the poem bears some analogical relationship to actual experience, even though it is obviously not, that the poem makes available the prospect for coming into contact with someone else's actual experience, even if it precludes identification or appropriation; that the poem, no matter how alien, extreme, or bizarre, has the potential to teach something; that the poem is a legitimate occasion for becoming aware of, even renegotiating the terms of, certain fundamental differences in our various social contracts—for while I cannot, obviously, "feel your pain," I can allow you to make

99

me feel a version of my own that is akin to yours; or, if not that, to make me feel my distance from yours and react to it. That's quite a lot.

In some cases—as in the example I use with Baraka—that begins with a sudden, seemingly unmediated sense of emotional commonality. Not at the level of detail, of course—Baraka's biography and mine couldn't have been more different at the moment I was reading that poem for the first time—but at the level of, "yes, I know what that feels like." Of course not all poems deliver this easily. I know how hard I had to work to "learn" to read, say, Baraka's later poems, with which I can't so easily say at the outset, "yes, I know what that feels like." I didn't. I still don't. I had similar difficulties with Adrienne Rich. It is very hard for me still to feel as if, while I'm reading her poems, I have an inkling about what their "world" is really like. But in each of these cases, I have been able to move from a sense of the poetry as off-putting, even opaque, to engaging and persuasive. I did, and do, this because the process "educates" me: as a poet; as a professor who is obliged to "know" his field; but more importantly to me, as a person with a life whose proper execution makes this sort of work necessary and interesting.

There are differences, though, that are intractable to even the most diligent work, the most generous spirit. We are all, for example, familiar with the sort of personal losses that arise from things said or done carelessly, thoughtlessly, or in haste. Innocent or unintentional as these gestures might be, they often break connections, disrupt relationships, in ways that can never be restored, in part at least because they call into question the whole array of assumptions that supported those connections and relationships in the first place. That's *not* the sort of loss that Baraka writes about. He is concerned with a kind of loss inscribed not by personal actions or circumstances but by cultural forces. While it may be true, as I try to argue above, that at the level of loss itself there is a possibility for connection, sympathy, between Baraka and me, identification is impossible. Our differences are marked not just personally but culturally.

100

At the center of Baraka's poem is a very specific kind of loss, unlike each of the other three I represent in the epigraphic poems. Hardy points to a sense of loss that is emotional in nature. Under the right circumstances, I can experience the same despair he does in response to that loss. Dickinson points to a loss that is spiritual in nature. Under the right circumstances, I can experience the same despair as she does in response to that loss. Berryman points to a sense of loss that is psychological in nature. Under the right circumstances, I can experience the same despair as he does in response to that loss. Baraka, though, points to a despair that is cultural in nature. His is an experience I simply cannot have on his terms. That is a crucial distinction, one that I have to acknowledge and respect as a readerly limit when race is an integral part of the stakes of a poem.

Toi and I were talking before class last week about the state of contemporary literary criticism, particularly the metaphor of "opening up a space" to look for alternatives to the dominant critical systems, to look for what's coming next. It's clear I think that the general cluster of critical approaches and theories that fall under the rubric of poststructuralism are now, and have been for a while, the orthodoxy of cultural studies in the academy. I have no idea of exactly when poststructuralism moved from the outside (as a radical critique of, and powerful alternative for, everything from the New Criticism to Humanism) to the inside (as just what everyone basically believes and is disciplined to practice). I do know exactly when it finally sank in for me that such a shift had occurred: It was about ten years ago, during departmental interviews of job candidates for a literature position. I can't remember specifically the critical approach that the candidate was promoting. Someone asked a question about the degree to which it was a response to or critique of some aspect of the New Criticism.

The candidate was baffled, as if he had never thought about his method in this way and as if he could see no reason to, as if the New Criticism were an artifact of ancient history that he need never attend to, let alone come to grips with. I knew right then that the argument that had defined the entry of my generation into the discipline—what became for many of us a pressing need to dismantle and replace the remaining vestiges of the institutional apparatus that the New Criticism had constructed—was entirely anachronistic. And I knew right then that poststructuralism was no longer a "radical" alternative to more "conservative" critical ideologies but was, rather, the current conservative critical ideology, what everybody did, was supposed to do, and would continue doing for quite a while. I started losing faith in it almost immediately.

Part of the reason for that is temperamental. My scholarly work usually begins with an oppositional move, and my teaching often does as well. I can think of no positive quality of personality or character to account for that tendency, so I'll leave it unnamed. By the same token, it's not so easy to just come up with something new when what's there is unsatisfactory. Poststructuralism in the nineties may be long in the tooth, but it is also so dominant that not many people have started systematically to seek, and lay the foundation for, its inevitable replacement, the next and the new.

There are several ongoing conversations that interest me in this regard, though none of them offers any immediate alternative for radically reconfiguring our professional lives. One is the discussion of the status of teaching in the university. I believe that the teaching/research binary to which we unreflectively subscribe in this profession needs to be called into question and renegotiated at the most fundamental level. The whole notion of a critique that begins with a binary is, though, so poststructuralist that this conversation is going to have to go a long way before it begins to look like an alternative. Still, it's not entirely out of the question that this line of inquiry—by focusing closely on practices and disturbing some of the most retrograde notions upon

103

which the equilibrium of the professoriate's internal pecking order has always depended in this country—can emerge in a whole new place.

There's also the discussion among writers in the academy about their preferred role in, and relations with, the English departments they inhabit. I first noticed this about five years ago, mostly in the kinds of articles appearing in the *AWP Chronicle* [now *The Writer's Chronicle*]. Writers were talking more and more about teaching, about teaching composition as well as creative writing, and about literary theory; they were reflecting on and criticizing their traditional roles, and those of their cross-area departmental colleagues. Part of this, I think, is a generational transition. Creative writing programs, like composition programs, were pretty much an invention of the 1970s. There was an sudden influx of writers into the academy during that decade, most of whom were not trained in university writing programs, since there really weren't any. This initial cadre now oversees large and diverse programs, most of whose faculty have, in fact, been trained by universities to teach in universities. The significance of this redefinition of the role and status of writers both in their immediate programs and in the broader habitat of the English department is, I think, being underestimated. The figure of the writer, the work that writers care about and do in and for the university, their sense of connection with and commitment to broader literacy issues, and to teaching, their sense of their literary pasts, their races and genders, all have been dramatically transformed. And all of this has gone on largely beside, and beneath, the notice of contemporary critical theories/theorists. Again, this conversation could be seen as merely a belated adjustment among writers to the dominant critical ideology. Or it could, by focusing on a different set of practices and disturbing a different set of retrograde notions, come out in a whole new place.

Third, there is the ongoing discussion among poets about form. I believe the concept of form has some potential for reshaping what poets do and why. But I think this movement needs to get much more sophisticated if it's to do anything more than generate a few "formal"

104

poems and serve as a platform for a more elitist notion of the poet. The move away from form in the early part of the century was, as I see it, one of the primary forces that contributed to the democratization, politicization, and diversification of American poetry. If you take the image, for example, as the primary marker for the poem—rather than form—apprenticeship, expertise, acculturation, education, social class, all become less important as prerequisites for claiming the title "poet." Both theoretically and practically, it becomes possible for a housewife, a migrant worker, even a child, to produce as "great" a poem as an elite-university-educated, well-connected male poet. Any move back to a formalism that threatens to remarginalize once again those "undisciplined" voices can't as far as I can see ever succeed, or if it does the expense is not worth paying. But what sorts of formalism aren't intrinsically elitist? Or are there various kinds of better or worse elitisms? Has the democratization of poetry created a genuinely democratic poetry, or just a much larger number of writers writing for each other? Has the exponential growth in the number of poems being written and published increased or decreased the amount of "great" work being done? Is greatness, in fact, in the sense of historically durable, even a useful concept any more? How, if at all, is the politics of poetry related to the poetry of politics? And has the academy, by providing a haven for writers, reduced the latter to the former? Again, this is a conversation that could just peter out, or it could end up in a whole new place.

And there are the various ongoing conversations that have, broadly, to do with a recuperation of the "self," a concept that poststructural critical systems have assiduously assailed over the last generation or so. The discourses that support this critique of our most commonplace notions about the self have to a large extent now become so entrenched in English Studies, so routine, so orthodox, that they seem most incontrovertible precisely at that site—the self—which becomes thereby an ideal place to originate a countercriticism. Compositionists are arguing now for example about the proper role and status of

"the personal," of "experience," not only in the writing they are calling upon their students to do, but also in the highly professionalized
discourses in which they are compelled to constrain their research.
The essays I've been writing this term could be seen—or at least I see
them—as participating in that argument. Part of what I'm trying to
do is to renegotiate for myself the role that I want my personal life to
play in my teaching.

More to the point are the issues that have welled up over and over
in the discussions we have had here. When someone feels marginalized, oppressed, demonized in some way by the dominant culture,
any critique of that person's selfhood, no matter how much it is
intended as empowering, will almost inevitably feel like just another
hegemonic move, another expression of the bad faith that is endemic
to majority. In other words, a critique of one's "self" will feel a lot different to someone who is confident that she already has one than to
someone who feels she doesn't, or isn't sure. This difference stands
out most clearly to me in relation to race. The poststructuralist critique of the self is likely to generate quite a bit of initial resistance
from someone white, straight, middle class, precisely because that person has a great deal invested in the self that is being called into question. Paradoxically, this very resistance becomes the engine to power
the critique. But what about, say, the inner-city African American male,
particularly one who either aspires to or abhors the conceptualization
of the self that seems to be most commonly at issue? That is a different, and more intractable sort of resistance, if we can even call it that,
and one, frankly, that needs to be respected in its political and personal
complexities. What distinctions poststructuralism has been capable
of making in this regard are not easily, or often, translated into our pedagogies, in part because they require such extensive and meticulous
circumspection. But there are ways in which this disjunction between
(critical) theory and (pedagogical) practice is pretty much inevitable: In
the baldest terms, the dominant critical ideology is almost always, by
dint of its routinized functions, elitist. And poststructuralism is today

106

just about where the New Criticism was in 1960. It's what we do. It has no significant competition. It is our orthodoxy. It is already dying.

Somewhere, the next new thing is taking shape. The formalistic and philological systems that dominated English departments in the early part of the century were imported from Germany and Russia. The New Criticism was largely British. Poststructuralism is decidedly French. That still leaves a lot of the world for us to borrow from. Like Africa, East Asia, South America. Maybe we will turn this time to neurobiology or consciousness studies for our impetus. Or maybe the poets will carry the day. Twenty years ago, what we have now couldn't come soon enough from my point of view. Given where we are in the profession, I'm just as impatient to see it go.

Other Voices

To Michelle Cliff from Mount St. Alphonsus—
. . . .

. . . This morning, I wrote some responses to students in my "Race and Gender in 20th Century American Poetry" class, who are concerned about some black writers who don't want white writers to "appropriate imaginal territory" (doesn't "imaginal" sound like "vaginal?"). I wrote that when black writers proclaim such boundaries, we are providing an opportunity to learn our lives and hearts from the inside: proposing white writers navigate the trembling spaces between impossibilities just as we have. After, I saw a man—no, I heard him—at the end of the long, still-dark, monastic corridor, approaching me as I went into the shower room. He stopped to try to catch his breath, bent over, so small I couldn't yet make out a human shape. He sounded like a dragon or a devil (if you can imagine my thoughts, all alone at five in the morning, suddenly apprehending a stooped rasping figure in the dark). Of course you don't stop, in spite of your fear, but you make tiny discriminations as you approach the thing you fear.

107

How frightening the sound of the breath—when it must be gasped like that! And I soon realized that it was a man having a hard time breathing—not a "devil"—and that he was ill, probably with emphysema. It was an interesting shade in my mind that slightly changed, turned from the fearful, the perception of the other as "monstrous," toward the compassionate. I realized that I wasn't afraid of the gasping sound of his breath because it was "weird," but because it reminded me of my own frailty. How frightened I am of the pain and relinquishments of the end of my life: As I approached, the man stood up, almost defensively, as if he didn't want to be seen in that humble position. Later, after I had made coffee, he came into the room and I looked up from your paper to say good morning. He answered like an executive, his shoulders pulled up so far that his thin body seemed to hang from his shoulders, as you might hang a tired piece of clothing on a huge wooden hanger. Then, grabbing hold of the table, he bent over almost as if he were praying to breathe. It was as if a part of me pulled back a layer of my "skin." It is sad that I can only trust such tenderness with the wounded—but I felt my "self" come forth—as one feels the sexual self, trusting, slowly emerge.

TOI DERRICOTTE

In reading Anne Sexton—her poems, letters, interviews and biographies—I can't help but think of her as a composite, as the outcome of a particular female/economic/American aesthetic—the great monolithic cultural force we all in some way subscribe to, even now. I am not dismissing free will, the right to choose the course of our lives, but I am questioning how those choices present themselves, make themselves known. I'm also wondering who is offering them and to what gain are these choices being offered?

108

. . . .

Yet within, or perhaps I should say outside this idea of the poet as product of their environment, there remains a voice and intellect and intention describing the poetics of the individual work. . . . I wanted to use this paper to represent Anne Sexton's voice and her poetics. In reading her letters and various interviews, I found that Anne Sexton was indeed aware of the "Anne Sexton" she was constructing for an audience.

. . . .

In a letter to Anthony Hecht (May 1, 1961): "Letters are false really—they are expressions of the way you wish you were instead of the way you are . . . (poems might come under this same category.)"

In an interview with Patricia Marx from the *Hudson Review* (Winter, 1966): "It's very hard to reveal yourself. Frankly, and anything I say to you is useless and probably more deceiving than revealing. I tell so much truth in my poetry that I'm a fool if I say any more. To really get at the truth of something is the poem, not the poet. . . . It's a very easy thing to say 'All poets lie.' It depends on what you call the truth, you see, and it's also a way of getting out of the literal fact of the poem. You can say there is truth in this, but it might not be the truth of my experience. Then again, if you say that you lie, you can get away with telling the awful truth. That's why it's an evasion. The poem counts for more than your life."

MARIA MCLEOD

Postscript

During my first year in graduate school at SUNY Albany—1972–3—a bunch of us, graduate assistants and younger faculty, used to gather pretty regularly in the afternoon at the cafeteria. One day the argument heated up about the status of "the self," that private, unique, originary, animate force (to use the Romantic discourse I felt naturally comfortable with then) I took for granted as constitutive of my personal identity. One of the faculty members argued, quite adamantly, that such notions were not merely intellectually simplistic but politically destructive, that there was in fact no such thing as this "self" we were calling "our own." It was the first time I had heard that argument. I thought he was nuts. I made a few mild passes at refutation and left, later, just shaking my head. Looking back, I see now that his position was not some crackpot theory he was just making up to shock us. He was a Marxist and had read a lot of structuralist social theory. I hadn't.

The following year, a friend, Frank Boylan, and I used to get together once a week or so in the evenings at my apartment. He was easily the best-read person I knew back then, maybe that I have ever known. We'd eat dinner and then, around 8, start to talk. My first wife, who thought we were intolerably boring, would either go out or go to bed. Frank and I would choose a starting point and then converse around it, in as rigorous a way as we could, for hours, until 2 or 3 in the morning sometimes. One night we were talking about the similarities and differences between the kinds of knowledge, as mode of "experience," garnered through actual living and those garnered from books, through reading. Which were better, more "real"? We had been talking back and forth about that for maybe an hour or two when Frank leaned back in his chair and smiled. "I've read all the great books," he said [and he had, more books than anyone I had ever met, and he knew them well, clearly loved many of them, spent most of his time reading more of them], " . . . and they're not so hot." Not so hot. I still remember how wise and funny I thought that sounded. At the time, I decided he meant something fairly direct and simple: that reading, even of the greatest books, is not a substitute for or the equivalent of or an alternative to the actual daily life in a human body in this world that all of us have to lead. Which *is* hot, in ways a book is, well, not.

110   I was persuaded then by the wisdom of his dictum, in part because it helped me to explain the disappointment I always felt when I finally read a book that I knew was "great" and that I hoped, futilely, would satisfy my urgent desire to know *something*, *anything*, clearly, finally, once and for all. I have recurred to Frank's dictum innumerable times

over the years to guide and moderate my readerly quest to earn the right someday to say, for myself: "I've read all the great books . . . and they're not so hot." But in the process, my reading of his expression has grown more complicated, more nuanced, in some ways more troubling, reminding me more and more in those respects of the character and personality of its inventor. I struggle still with the problem of what to make of and do with the many great books I read and reread, with continuing perplexity; I struggle still with the problem of what to make of the actual life I find myself living, with persistent astonishment. At the intersections between these two kinds of texts, books and life must somehow e / merge. But how?

Self. I do not know exactly now what to make of this concept. I'm not sure, at heart, my own "personal" [Ah! the quotation marks, which have saved me over and over during these reflections, allowing me to use the words I feel comfortable using at the same time I can indicate that I know everything that is "wrong" with them. Ah: the quotation marks.] position on the matter of its existence and practical, everyday function in my actual everyday life is any different than it was in 1973. I wrote in my very first essay to the class about how the modes of reading I learned first continued to exist for me, under something like the poststructuralist mode of erasure. I think all learning, like all memory, is like that—down in the nervous system, at the synaptical level, where it most matters. We can cross things out, overlay them, attach all kinds of qualifiers to them, but we can't make them go away, like they were never there in the first place. And under that mode of erasure, they continue to assert a powerful influence on what and how we think and feel. I've been reading criticism and theory now for over twenty years. I know something now about the problems with essentialist concepts of the self. I know something now about the problems with humanist social and ethical systems. I know something now about the problems with formalist approaches to literary texts. I have no interest in recuperating, or even revisiting, any of that. But I wonder if where I am today isn't, despite all my work,

111

pretty much where I was twenty-five years ago, except under a mode of erasure. All those great books. Still not so hot.

What better author is there to complicate a discussion of the role of "self" in acts of composition than Anne Sexton, whose *Complete Works* we began discussing during this class session. I've taught Sexton's work a number of times in a variety of different kinds of courses. Almost inevitably, no matter how hard I work to resist it, the conversation gravitates to her flamboyant and tragic biography, a watered-down version of "The Savage God" approach to poetry. That did not happen in our discussions here, for which I was immensely grateful.

By this point in the term, the class had pretty much taken over the initiative for our discussions. Small groups were moderating large portions of the class time. We negotiated the self-into-text conundrum in this discussion in quite a sophisticated way, helped in part by the handout of the above material from Maria McLeod. This had been, as I have been saying, an ongoing difficulty in our negotiations not only with the materials of the course but with its method. The obvious temptation with Sexton is to get into the juicy details of her biography, using that material as a kind of lurid gloss for the poems. The rubric "confessional" under which her poetry was originally pigeonholed made this sort of reading almost de rigeur for nearly a generation. Even today her work remains caught up in the propriety, legal or otherwise, of the exposés that have been written about her private life. This is, of course, the sort of response that Sexton tempted; it is important to remember, though, that it is a response that she also sought to deflect. It was a respectful balance between temptation and deflection that the discussants were able to maintain in their treatment both of specific poems and of Sexton as their author.

This discussion called attention, at a very specific level, to Sexton's sense of humor, dark as it might have been, as well as to her sense of (melo)drama; to the manner in which the poems were obviously

112

crafted and not just bled out onto the page; to the gentle poignancy of her affections as well as the hyperbole of her psychic crises. She emerged in my mind as, really, a poet of the first order, more interesting and influential ultimately as the pioneer into a "body" of material for writing poetry "about" women than Sylvia Plath, whom I had beforehand presumed to be her better. And, perhaps as a consequence of this, her work seemed to me much more sedate than it did when I encountered it in the late sixties, a first reading that tended to dominate all of my subsequent returns to her work. In some ways, in fact, her work looked tame by contemporary standards, more like a tentative move to open up a vast, volatile, and vital terrain than the tour de force that closed that terrain down forever by its own explosive force.

I really did get a new take on Sexton, and more through the work of the class than through my own initiative—as was, for example, the case with my retake on Baraka a couple of weeks before. If there was a moment when I began to realize in a very practical way what this class—as a group of people—had taught me, this was it.

NOVEMBER 16

For every action there is an equal and opposite reaction.

That's a basic law of Newtonian mechanics. A similar law applies to teaching; though, since it is difficult to accurately predict the precise effects of any of our pedagogical actions—at least not as accurately as, say, the effect of a cue ball striking another ball with a specific force at a specific angle—it is equally difficult to accurately predict the reactions they will generate. Anyone who has taught multiple sections of the same course, especially when they are scheduled back-to-back, knows the dangers inherent in trying to translate what seems to work in one class directly into another. And there is also the simple matter of fact that, if nothing else, everything we do as teachers makes it impossible to do everything else that might be done with the time it takes to do it. And what will be most obvious by its absence is, of course, by the law of opposites, the thing our action seems expressly designed to preclude (though the perception of the value of this latter thing might vary a great deal from person to person). The discussion during the final hour of last week's class has led me to reconsider this problem, and I'd like to use this occasion to think through a brief genealogy of the one very specific classroom practice that became the focal point of our discussion: the read-without-response format of our class openings, especially the post-reading silences that regulate the movement from one piece to the next.

Let me begin with a confession: In the pre-course discussion that Toi and I had about whether to do a pre-class read-around with or without response; in all of our considerations about it since then; in all the time I've sat in my own silence between readings; it never once crossed my mind, not even fleetingly, that these silences might also be perceived as silenc*ing*, as many of you said last time you felt they were. I have no way of completely accounting for how I could not have seen such an obvious thing, which I recognized it was within the first few minutes of our discussion. Prescribed silences, while they may be extremely useful and productive, are also, well, silences. They are designed precisely to hide what they produce. It goes without saying . . . without saying . . . all that time going . . . without saying. If this were the first time I had missed something so obvious as a teacher, I would have an easier time justifying it. But, as I indicated above, such problems are so endemic to teaching, at least to my teaching, that I should have foreseen this one. I've had my share of classes go badly because I failed to foresee, or just miscalculated, the inevitable mechanics of that equation: Every thing you choose to do precludes everything else you might have done with that time, and calls attention to, most especially, the very thing you seem to be trying *not* to do. It goes without saying. But even if I could have, or had, foreseen the antithesis of my actions, that still would not have secured me or the course from the inevitable consequences of choice. It's impossible, in my experience at least, to be a perfect teacher. It's impossible to have everyone like or approve of or even learn from whatever it is you

115

happen to be doing. And good intentions really don't much matter when push comes to shove. From my point of view, those are some of the most difficult psychological realities about teaching for me to cope with. The inevitable miscalculations, the missed opportunities, the misunderstandings. One can derail a class. A few can derail a course. Or at least make it very difficult to get through.

I know that your silence and mine are entirely different things. To the extent that this course silences me—as a generic teacher-figure—it is at my own discretion. When I choose not to speak, as I do over and over, it is not because I feel I can't. At the graduate level, a big part of my job is, as I see it, to be quiet, not to take up the time with my talk, but I rarely feel silenced, even during the opening read-around. Let me leave my other self-imposed silences aside and just talk in an off-the-top-of-my-head way about my reactions to those silences between the pieces that constitute the opening read-around. I've been really impressed by, and grateful for, what I have been able to hear and learn from your offerings. And, for me at least, the silences between them have been as provocative and fascinating as the readings themselves. I find myself doing many different things in that space: Sometimes my mind races to assimilate and try to evaluate a primarily intellectual response; sometimes my nervous system races to sort out and make a decision about a primarily emotional response; sometimes I find my mind turning outward to the group, guessing, gauging, what you, as individuals, small interest groups, are thinking and feeling (eyes move up or down or make momentary contact with the reader or a colleague elsewhere at the table, a smile or lack of one, etc.); sometimes I find myself trying to decide what to add to my overall impression or assessment of the one who has read; sometimes I'm just wondering how and when someone else, or me, will break the silence with another entry. In one respect then, that period of silence is a sort of safe moment for me to have an uncensored time to sort out my reactions

116

with no opportunity, and therefore no obligation, to share those reactions with the group. By the same token—and this begins to get at the degree to which that safety is fundamentally illusory—we all know that we are always in the process of judging one another and being judged.

Both Toi and I wanted to foster an environment in class that would allow everyone to bring what they have written to the table, at least partially and at least part of the time. The open forum at the beginning of class, it seemed to us, was one of the best and easiest ways of doing some of that work. We decided to have no pre-set limits on genre or time or position, while, by eliminating response, allowing all entries to have a relatively equal status in that space. Right from the start, both of us worried about creating such a seemingly "safe" space (one in which a position could be rendered without the opportunity for, or threat of, immediate response, let alone critique or opposition) for each of you to have direct access to the discourse of the class. And Toi—I think I remember correctly—was concerned more generally that such a "safe" place might keep us from engaging with some of the issues of the course in their most volatile, conflictual forms, which she felt was necessary. We certainly had no intentions of silencing the very basic arguments that a course of this sort must address. Whether or not we have—or if the non-response format of the read-around has served more to inhibit than advance those arguments—is probably an argument in its own right. One which we started last time.

I remember once in another seminar someone prefacing a remark with the expression, "This is off the record . . ." and what struck me suddenly was the general truth that, in the academy anyway, nothing spoken or written is ever fully off the record. I'm not sure precisely why that is. Maybe because we don't make things or money with our time. We marshal, manage, seek to extend, to capitalize on, to assert, our authority, our credibility, our status, our position(s), upon which

117

depend our capacity to move people and systems in the ways we believe are right or preferable. I suspect we have all had experiences as teachers, as readers, as speakers, where we felt the exhilaration of engaging, even moving, an audience, of gaining the control and the capital that accompanies being heard and appreciated and respected and just plain listened to. Likewise, we have probably all had experiences as teachers, readers, speakers, where we have performed badly, or have simply been badly misunderstood, and have realized immediately that our loss of control, of capital, with that audience, that person, that group was unrecoverable. This is a business that runs on the fuel of language, discourse, information. Nothing confidential remains so for long; nothing off the record remains there for long. In fact, it is often precisely those bits that we most covet, not simply to have the power that goes with knowing the secrets, but the even greater power that goes with being able to tell them to someone else. An anthropologist from an alien world, in examining the economy of our system, might well presume that the general hierarchy of power, the pecking order, is governed more by the things one is able to find out, and then parcel out to others—whether it's the newest, most exotic theorist, the trendiest nomenclature, the latest gossip, some behind-the-scenes secret—than by the amount or quality of what one knows and is willing to freely share. I know how cynical that sounds. But it is simply to say: There is no safe place in this arena; status is being accorded or withheld, gained or lost, every time we utter or write a word. And Toi and I didn't want to create the illusion that in this place things would somehow be otherwise.

118   Other Voices

In the last few years of our lives, I moved to the city where my grandmother lived. In more than two years, she never called, never stopped by. I thought about her a lot, when people asked where my family lived. Here, right here, but we no longer speak. My grandmother never told me that I wouldn't "amount to much" but it was evident that I did not amount to much for her. This was okay, I consoled myself, people in your life often become peripheral: relationships dwindle to nostalgia. This, I told myself, may be normal.

The silence between us bothered my mother. The aunts started talking about why I wouldn't call her, that my whereabouts were unfamiliar to her, that the arriving party is expected to foster the reunion. It was late by the time such talk started—our habit of silence grew less alarming to me, but never normal. It felt like a grudge based on void: no feud, no effort, no dueling convictions.

At the viewing last week, the first words my grandfather said to me were: You should've gotten in touch with her, really. She wondered why you never called.

. . . .

Last week I was thinking about confession.

This week I am thinking about omission. How I worked around the silence between my grandmother and myself by ignoring it, denying it, writing around a very present anger. I think of how writing a decent poem without including the all of it is a penance that people understand. I've been thinking that by writing around the truth, you can conceal it on the surface. But deep down, absence is always apparent.

KATHLEEN A. VESLANY

I haven't been on the bus for five minutes before the group starts talking about who their favorite driver is. "I like the colored girl," a woman says. "She's good."

"Not 'colored,'" Tony corrects her. "Black. Black or white."

Two minutes later he turns to me. "What are you?" Often I'm asked if I'm Greek or Italian. I know it's meant to establish a connection, to be a compliment.

"Black," I answer.

He looks blank, as if I hadn't said anything.

119

"Black," I try again.

Now he looks as if he got a fly caught in his ear and he has to knock it out. "What?" he asks. "Black? No," he answers himself.

"I know what I am."

TOI DERRICOTTE

The dialogue for many of my issues around gender . . . did not exist in this class. "You could have created one"—I can hear some well-intentioned straight person say, but it's not a dialogue I want to have all by myself. This class performed its role, as part of the hetero-sexist powerstructure. For the most part, questions of gender operated around the male/female polarity, as opposed to say butch/femme lesbian issues or trans-gendered biological issues. Power and privi-lege dictated what the class brought to the table as well as who sat at the table.

EVE ALEXANDRA

Postscript

What I wanted to suggest in the piece that opens this chapter was the degree to which the actual practices that Toi and I chose for this course were carefully considered, how teaching often involves a scrupulous attention to detail, beyond the level of method that education text-books tend to start and stop with, beyond a course's proper "materi-als," beyond the obligatory research to master beforehand a body of knowledge. I'm talking about the level of detail that is so specific it seems, in practice, to be natural, something that just happened that way. Like effective details in a poem or story seem just to be present-ing things the way they are. And I'm talking about the level of detail at which risk turns to action, moral in its imperative, political in its effects.

Toi and I had talked a lot during the course about the importance

120

of the class-opening read-around, about how having each of the ren-
derings framed by silence was really the best way that the diversity
among them could be foregrounded. I was, therefore, astounded when
several participants in the seminar construed that silence—which had
seemed to me so generative, so gentle, so generous—as an imposition,
a form of silencing, an oppression. Toi and I. Who had been, in the
perfection of my own inner narrative, so patient, so attentive, so careful not to inhibit or exclude. I felt their anger and I felt an anger of my
own well up in response. Now, these are emotions I rarely reveal even
the slightest hint of, let alone express. I just hate to lose my "temper."
When I do in the classroom, or almost anywhere, it is usually staged,
rooted in some recent fit of pique, but sublimated in the meantime,
disciplined, to serve a purpose. So in this class I just sat in silence and
listened, trying to fight the dumbfoundedness, the nausea—the fear
that we, that I, had failed in our most important enterprise and hadn't
even known it until now.

I listened for quite a while as the conversation developed. And
gradually it all turned. I couldn't be angry at "them." They were, from
their vantage point, entirely right. They had been silenced. We had by
definition precluded verbal response to the pieces being read. This
can be hard on a listener with an urge to disagree with or critique what
she hears, or who just wants to laud or commend it. And it can be
hard on the presenter, too, who feels a need to get feedback on this
risk she has taken. The conversation was being animated by all of this
pent-up energy. But I couldn't be angry at "us" either. What Toi and I
had chosen to do with our time was so obviously, from our vantage
point, the right thing, had generated so many benefits, how could we
blame ourselves for doing it? After the third or fourth week of the
term, the read-around was consuming about thirty minutes of class
time, sometimes more. If we had opened up each piece (there were
maybe six to eight per session) to responses, class would be over
before we had even finished the readings, let alone gotten to the "required" readings for the course. No one would have been happy with

121

a "course" of that sort. Which is to say again: Anything that takes up class time does so at the expense of everything else you might have done with that time. Toi and/or I explained this to the group. And there were many in the group who actually enjoyed the freedom of being able to read their work and move on. In any case, by this discussion's end, everyone's mood had improved, including mine, and we all moved on.

The discussion made me think again about the ways in which the role of the teacher, no matter how it's implemented, is, by dint of its institutionally sanctioned authority, oppressive. And it will be perceived as so by some people some of the time. Every teacher knows *that* much of course. What I hadn't thought through far enough was the degree to which the figure of the teacher that I inhabit bodily is being inflected in powerful ways by race and gender. Enacted through this white, male body, the one I was so concerned about bringing into this forum in the first place, my practices become to some extent "his" practices: the desire to be "democratic," for example—which I usually think of in terms of egalitarianism but am compelled to see here also in terms of homogenization; the urge to "moderate"— which I usually think of in terms of orchestration but am compelled to see here also in terms of toning down or leveling; the underlying ethic of "tolerance"—which I usually think of in terms of generosity but am compelled to see here also in terms of putting up with; and, above all, the tendency to "temper"—sometimes with silence—the very exchanges that my practices seem to warrant. Enacted through my body, this tendency can easily be perceived as, though I'm not persuaded it becomes, just another strategy for enforcing the status quo. I will try to remember that.

DECEMBER 7

Hard is it on the one hand to become
A good man truly, hands and feet and mind
Foursquare, wrought without blame.

. . . .

Nor do I count as sure the oft-quoted word
Of Pittacus, though wise indeed he was
Who spoke it. To be noble, said the sage,
is hard. . . .

This is an excerpt from a poem, by the Greek poet Simonides, that Socrates discusses with Protagoras and Prodicus in Plato's *Protagoras*, one of my favorite dialogues, in part at least because it is in much of its give and take, including this long bit of philological hairsplitting about poetry, both profound and funny. The argument turns on the question of whether the first and last lines of the quoted passage are consistent or contradictory, specifically, whether "to become" and "to be" are the same or different.

123

The discussion during the last class led me back to what has been, for me at least, a term-long concern with problems related to change. In one of my earlier pieces I offered a description of the way in which I tried, when I was in college, to train myself not just to "do" what I thought was good, but to "be" good. I know that the terms here—the distinction between doing and being—are not quite consonant with the ones Simonides/Plato are working with. But the problem they pose, and the stakes in working it out, are structurally similar. What I want to do here is see if I can come at this issue along the tangent of the "positionality of the reader" that I proposed last class as a counterpart to the "positionality of the writer," the concept that has emerged from you in our recent discussions. In the most practical sense this is to ask: Are we obliged in some way to assume and maintain our cultural position—in race/gender/class terms for example—when we read a text? If so, how do we know precisely what our position is? Or maybe more accurately, how do we know where to draw the boundaries around the part of our position that is pertinent? In this process of drawing the appropriate boundaries, to what extent must we respect the desires or the will of the writer in assuming the readerly position she seems to prefer for us? And when we do that, how, if at all, can we make common readerly claims about identifying with, or empathizing with, or even comprehending the position of the writer, the other, of the text?

We all, of course, inhabit our positions in very complex ways, some of which intersect neatly with cultural stereotypes, some of which run against the grain. When we read, the questions become (1) which of these positions is applicable at the point of contact with the text and (2) who gets to have primary control in making those decisions: the writer, who provides many obvious cues to name and locate his audience; or the reader, who decides how to respond to those cues. I'll try to be as plain as I can about this, because I do think it's fairly straightforward, at least at the level of readerly practices in the face of a political poem. Any poem that is overtly political not only foregrounds the position of the writer in terms of some familiar, broad cultural categories—like race/gender/class—it also moves explicitly to position its readers in those same, or comparable, kinds of categories. As readers, we have a wide array of choices we can make in response to those moves. We can accede to them completely, we can resist them, we can refuse them, we can seek to modulate or modify them, or we can even just walk away after the first line of the first poem we read. If we are *required* to continue reading, as in a course like this, we can simply continue to read while withholding any real emotional or intellectual investment in the work. We all know how to read like that, like it doesn't matter or we don't care, or won't put ourselves into play, at risk.

Art is not life. The slightest hangnail can compel us to attend to it in ways that the greatest poem can never match. The differences in magnitude and significance of the metaphors "turning the page" and "closing the book" when they are applied to life rather than to reading are ample evidence, for me at least, of that fundamental truth. And anyone who has had to cope with a death in the family, a divorce, a serious physical or mental disorder, any great difficulty, knows that no amount of reading or writing can fully prepare one for, or get one through, or render afterward, all of the life that goes into and comes out of even such relatively common events. Maintaining a sharp distinction between art and life has been important to me ever since I first began to think of myself as a writer, at the precise historical moment— in the late sixties, at the peak of the "confessional" movement—that poetry and suicide were considered almost synonymous. I found myself occasionally thinking that I was obliged to take the sort of risks with my mind and my life that many poets and critics then were talking about as either essential to, or the inevitable consequence of, the production of great art. And I finally decided that that was just plain stupid—for me, at least—and quit writing poetry. Poetry, as central and urgent and important as it had always been to me, really paled by comparison with what I most wanted out of my life—which I won't

125

put a name on here. After a few months I just started writing again, differently. I have quit writing poems two other times, for similar reasons. But I always, after a few months or a year, started up again, with poems that were, from my point of view at least, different from, more in keeping with, what I wanted to make of myself. When the choice comes down to my poems or my life, you can take my poems. Please. I want to emphasize that this is simply my choice. I have read many (and known a few) poets who have made the opposite choice, and made it quite consciously and confidently, more than willing to risk paying the price it entailed. I have made a variety of other consequential choices about the place of poetry in my life. I don't want to recommend any of them to anyone else. In some cases, in fact, I would recommend doing exactly the opposite. What I do want to say is that we all can make all of these kinds of choices, as writers, as readers, as people, in whatever way we want to, no matter what the institutional or textual imperatives seem to be calling for. There are consequences, sometimes painful ones, to those choices. But there are consequences to pretending that they are not our choices to make. Or worse, that they are not open to choice at all.

Which gets me back to Plato. Well, actually, it doesn't. This is nowhere near where I was expecting to end up when I started this. But it's amazing how big a gap between two textual points you can cover over simply by asserting that it's not there. In any case, in the argument between Socrates and Protagoras/Prodicus the overriding issue is whether or not virtue can be taught. At the beginning of the dialogue, Socrates says no and Prodicus says yes. By the end, they have reversed positions. In my reading, this is Plato's way of saying that the specific question posed about virtue's teachability is not the one to be asking, at least not in quite those terms. The conversation about being and becoming in Simonides' poem—about as good a lampoon of literary criticism as you'll find in classical philosophy—is, ironically, as I see it, closer to the problem Plato wants us to explore. To be or to become, that is the question. I have to go with Socrates on this one: Being and becoming are two different things. More particularly, to *be*

126

good is impossible, though to *become* good is not only possible but what we are here for. And the way I now believe this process advances is by the good we *do*, an inversion of the personal regimen I described earlier and alluded to above. In this context, virtue, while it may be unteachable as a specific body of knowledge or set of practices, is certainly learnable, a process that can be facilitated by certain kinds of pedagogy, both within and without the academy. More broadly, the value of teaching and learning in this view is measured in terms of what changes and how much, not in terms of the knowledge-as-commodity that is generated, exchanged, or replicated.

This is pretty close to where I started the term in these reflections. With change. Mine mostly; maybe yours. So I think this is where I'll end. I'll leave it for another time to assess for myself whether the distance between those two points was worth the energy and effort it took to traverse it.

Other Voices

Maybe I just want to end on a light note, but I keep thinking of my naive, young feminist hopes that I brought to my first trip to a legendary N.Y. lesbian bar on a Friday night. I was twenty-one and just out. I got all decked out with my best friend, who brought her boyfriend—trying to pass him off as gay, we put lipstick on him and ordered him not to look at any women. I was wearing a black bustier. A beautiful, older woman approached me and asked if she could touch my breasts, because she and her friends—pointing out two women in leather at the bar—had a bet: the woman I let touch my breasts would win fifty dollars. I was somewhere between thrilled and horrified, but that moment shattered my perceptions of gender and the lesbian sisterhood I'd envisioned. I encourage you to expand the possibilities for dialogue and shatter your perceptions as well.

EVE ALEXANDRA

127

Postscript

We concluded our readings for the course with Rita Dove's *Grace Notes*. The mood this night, as is common for end-of-term classes, was generally happy, even celebratory, and both Dove and her book are ideal vehicles to translate such a mood into conversation. As we planned the course, I thought we could use this book—such beautiful, perfect poems—and Dove's career—such a rapid and well-deserved rise not only to prominence but to eminence—as an instrument to get, again, at certain crucial knots in the "race" and "gender" categories. As I imagined it, we would begin by juxtaposing Dove with Baraka to consider whether/how the role of gender as a difference-marker for African American writers is functionally comparable to its role for white writers. I think this is an important question, not only in political but in poetic terms. Our course took place before the Simpson murder trial, before the Jonny Gammage incident in Pittsburgh, before the Million Man March, which brought to the fore, each in a different way, the place, and the plight, of the African American male in our society. I was hoping to translate this issue into an authorial, even a poetic, matter. I may or may not—given the mood of the class—have raised this concern. But I know we didn't end up talking about it.

I was hoping as well to call attention to the fact that the "major" poets of my generation—and even to some extent the generation just before mine—are mostly women. This is true across racial/ethnic boundaries as well. I was hoping to talk about the unprecedented "diversification" of American poetry at the end of our century, this plethora of such various and distinct voices that have, if only by force of numbers, redefined for us what poetry is, who can claim the title poet, where poetry's audience comes from; that seem in their diversity to finally threaten in a serious way the concept of the canon as a means of differentiating between such things as major and minor poets, great and popular poetry, academic and avant garde poetics. Again, I may or may not have raised this issue that night. But I know we didn't end up talking about it.

So much for the teacherly plan. Like so many other well-planned classes, this one took on an entirely other life of its own. Fortunately I have learned enough over the years to sometimes just let that happen, to accept and participate in the discussion and the lesson that the group happens to offer me, even when it's not the one I had anticipated. And especially when it's better than the one I planned. It has become now one of the things I most enjoy about teaching: the great class that emerges from the group to displace, for the better, the one I intended to impose. This night, we spent two hours reading aloud, and then performing spontaneous close readings of, many of Dove's poems. The interesting thing about these readings was that even in their scrupulous attention to text on the page, they were full of emotion, sadness, anger, joy. Such precise and crafted poems lend themselves to and deserve that sort of care. They would have slipped silently beneath the surface of the conversation, the argument, I was imagining in my script. And that would have been a great loss to us all.

In a seminar, one of my ambitions is to become irrelevant to the work of the class. If, at the end of the term, I can just sit and listen to a focused and carefully documented discussion of the texts at hand without having to initiate, direct, or moderate it, I feel I have succeeded in at least part my mission: which is to demonstrate that intellectual work, the life of the mind, for both the individual and the group, does not require the services of a professor to proceed at a high level. During this class I was largely a silent participant. That may seem oxymoronic: How can one participate with silence? I know when I first started to teach—in entry-level composition courses for which I always made "participation" a significant portion of the grade—I tended to equate participation with talking. Students who talked, participated; those who didn't, didn't. It didn't take me long to see the problem with this economy, especially in situations where one or two inordinately loquacious students consumed most of the discussion time unproductively. So I developed the usual techniques for getting more and more voices involved—calling on students, in-class writing as a preface to discussion, small-group work, and so on. Still, there were some stu-

129

dents who were tenaciously taciturn, seeming to prefer silence no matter the expense. Gradually, I started to notice something about at least
some of these students: when they were absent, discussion didn't go
as well. When they returned, it perked up noticeably. Why? What I
finally realized is that these students, while they might not be great
talkers, were wonderful listeners—to me and to their colleagues. They
were not in fact absent from our discussions, not for a second. They
were right with us, paying close attention, nodding heads, raising eye-
brows, smiling, looking puzzled. They were participating, with quite
powerful effects. All of us were performing better because at least part
of our audience was visibly, if not verbally, responsive, even support-
ive. Since then, I've tried always to recognize those "silent participants," to give them credit for their work and to tell them why I am
doing so.

Silence can have many modes in the classroom. And teacherly silence, because it is chosen, can often be a powerful pedagogical tool.
A teacher, of course, cannot afford to adopt this strategy from the outset. But it can be a goal, achieved gradually over the course of a semester, as the other voices present achieve their own "authority" with the
course's material. If a big part of our work in this venue is to produce
colleagues—rather than, say, disciples—then our own authority needs
to be attenuated in order for student authority to develop. For me,
this process begins with finding ways to listen productively to others.
And it ends, ideally, as this seminar ended, with my being able to listen productively for myself. Authority is, of course, endemic to the
position of the teacher. There is really no escape from the social dynamics it initiates, no ground to stand on that is outside its purview.
So over and over when I teach I find myself struggling to evade my
authority even as I evince it. Sometimes that makes how I teach seem
maddeningly convoluted, my statements overly mitigated, my comments multiply qualified, like this sentence. "Why can't you just tell
us what you know?" "Why won't you just tell us what you want *us* to
know?" I often hear students ask me. "You should have come to the

last class of this seminar with me," I want to answer them, "or of other seminars that end like this. Then you would know."

I'm sure many share the feeling that I've had, quite often, after I've finished teaching a course for the first time: that I wish I could go back and do it over, but with the knowledge I have right now. Not next term or next year, but to go back in time with the same people, the same books. Smarter, this time, though. Ready, finally—having taken the course and realized some of the important things I don't know, say, about race and gender—to "expand the possibilities for dialogue . . . shatter [my] perceptions." That's impossible, of course— the going back in time, I mean. But it's important to recognize the degree to which what a course actually teaches is not necessarily confined to the time it takes to complete it. This course for example initiated a process of reflection for me that goes on now still, years later. I type out Eve Alexandra's passage above and think: It would have been so much fun to open up the dialogue she wanted us to have. But I just didn't know enough then about how to do it. Now, perhaps, I do. Then again, which conversations that we *did* have would this one have displaced or made impossible? Somewhere down the line my thinking about this will make a difference.

There is a way in which many of the courses I teach tend to go on in my mind for years after they're over. I remember people, comments, incidents, images, conversations, and I use them to think about things that concern me. I choose to believe that those courses continue in a similar way in the minds of the others who shared that time together with me. Every now and then some bit of evidence arises—an unexpected letter, a passing comment—that such is the case with at least one other person. Those moments are gratifying to me, but they are not essential. To teach is to change. That's where I started this book. And that's what I believe. Not that a teacher must somehow transform his own life over and over or transform the lives of everyone

131

that comes into contact with him/her. I wouldn't want all that up-heaval or all that responsibility, even if I thought such things were possible—and I don't. But teaching does, I believe, open up a process that doesn't stop when the final papers come in, the final grades go out. Every day out there, there are, as I imagine it, hundreds of people thinking about things I, or one of their colleagues, got them started thinking about in one of my classes. Just as I am working through things they got me started thinking about. Things I might never have come to be thinking about without them. I am grateful to them for that, as I imagine them to be grateful for the ongoing traces of their contact with me.

Would I teach this course again in the real world, where you don't get to just start all over again? And, as a corollary, should I have taught this course in the first place? My answer is, well, probably yes and probably no. Probably yes to the second question and probably no to the first. This mixed answer derives directly from where I started think-ing about my teacherly position in this course: not, for example, as an "authority" but as a generic white, straight, male. I had previously read most of the texts we taught, I had written professionally about twentieth-century American poets and poetry, I had written a lot of poetry. But—and this runs counter to the logic of our profession—the primary legitimizing factor for my effective *participation* in the work of the course was my lack of *credentialed* expertise on its express subject: the literatures of race and gender. It was, I believe, this deficit that neutralized my majority status sufficiently for me to engage "personally," along with the rest of the group, with the course's en-terprise. In short, my lack of authority on the subject of the course is what made it possible for me to teach it. And it is, ironically, what al-lowed me to write about it in the many diverse, exotic, and unex-pected ways that I did in these essays. They were never intended to function as, to become, or even to look like, scholarship or research.

Had I planned to publish them, they would never have been written, at least not in anything like these forms and discourses. What they become by the fact of publication is, as I said in my preface, dependent more on what readers choose to expect from them, from me, than on anything I can now say about them.

I have few doubts, and no regrets, about the decision I made to participate in this course the first time. But, were I asked to teach it again, I think I would say "no." I'm not sure I can ever fully account for the knot of contradictions that is at play here. But one way of putting it is that I lost my place in any future version of this course because of what I learned by teaching it. And for me, that was a very worthy result. I close with Rita Dove's "Arrow," which I think gets at, from the point of view of the audience, the contradiction I am talking about:

> The eminent scholar "took the bull by the horns,"
> substituting urban black speech for the voice
> of an illiterate cop in Aristophanes' *Thesmophoriazusae.*
> And we sat there.
> Dana's purple eyes deepened, Becky
> twitched to her hairtips
> and Janice in her red shoes
> scribbled *he's an arschloch; do you want*
> *to leave? He's a model product of his*
> *education,* I scribbled back; *we can learn from this.*
>
> So we sat through the applause
> and my chest flashed hot, a void
> sucking at my guts until I was all
> flamed surface. I would have to speak up.
> Then the scholar progressed
>
> to his prize-winning translations of
> the Italian Nobel Laureate. He explained the poet

to us: immense difficulty
with human relationships; sensitive;
women were a scrim through which he could see
heaven.
We sat through it. Quite lovely, these poems.
We could learn from them although they were saying
you women are nothing, nothing at all.

When the moment came I raised my hand,
phrased my question as I had to: sardonic,
eminently civil my condemnation
phrased in the language of fathers—
felt the room freeze behind me.
And the answer came as it had to:
humanity—celebrate our differences—
the virility of ethnicity. My students
sat there already devising

their different ways of coping:
Dana knowing it best to have
the migraine at once, get the poison out quickly
Becky holding it back for five hours   and Janice
making it to evening reading and
party afterwards
in black pants and tunic with silver mirrors
her shoes pointed and studded, wicked witch shoes:
Janice who will wear red for three days or
yellow brighter
than her hair so she can't be
seen   at all (49–50)

I'm can't quite pin down exactly the sort of "silence" this poem makes
me want to achieve—but I know it is an achievement and not a failure.
I find myself sympathizing with, even envying, Janice, so flamboyant

in dress "she can't be / seen   at all," not so much silent for these three days as hidden—but powerfully, therapeutically. Perhaps "absence" is the better term for what I'm after here, and it's one I talk about quite a bit in the second half of the book. I do not believe that I am such an "arschloch" as this professor, at least not yet, or to most people. But from where I am standing—foursquare in my majority-laced shoes, so unlike Janice's, those "pointed and studded, wicked witch shoes"— I have reason to fear the threat of that "sardonic, eminently civil" question, the temptation toward that bland and stupid answer.

135

An Interchapter for Two Parts

Part I

> The past and present wilt . . . I have filled them and emptied them,
> And proceed to fill my next fold of the future.
>
> Listener up there! Here you . . . what have you to confide to me?
> Look in my face while I snuff the sidle of evening.
> Talk honestly, for no one else hears you, and I stay only a minute longer.
>
> Do I contradict myself?
> Very well then . . . I contradict myself;
> I am large . . . I contain multitudes.
>
> I concentrate toward them that are nigh . . . I wait on the door-slab.[1]   137
>
> WALT WHITMAN

When I first put the two halves of this book together, there
was a gap right here. You would be turning the page over it now to

begin the essays that compose, from my point of view, the inevitable second half of the argument—which is what this book is about to become, as a function of its two parts being so violently yoked here, across this gap. Every reader of this manuscript in its early drafts turned that page either with great anticipation, eager to keep reading, or with great irritation, wanting to turn back. There have been no neutral readings of its significance. A friend finally suggested to me that I write a transitional piece here, by which I took him to mean that it might be a good idea for me to try to write into that gap—not so much to fill it up (that, you will soon see, would take more language than I am capable of generating), or even to bridge its two sides (that, you will soon see, would take a kind of verbal engineering of which I am incapable), but to call attention to it, to say something about what it's here for, to make it do some work, its fair share at least, on behalf of the agenda of this book.

Now that you have read that paragraph, the gap is no longer an empty space that you can fill as you wish. I must say something to you about why my book did not stop a page ago, a proper monograph in, say, a pedagogy series; with the next half starting up somewhere else, between its own two covers, as another proper monograph in, say, a rhetoric series. These are, after all, quite different, even incommensurable, kinds of texts: each of them, taken separately, interesting (I think), publishable (possibly); together, though, each turns the other on its ear, wrenching it out of the comfort of its discursive voice, forcing it to face a whole set of questions in its defense that it would have been insulated from, if (only) it had (properly) chosen to go its own way.

And, there, surprisingly (even to me as I'm writing this) is the point I want to make—again, following my preface, but from a new angle now—about this "position of the teacher" from which I am writing. This is not a semiautobiographical half-a-book about a course I co-taught back in 1994 followed by a semischolarly half-a-book about Plato. This is a book, one whole book, in which I write *through* my

138

two subjects into the text of the classroom. Separately, in relation to the texts that belong to their provinces, the discursive systems that support each one of these authorial enterprises—autobiography and scholarship—are equally valid. Together, in relation to the text of the classroom, they become equally provisional. Do they contradict one another? Not exactly: they are each too single-minded for that. It is more as if they make it possible for you to contradict me—who chooses to put them together here—in potentially productive ways. If this were an autobiographical book about me, would you be able to do that? From what position? If this were a scholarly book about Plato, would you be able to do that? From what position? In both of those transactions, you and I remain small, relatively "self"-contained. Here, moving through this space on our way to the next half of my book we are large . . . we contain multitudes. This gap accords you an authority to question and criticize everything I do, or to learn from it, in ways that either half, by itself, would largely occlude. By which I mean, in part, that from the position of the teacher all discourses are equally available, equally powerful, and there are not just a few of them, the ones I choose to use here; there are multitudes of them. You will, I hope, be thinking already about the ones you typically use to define the position of the teacher for yourself, and the ones you might use to write from that position.

So I am saying that this gap, which until a few minutes ago had no language in it, is what makes this bifurcated text a "book." There is no way around it. You must go through it to get to the other side. Perhaps, as in the case of some of my readers thus far, this will seem a sensible, even inviting prospect. Perhaps, as it has been already for others, this will seem an impertinent, even unacceptable one. And there I am again, in this gap that seems to be dividing not only my text but also now my readers: those who read its two halves as one hopeful book; those who read it as two half-books hoping to be one.

139

Part 2

> *I have depicted the between as temporary, a transitional moment,*
> *somewhere between here and there, between self and other. I wrote,*
> *"When a person experiences the sensation of being between, she*
> *neither belongs to one world or the other. Her previous moorings*
> *loosened and disrupted, she temporarily drifts in a liminal sea be-*
> *tween worlds." But for Avery (unlike myself and most of the stu-*
> *dents I have described in this book), there are no previous moorings;*
> *the between is not a state Avery is merely passing through on her*
> *way to somewhere else; she lives there and has always lived there.*
>
> DONNA QUALLEY[2]

Donna Qualley yokes Anne McCaffrey's metaphor of "the between,"
—"a transitional space of nothingness and sensory deprivation"—
with Victor Turner's "notion of liminality"—"a mood of maybe,
might be, as if, hypothesis, fantasy, conjecture, desire"—to define for
herself "the liminal space of the between" that "invites reflexive
thinking" (10–11). To me, the position of the teacher is one of the liminal spaces of the between that invites reflexivity in my professional
life. It is not a "state [I am] merely passing through on [my] way to
somewhere else; [I] live there," trying to chart a course "between
here and there"—by my own best lights, in the name of my institution and discipline, with and on behalf of the students who join me
on the way; trying to negotiate transactions between "self and other"
—where each party is simultaneously "other" to her surrounding
"selves" and "self" to her surrounding "others." This "between" is
amply represented here by the unfillable/unbridgeable gap I am trying to write into.

140

Now that I am getting more comfortable writing to you from this
space, I am beginning to see even more ways in which it is like the
position of the teacher. You will see as the next half of the book
proceeds—most especially in "Author/ity in the Classroom"—that I

liken classroom discourse to a kind of loosely orchestrated Bakhtin-ian polyphony: all of us there, teachers and students alike, ventrilo-quizing "ourselves" through the myriad of "other" voices we inherent by dint of our assigned positions in this arena. All of us con-tain multitudes. The figure of the teacher is easier to analyze in this respect because "our" voices from that position—especially when we teach entry-level required courses—are so obviously inflected by in-stitutional and disciplinary agendas that are not of our own making. Unlike the most prominent sophists, who were relative free agents in the academic marketplace, we don't get to make up the curriculum, or even decide where to place ourselves in it, let alone how much to charge for our services. We are citizens of a much larger institutional system that melds our voices into consensus, which we all then, more or less, bespeak. Likewise, most of us don't have the imaginative genius to invent even our own "approach," let alone an original criti-cal system, for teaching our assigned courses. We borrow or filter or sift methods from the current disciplinary arsenal—reader-response, process, deconstruction, whatever—tweaking them to our own pur-poses. And many of us don't always even design our own course ma-terials, using extant staff materials or developing such materials in a collective. That is especially so in composition, which has a long his-tory of intra-institutional collaboration and conformity. From my point of view, all of these inflections to our teacherly voice serve to dislocate the center of our pedagogical authority in ways that can be productive. For example, I often *prefer* to use other people's materials, especially when I teach composition courses. Standing before my class as a spokesman for, rather than the author of, my primary materials reminds me persistently of the medial position—the betweenness—I want, and feel I need, to inhabit in such a classroom.   141

As it pertains to the university-level classroom at least, teaching does not belong to any specific department or area as a writing subject. Few of us were trained much in teaching. Few of us spend much of our time *teaching* teaching. Few of us write much for publication con-cerning teaching (though we write an enormous amount in order to, and as we, teach.) Teaching is not, after all, our discipline, our field, our specialty. Teaching tends to fall *between* the disciplinary cracks, where it sort of belongs to all of us, or none of us. So it's between those cracks where I go to look for it. There's a lot of talk these days, has been for a while, about the generative possibilities of interdisciplinarity. I want to call attention to the prefix *inter* here and use it to characterize further what I mean by the between that teaching represents in our professional lives. Typically, when we think of interdisciplinary work, we think of combining discourses or methods from two distinct disciplines into a sort of hybrid in order to perform a new or divergent kind of work. But there is another way of thinking about that prefix: as the empty spaces *between* disciplines that are generally not even perceived let alone traversed or cultivated—like the gap *between* the two halves of my book that I am now gradually writing this *inter*-chapter into. It is into a gap of exactly that sort, that crack *in between* disciplines, that I keep going to write from the position of the teacher, that I am about to go now to engage with Plato.

Part 3

> *The genuine life of the personality is made available only through a dialogic penetration of that personality, during which it freely and reciprocally reveals itself.*
>
> MIKHAIL BAKHTIN[3]

I think I understand more fully now why I have felt, almost from the start, that the first half of this book should not be left to stand on its own, as a (proper) monograph, say. The two genres that I most rely on there—autobiography and literary criticism—might lead you to misunderstand that I believe the position of the teacher is constituted from two primary sources: who you are (as a function of personal

142

history) and what you know (as a function of disciplinary training). There is a long historical tradition of constructing teacherly facility, at the university level, as a combination of talent with technique.[4] Under the first of these terms, teaching is unteachable. Talent cannot after all be instilled. Under the second, it is not worth teaching, at least in a sustained curricular way. Technique can be "picked up" kind of piecemeal, along the way. Subtending this tradition is the assumption that if the right knowledge, and enough of it, is added to who you are, the pedagogy part will, sooner or later (with "experience" and the consequent on-the-fly acquisition of technique) take care of itself. Were I to stop my argument right here, I would risk leaving my own conception of the position of the teacher dangerously in the path of that tradition. And I don't want to. For without a theorizing framework, both talent and technique remain potentially vacuous.

That is where, for me, Plato came into it, back in 1994, and where he (properly) comes into it now. Much of the work I have done to this point has been to approach the position of the teacher in a writerly way. But it is just as important to develop that position in a readerly way. I understand, and respect, the need to accommodate "scholarly" work to the framework of established disciplinary conversations. I do a great deal of that kind of work in the essays that follow here. But in the case of Plato, I intend also to do something other than that. Not more or less. Other.

As they pertain to teaching, for example, the Platonic dialogues belong not just to experts in philosophy or rhetoric. They belong to us all, and most especially to any teacher who seeks to give serious thought to the *personal* stake he has in his own professional life. I am, after all, a professor teaching at a major university. I want to come to think about that work with the masters; I want to imagine myself as warranted, by the authority intrinsic to my position, to contend with them on *my* terms. From that vantage point I have some things that I think are quite original to offer. Chief among them is the demonstration—and tacit promise to other teachers and all students—that you

143

don't necessarily have to inundate yourself in the apparatus of academic discourses (though I do a great deal of that in any case) to have something rich and useful to say about Plato.

What all of this is to say is that there are certain kinds of texts that we have considerable experience approaching from the customary readerly positions of our disciplinary systems. The reader we play in that work is generally constructed along the lines of the "scholar" or the "researcher." I have nothing against those two modes of prefiguring reading in the profession. I engage in them all the time. But what I argue on behalf of here is the reader-as-teacher: a figurative position from which we can engage all kinds of texts that are written *by* teachers, in order *to* teach, and that *enact* their pedagogy. Which is why, I now see, it would be equally misleading to let the second half of the book stand on its own, as a (proper) monograph, say. It would be almost impossible to read it as anything more or less than disciplinary scholarship "on" Plato. And it's not. It's *inter*-disciplinary scholarship on Plato. I have written it from "between" the disciplines that have staked a claim to Plato, which is where I most hope to find other teachers interested in these texts for the reasons I am. The fact that I approach these dialogues (recalling Kathleen Blake Yancey) "first, always, as teacher," inflects my reading of them in every way I can think to name.

I'm sure every teacher reading this is pretty much like me in that certain writers and texts have become highly significant "voices" in the construction of your teacherly position. After enough re-readings, you start to carry those voices into the classroom with you—not so much as in conscious thinking but more in the mode of productive, inaudible bickering over what exactly to do, and why, and how, and when. My A-list encompasses a diverse array of often contradictory voices: the confident, iconoclastic Whitman of the 1855 version of "Song of Myself"; a chiding, dry Ecclesiastes calling me back with his matter-of-fact awareness of what most matters in the long run and what doesn't matter at all; a brash Francis Bacon ready to restart the whole enterprise from scratch, on his own terms; the wise, harmo-

144

nizing, sermonic Emerson, earnest, ethical, almost serene; an oddly down-to-earth Einstein coming up with those thought experiments with elevators moving near the speed of light; and of course, Plato, about whom I have chosen to write the second half of this book. This is not to say that I emulate, or even vaguely resemble, any of these teacherly figures. I don't. Only that I read these writers, and many others like them, as often as I can, from the position of the teacher: as one teacher engaging with another, trying not just to learn "technique" from these masters, but to converse with them, to contend with them, as if I, because I am a teacher, have a right to be there, just as you do with those figures you have chosen to listen to and argue with about the teacherly things that preoccupy you.

I offer my list to suggest that I could (possibly) have written the rest of my book about one or more of them, instead—with the same ambition, toward the same end, and with the same effect. I chose Plato because he is the one I have been the most intrigued and aggravated and compelled by over the last several years, because he was the one I was writing about at the time, and because he clearly has the credentials to serve in the capacity I am asking him to serve in here: as the teacher I am reading in order to suggest that more goes into the construction of the position of the teacher than just who you are and what you know. By reading Plato, I can theorize my conception of the position of the teacher in a way that I have not been able to in the first half of the book, and in the way that I have to in order for my argument to be complete. And in my role as teacher, I am, like any teacher, perfectly well-qualified to read him, and all the authors I mention above, and many more besides, in exactly the ways I need to in order to work out my own teacherly position. Once all of these other voices get into the mix—and they do for every teacher who takes work in the classroom seriously—things like who I am and what I know, like talent and technique, take on a whole different significance, or perhaps it is more accurate to say that it is only in that mix that they can begin to take on their *proper* significance.

In the same way that I am writing about Plato from *my* position as

teacher, I want to write about him in terms of *his* position as teacher
—rather than, for example, his disciplinary position as philosopher/
rhetorician, or his historical position as a real person, about whom we
might know maybe as much as you now know about me, from having
read the first half of this book. So how do I locate him in his position
as teacher? He never speaks in his own name, through his own voice.
Where is he then? Contained entirely in the figure of Socrates, at a
one-to-one correspondence, as some readers believe? Then who and
where is Socrates, that other real, historical philosopher/person that
needs to be accounted for in this equation? I will offer as I go ways of
answering these questions. For now, it is enough to say that my Plato,
the Plato-as-teacher, is in the same sort of between that I am, that all
teachers are. Because he is not himself contained in the dialogues, he
can contain multitudes. Of voices, that is. Some of which he is interested in standing foursquare inside of, some of which he tries on just
to walk around in for a while, some of which he merely hangs in front
of himself fleetingly and then discards as unfit. That is the Plato I am
looking for. The one who contradicts himself. The one I feel is willing
to join me in the position from which I am trying to write this interchapter—neither here nor there, neither self nor other—to get you to
the next half of my book. It's from that position that the teacher is always writing.

2

In Dialogue with Plato

INTRODUCTION TO PART 2

And every respectable scholar will know right away when a suppos-
edly scholarly text is not behaving itself or when it is not generating
any knowledge. Any good scholar will see that a sophistical text is a
little too playful, a little too self-indulgent, a little too angry, a little
too slipshod, a little too situated in the purely personal, a little too
unsure of itself. It keeps coming apart all the time. It never seems to
end or to know where to end.

JASPER NEEL[1]

Not to write a line (like Socrates) is perhaps not to privilege speech,
but to write by default and in advance, since, in this abstention, the
space of writing in which Plato already works is prepared and is
decided.

149

MAURICE BLANCHOT[2]

Thus in Plato's Socratic dialogues . . . laughter . . . remains in the
structure of the image of the major hero (Socrates), in the methods

for carrying on the dialogue, and—most importantly—in authentic
(not rhetorical) dialogicality itself, immersing thought itself in the
joyful relativity of evolving existence and not permitting it to con-
geal in abstractly dogmatic (monologic) ossification.

MIKHAIL BAKHTIN[3]

The following essays originate from texts that are quite a bit different from the ones I began with in "Race, Gender, and (Teaching a) Class," those relatively immediate, and clearly uncanonical, personal stories. Here I consider the much more historically remote and culturally valorized dialogues of Plato (particularly *Protagoras* and *Phaedrus*). We tend, though, to meet comparable difficulties when we try to use either of these two kinds of sources to get at matters of pedagogy. The former tend to be so enmeshed in the emotional contexts that constitute their significance *to us* that the inertia of the "personal" can be hard to overcome. The latter tend to be so enmeshed in the modes of authorization that constitute their significance *to others* that the momentum of the "scholarly" can be hard to resist.

My first move toward such resistance in the case of Plato has always been to imagine a Plato who is basically like me, to the limited extent at least that he is perplexed by, attracted to, disturbed about, certain kinds of problems related to teaching and learning. I read his dialogues on these matters as workings-out, through his various interlocutors, not so much of solutions to problems as surveys of their range and contours. And they help me immeasurably in my workings-out of my own perplexity with, my own attraction to, my own sense of disturbance about, a similar set of problems in a vastly different historical setting. In short, this Plato of mine becomes someone with whom I can actually engage in a dialogue that is productive for me because he is interested in the things that interest me in some of the same ways that they interest me. I am especially compelled by the forthrightness with which he faces the moral implications of the issues before him, and by the playfully ironic wit he uses to forestall,

150

even to foreclose, easy resolution. I start a conversation with this Plato—and then I go on to my situation, my concerns, my intellectual agenda. I tend not to feel very obligated therefore to the "real" historical Plato, or to his "real" historical characters; nor do I feel overly obligated to the various "Platos" that have arisen under the disciplinary aegis of philosophy or history of rhetoric in the contemporary academy. It is not my intention to subvert or deny any of those Platos. There are very precise ways in which I acknowledge, respect, and enjoy them. But I am interested, finally, in the Plato who lends himself to the position of the teacher.

A number of years ago I wrote a long essay on Coleridge's "Essays on Method." I became fascinated, as I worked through my reading of Coleridge, by his Plato, the one he refers to over and over again, the one who lends himself to his purposes. As part of that project I read a lot of Francis Bacon, whom Coleridge also deploys toward his purposes. And I noticed in reading Bacon how different was his Plato from Coleridge's. I noticed, too, how different was my Bacon from Coleridge's, as well as how different was my Plato from either of theirs. I mention all of this to suggest what I believe to be a fundamental reality of scholarly enterprise: We participate in an odd symbiotic relationship with the figures from the past upon whom we call to animate our/their arguments. While we help them in some respects to extend their influence into new settings, while their usefulness to us will inevitably be constrained by the ways in which they have been culturally received, they are, ultimately, what we are willing and able to make of them within the framework of the motives and interests we bring to the task. In short, they become part of a project that is, in the final analysis, quite "personal."

There are, of course, ongoing disciplinary conversations that inform what I have to say in these essays. We in composition studies, for example, have both witnessed and helped to foster an extraordinary recuperation of classical rhetoric over the last generation or so. The progress of this history began first, as I read it, with an earnest turn toward Aristotle's *Rhetoric*, who became, through the work of both

151

classicists and cognitivists, one of the gurus for the early process theories of composition. The original countercurrent to this general drift toward the respectability of disciplinarity was rooted in a particular take on Plato's rhetoric-related dialogues, excerpts from which I used to frame a number of my own public arguments during the mid-1980s. This countercurrent receded pretty quickly though, to be replaced more lately by a dramatic resurgence of interest in the sophists. Scholars like Victor Vitanza, Sharon Crowley, Susan Jarrett, to name only a few from our field—not to mention Jasper Neel, from whose remarkable book I borrow my epigraph—all have worked assiduously to promote alternatives to the more hegemonic texts of Plato and his pupil.[4] To the extent that I enter this conversation, it is more on a tangent than directly—through footnotes and asides—as a sophist might, I suppose.

Frankly, I came to Plato originally, and to a large extent still prefer to come, as a "general" reader. I read Plato—and drew many of the conclusions about his work that animate these essays—over a period of years before I turned my attention seriously to the various kinds of disciplinary scholarship that I acknowledge, sometimes quite assiduously, along the way here. In other words, I altered the temporal sequence that we usually imagine scholarly work following: I read and reread the "primary" text, using it to think through a set of issues that interested me "personally" without much concern for ongoing disciplinary discussions, let alone publication; and I did this primarily because my intellectual focus was on teaching, on my work in the classroom. When I first began to read what the "secondary" texts had to say, it was, again, to help me to think through pedagogical matters, from the interdisciplinary "between" I describe in my interchapter. Even here, I see the principal debate that I want these essays to enter as the one we are finally having in our discipline about teaching. In some ways then I have struggled, and continue to struggle, against the inevitable imperatives of established scholarly traditions in an effort to come at Plato, over and over again, anew, with my teacherly eyes dominating the view. The more scholarship I read, of course, the

152

more my Plato becomes "disciplined" by the regimens of academic specialisms. I understand that this process of professionalization is necessary and useful. For some reason, though, in the case of Plato in particular, I want as much as I can to conserve the prospect that is there for a general reader, to remain capable of imagining these texts as not simply important, or even teachable, cultural artifacts but as immediately pertinent to useful purposes right here and right now, both for me and for students.

But while I am neither a philosopher nor a historian of rhetoric, my work has inevitably engaged me with some of the discussions they are having. Originally, that engagement was vested in finding a counter to the appropriations of Aristotle that were, as I said, all the rage twenty years ago. While I have no problem assenting to most of Neel's dismantling of Aristotle's "voice," my own reservations were, initially, far more modest. I simply believed that grounding a rhetoric on audience-based concerns was conceptually problematic in ways that were being ignored and needed to be examined; and that, further, grounding the concept of *ethos* itself in textual constructions that are independent from the values and positions of the speaker was ethically problematic. And how could one find a more strident moralist to counter this view than Socrates? But as I read the Platonic texts to develop a set of more agreeable alternatives, I very quickly realized that Socrates was no better bargain than Aristotle. Who would want to recommend, either philosophically or pedagogically, a figure who, despite his obvious brilliance, was so often rude, incomprehensible, arrogant, even abusive in his domineering relationships with his peers, let alone his students and acolytes? He represented in these respects precisely what I thought it was urgent for a "professor" to avoid, what I saw all around me it was so easy to drift into, the self-satisfied belligerence of the indignant and self-righteous critic—the fate that all the time threatens to engulf me, that threatens anyone in a position whose power is, like ours, simultaneously both valorized and marginalized by the culture at large.

Right around this time, in the early 1980s, I attended a Lilly Founda-

153

tion Summer Seminar in Colorado Springs. The University of Pittsburgh sent me there to think about, and make recommendations concerning, our recently approved writing-across-the-curriculum requirement. Among the available options for a mandatory reading group was one on Plato's dialogues, which I chose with great delight. The first thing I noticed about the reading group's director was that, like me, he had fun reading Plato, that he saw playfulness, even farce, all over the place. He read the dialogues as constructions, authored texts, as literature. And I realized: this is what *I* want to do; this is what I *know* how to do. The effect of that recognition was to jar loose in my mind, completely and permanently, Plato-as-author from the various characters that populated his dialogues—among whom Socrates might be an especially privileged one, but a character nonetheless. I found this shift in perspective liberating; it opened up these texts for a sort of work that I had not before felt authorized to undertake. What follows here is another stage in that work. And I want specifically to represent it as a stage, as a set of provisional readings that change in some ways even through the progress of these essays, that will most assuredly change, perhaps even in radical ways, the next time I come back to these dialogues, to read them, to teach them, to write about them. This may seem a scandalous sort of reservation for any "scholar" to declare at the outset concerning the status of the "knowledge" he has to offer. I make no apologies for it, but I offer an explanation.

I am willing at this point in my progress through Greek rhetoric to concur in most respects with the neo-sophistic-ates, some of whom I name above, about both Aristotle and Socrates. But I remain convinced that it is a mistake to presume that the Platonic system is essentially Socratic in either letter or spirit. As Neel notes, and as any reader of Plato must admit:

154

> One need do no more than read *Phaedrus* to see both that Plato tries
> to exclude certain maneuvers under the name sophist and that he
> uses each of those maneuvers in his attempted exclusion. (191)

What are we to make of a writer who does such a thing? Is he, as is I suppose possible, simply blind to his own self-contradictions, so transfixed by the oratorical mystifications of his silver/sliver-tongued mentor that he cannot see their absurdity in his textual representations? Is he aware of his duplicity, but confident that he is a slick enough craftsman to elide the difficulties they present long enough to keep his readers blind to them? Or is he, as I prefer to think, not only quite aware of the manner in which what is being *said* is so often at direct odds with how it is being *written,* but intensely *working* to make his readers aware of those disjunctions also? These pieces are just too complex and crafted to have been designed by the sort of self-deluded buffoon (or gifted manipulator) who would fall prey (or would have us do so) to the stupidities we need to attribute to him (or to ourselves) in order to imagine him as unabashedly Socratic in his philosophic system. Or maybe I just want him to be that way, as I once hoped Aristotle, or Socrates himself, would be what I was looking for.

The difference between them and Plato, though, from my point of view, is that Plato provides systemically an array of gaps and fissures through which a reader can enter highly ambiguous spaces in relation to the declared significance of the texts. With Socrates and Aristotle, no matter how hard *I* try at least, I simply can't find such room for play. In these essays, I have chosen to navigate those spaces. And I have enjoyed that work immensely. By the same token, I recognize the degree to which I am, in the process, taking issue with the dominant view of how Plato stood in relation to the positions he allows Socrates, most often, to deliver to us.

John Poulakos, for example, argues for this reading of the agenda driving Plato's dialogic form:

Unlike an oration, a form of discourse making up one part of a larger setting, many Platonic dialogues include a setting making up one part of a larger discourse. The setting itself . . ., the affairs of the characters . . ., their circumstances . . ., their reputation . . ., as well as their conduct during the course of the dialogue . . . are all targets

155

for commentary. But as the dialogue proceeds, all these circumstantial elements fade into the background and the main idea begins to emerge and take center stage. By the end of the dialogue, say the *Gorgias*, the focus is not on Gorgias' fame as a brilliant declaimer, Polus' youthful immaturity, or Callicles' impolite behavior; rather, it is on a set of significant questions: What is rhetoric? Is it better to commit or to suffer wrong? What does it mean to be powerful? Which life is superior, the active or the contemplative? In this way, the circumstantial elements represented in and occasioning or facilitating the internal workings of the dialogue are ultimately subordinated to the ideas the dialogue expounds. But if this is so, the reader must acknowledge (along with Gorgias, Polus, and Callicles) that in the final analysis, rhetoric needs to concern itself with justice; that to be powerful means to be in control of one's appetites; and that the contemplative life is superior to a life of action.[5]

For me, the opposite readerly reaction is effected by the inclusion of context in Plato's form: The ideas the dialogue expounds are ultimately subordinated to its internal workings. A good example of this is, in fact, the *Gorgias*, in which the argument, in the final analysis, degrades from a stable binary into such a state of bitter irresolution that it is nearly impossible for me to draw firm conclusions about justice or controlling one's appetites or the kind of life I might lead, or anything else for that matter. An "oration" would, in fact, have been much more effective at accomplishing that sort of pedagogical work.

Poulakos goes on:

> Plato's dialogical discourses did not vary substantively from their sophistical counterparts—they, too, were seeking to stage playful discursive encounters, the kind that would guide their readers through a specific path and point them to a specific goal. But unlike sophistical rhetoric, which had relied on the susceptibility of large crowds to enchanting language performed in a public place, Plato's dialogues aimed at the singular reader who could follow an intelligent conversation and adopt its lessons for life. (104)

156

Again, I find myself moving the opposite way on this. It is, for me, precisely via the multivocality and the intracontextuality of the dialogic form that the reader is drawn, figuratively of course, into the public space of the crowd. The reader is thereby precluded from functioning as a singularity but is compelled, as I try to show, into positions that are doubled (in *Protagoras*), even trebled and quadrupled (in certain parts of *Phaedrus*). It becomes from such positions virtually impossible to "adopt . . . lessons for life," at least if those lessons are imagined to be identical with what Socrates has to teach.

It is true that oration is a "form of discourse making up one part of a larger setting," and in that respect it has certain obvious advantages over a written text. But that setting, which is so constructive of the rhetorical context for one who is present at the actual delivery, is lost in the act of textualization. It can, of course, be recovered. But in the case of remote contexts, like Athens in the fifth century B.C., that recovery requires extensive historical scholarship, for most of which one must rely on others—experts—to provide, in which case the act of reading becomes highly mediated by academic and professional convention. The advantage of the dialogue, at least in the literary form that Plato deployed it, is precisely the fact that it carries so much of its baggage—setting, characters, their conduct and concerns— with it. It is possible then for a reader to find a position to stand in, and to work from in a sophisticated readerly way, without years of training or the subordination of her readerly project to professional mediators.

It is with respect to this paradox—my simultaneous declaration as a general reader and as a participant in the larger arguments ongoing about Plato's place in the contemporary academy—that I cast these essays as provisional. I may reach the point where I become as ungenerous in my reading of Plato, vis-à-vis the sophists for example, as I am now toward Aristotle and Socrates, as so many of my colleagues in and out of the discipline are these days. But I am not there now, and I want to make the case for my Plato before I/they/he can change my mind.

157

PROTAGORAS AND PEDAGOGY

When we were inside, we came upon Protagoras walking in the portico, and walking with him in a long line were, on one side Callias, son of Hipponicus; his stepbrother Paralus, the son of Pericles; and Charmides, son of Glaucon; and on the other side Pericles' other son, Xanthippus; Philippides, son of Philomelus; and Antimoerus of Mende, the most eminent of Protagoras' pupils, who is studying professionally, to become a Sophist. Those who followed behind listening to their conversation seemed to be for the most part foreigners—Protagoras draws them from every city that he passes through, charming them with his voice like Orpheus, and they follow spellbound—but there were some Athenians in the band as well. As I looked at the party I was delighted to notice what special care they took never to get in front or to be in Protagoras' way. When he and those with him turned round, the listeners divided this way and that in perfect order, and executing a circular movement took their places each time in the rear. It was beautiful.[1]

158

Beautiful, indeed. The choreography of this procession, as Plato renders it through the eyes of Socrates, is both balletic and burlesque, deftly depicting in one sweeping turn the range of contradictions that riddle teacher-student relationships, especially those geared toward "studying professionally."[2] This image of the professor as the solar figure—around whom many satellites carefully circulate—is strongly entrenched in the contemporary academy, reinforced by a wide array of both disciplinary and institutional forces, not to mention the broader cultural forces that serve to regulate the roles and relationships available to professors and "their" students. Protagoras is a living emblem of the multiple ambiguities that result from the confluence of these forces in a pedagogical transaction. Is Protagoras seeking some form of multiple self-replication? imparting a useful and important body of knowledge? training his listeners to be better and more productive citizens? pursuing some modicum of shared truth? Is he, in other words, arrogant and egocentric? wise and helpful? earnest and responsible? curious and pure-minded? And are his "followers" (here in the literal as well as the figurative sense) staying to his rear and out of the way out of deference to his authority? respect for his knowledge? fear of his power? love for his wisdom? Is Protagoras a noble leader or a domineering tyrant? Are his students servile sycophants or devoted disciples? I do not ask these questions with the intention of picking out, by careful analysis of the image Plato offers us, or even the subsequent dialogue, the correct answers and dismissing the others. Certainly, Plato is making fun of Protagoras—as he lampoons Hippias for giving "his explanation ex cathedra" (314; 314c) and Prodicus, who "has such a deep voice that there was a kind of booming noise in the room which drowned the words" (314; 316a). Certainly, Protagoras and his audience would defend themselves if given the opportunity, as to some extent they are in the dialogue that follows this opening scene. What I want to suggest at the outset is simply how difficult it can be to determine what is driving a pedagogical relationship and what is being given or gotten, sought or proffered, accomplished or avoided, in its playings-out.

159

The tensions Plato explores in this dialogue are endemic to all ped-agogical relationships, but especially so at the graduate level: Here our roles as masters and mentors, as gate-minders and door-openers, are riven by contradictory combinations of power and humility, au-thority and deference, knowledge and reputation. And graduate stu-dents come driven by their own contradictory desires for emulation and mastery, originality and conformity, rebellion and compliance, often choosing a program specifically for the opportunity to "work with" or even "under" (and inevitably to some extent, "against") a par-ticular professor. In this professorial role, whether or not we are promi-nent or notorious enough to attract Protagoras's sort of "following," we work to construct our own future colleagues and replacements—most especially in a discipline like English, where "studying profes-sionally" means, most often, preparing to become a professor. When we begin to see our mission in such a wider scope, it is clear that we serve, either tacitly or expressly, as "disciplinarians" in both of the ap-plicable senses of that word, being called upon to share and cultivate our highly specialized modes of inquiry, but also to enforce the "rules" of the discourses, and the institutions, that allow those modes of in-quiry to do the work they are expected to do.

A position inclined to these ways of marshalling authority is rich with possibilities but also fraught with dangers. While graduate students are not quite our colleagues, they will be shortly. Thus, one might say, our mission is to teach them to be our equals, a pedagogi-cal oxymoron, to the extent at least that the location of authority in the teacher-student relationship is left highly vexed. So where do we turn for a way of thinking about a pedagogical relationship that is being pulled and pushed in so many contrary directions by so many different forces? One such place is a text like the *Protagoras*, which I want to use not so much to ask any startling new questions, but more to ask questions so basic to the pedagogical enterprise that we simply do not keep them clearly enough, or consistently enough, in our view, often allowing them to be answered already for us, tacitly, by the dis-ciplinary and institutional systems within which we must function.

These are not questions, finally, of technique or persona, but both precede and construct such matters of practice, in terms that we can, to some extent, establish for ourselves. When we don't, we simply allow them to be constructed for us by our ambient professional surroundings.

Let me begin where Socrates himself begins, shortly after the above vignette, when he says, on behalf of Hippocrates, who wants to "study professionally" with the eminent Protagoras: "he would be glad to be told what effect it will have on him" (316; 318a).[3] What effect will it have? How will he be changed? By his teacher. Specifically. What strikes me about this question is how obvious and basic a one it seems to be for a teacher to be asking. And how rarely it is asked. What effect will it have? Important particularly in the part of our work that prepares others to become professionals at what we do. For such a question places the pedagogical transaction at the center of the problematic, rather than, for example, the professor or the discipline, both of which have developed already for themselves highly overdetermined senses of their authority. This shift of focus allows us to address much more directly, and perhaps begin to redress, one of the more troubling conundrums of academic life: The qualities that we often tacitly encourage by our teaching practices diminish rather than enhance the prospect for a student to develop precisely the kinds of "authority" we not only admire but demand from our peers and colleagues.

I have used the term *project* in a number of different ways thus far. In the preface, for example, I use it specifically in relation to this book, distinguishing between the "material" projects of its two halves and the "ideological" project that their jointure makes possible. In my essay of October 5 to the Race and Gender class I use it to name the ground or framework out of which, to me, genuine intellectual work emerges. I use it in the introduction to this part of the book to suggest the sort of contention that inevitably arises from engaged reading— in this case between Socrates or Plato and me, primarily; but also, to some extent, between my approach toward Plato and the dominant contemporary disciplinary approaches to his work. It is a word I use in every course I teach, from freshman writing to graduate seminars, to persuade students that they need to find ways to become fully vested in the writing, the reading, the research, the intellectual work, I am calling upon them to do.

In each of these instances, I am raising a different kind of question concerning relative authority in unbalanced power relationships, like those between teacher and student, between reader and author, between individual scholar and disciplinary convention. In the case of this dialogue, there are two distinct "authorities" expressly in contest: Socrates' and Protagoras's. Hippocrates, putatively the primary beneficiary of this argument, can only become an authorized contestant in the dispute if we do all the work that is necessary to stake his claim. The question—if we want to imagine Hippocrates as a potential colleague rather than a dependent minion—is how can we make it possible, necessary even, for him to do this work for himself? It's not enough, really, just to authorize him to speak. He needs to have something that he genuinely wants to say, and he needs to be able to enter the conversation with the prospect of actually being heard. That is not an easy task when the ongoing conversation is being controlled by figures as dominant as Socrates and Protagoras. But in some ways, Hippocrates' problem is not unlike the problem that all graduate students face in their progress toward collegiality with us. Certainly most new graduate students feel they are at a huge disadvantage in that they are not yet proficient with the specialized discourses of the discipline that we tend to take for granted. I teach a lot of first-year graduate students, and I know the frustration they experience because of that perceived deficit. When they ask for help with a place to start, we have a variety of quite different choices, each of which sends a different message about how authority is achieved and, of course, produces a different "effect."

We can direct them to a variety of currently dominant theorists and urge them to master, with our help perhaps, those discourses. This is something like what I imagine Protagoras might do. We can "take

162

them under our wing" and inculcate them with our own preferred critical approach/ideology. This is something like what I imagine Socrates might do. Each of these "professorial" tacks has a long cultural history and I don't want to dismiss or even demean them. But what they have in common is the ongoing, enforced "absence" of the student, who must delay and defer—sometimes for years—her own authority in favor of those that are already sanctioned. Collegiality is precluded.

But there is, I think, an alternative that allows for immediate participation in the conversation, and I find the term *project* useful in making that alternative visible. Every graduate student, no matter how new they are to the profession, already has a set of ambitions and desires and needs, as well as a material focus—something specific they really want to read and think about—that brought them here. This is not, after all, the sort of profession that people tend to enter without some prior reflection. That's basically all I mean by a project in this context: a kind of rough statement of what you are here in a committed way to do—through your reading and writing and teaching—for your own good reasons, and why. Anyone who has that has a place to start: which is with whatever is right in front of them at the moment. One needn't, for example, become fluent with a professional discourse to have something of immediate interest and consequence to say about Plato, or Adrienne Rich, or Amiri Baraka. I have freshmen who read those kinds of texts with great energy and wisdom all the time, even though they don't come into the enterprise with any prior experience with these writers. I urge them to reflect on their readerly positions, and to extend that process of reflection, through the considered use of their sources, into a project they genuinely want to think about. And they often do it quite well. In other words, if you are reading a text in an engaged way, you are automatically authorized to speak about it. Neither must one have taught for years and years to begin to frame, on and for one's own sake, good, useful questions about classroom practices or processes. If you are teaching a class

163

in an engaged way, you are automatically authorized to speak about it. Expertise, in its aspect of facility with the current specialized discourses, inevitably follows engagement; and not vice versa.

We can both allow and expect all graduate students to function, at this most fundamental level, as our colleagues and peers—right from the start and not simply during the final stages of work on a dissertation. All it requires is shifting the weight of authority (and responsibility) around, both in the individual courses we teach and over the longer duration of our programs of study. This is not to say that then we ourselves don't get to speak. Just the opposite. Once we authorize students to their own projects, we also authorize our own. At the graduate level, this collegiality produces then the same range of effects as our other professional peer relationships produce: There is some generative collaboration, there is some productive contest, and there is some disruptive conflict, each of which has specific effects on the decorum of the classroom and on the kind of relationship(s) we can have with students. I wrote about all three of these effects, through metaphors of silence, in the last two sections of the first half of the book: the renegotiation of my reading of the silences in the class-opening read-arounds in response to the group's objections to them; and my own experience of accomplished silence during our final class session. Because pedagogical moves of the sort I describe tend to diffuse, if not extinguish, the customary aura of professorial eminence that a number of institutional structures—some of which involve graduate students as complicitous partners—engender and support, they will produce a range of side effects as varied as the individuals affected by them: excitement or irritation, motivation or frustration, respect or anger, relief or fear.

164   One of the consequences of this shift in balance is, then, to raise the level of risk, for both parties, but especially for the student. As Socrates sees it the stakes for the student are high in the enterprise of "purchasing knowledge" from an expert, because you are "gambling dangerously with all of you that is dearest to you" (313; 313e–314a). This may seem an almost paranoiac hyperbole from our highly pro-

fessionalized perspective. It is important to remember though that for Socrates "knowledge cannot be taken away in a parcel. When you have paid for it you must receive it straight into the soul. You go away having learned it and are benefited or harmed accordingly" (313; 314a–b). The sense not only of immediacy but also of urgency that this lends to pedagogy is one that is alien to our customary notions of what kind of work we do—largely, I believe, because the entrenched conceptualizations of teaching in our everyday professional and insti-tutional lives would, from Socrates' perspective, seem disturbingly ill-defined, at least by contrast with its highly developed academic counterpart, research. It may be hard for us to imagine anyone being anything other than improved by the knowledge we have to offer. And even when we can, we may end up with profound differences of opinion, among ourselves or with students, about what, if any, those improvements are. But that may have less to do with our own arro-gance or myopia than with the manner in which what counts as knowledge in the university—especially so at the graduate level where concepts of "specialized" "expertise" control its propagation—has been scrubbed clean of its "value" (in its moral sense rather than, for example, its economic sense—though, ironically, Socrates keeps using marketplace metaphors to flesh out his position) by so many kinds of commodification. Socrates would probably have the same general complaint about us as he had about his sophistic contemporaries: "that some of these men also are ignorant of the beneficial or harm-ful effects on the soul of what they have for sale, and so too are those who buy from them" (313; 313d–e).

Now we can't just start warning our students about the potential consequences of study to their "souls"—at least not in most public universities—without risking some unwanted side effects. But it is important for us to look beyond these problems of nomenclature to see what application the concerns of Socrates and Protagoras—and more importantly of Plato, who orchestrates this conversation from a distance with his customary combination of dignified aplomb and wry irony—have to our own. In this light, as far as I can see anyway,

165

one of the things Plato wants to get at is the relatively practical matter of benefit or harm, better or worse. To the degree that this is also
a matter of good and evil is open to a wide range of applications, including, of course, those of both Socrates and Protagoras. In short,
Plato is prospecting for an instrument of measurement, a yardstick
if you will, that will provide a guidepost for both valuation (from an
intrinsic vantage point) and e-valuation (from an extrinsic vantage
point) in the pedagogical enterprise.[4] "Faced with these considerations," Socrates asks, "would people agree that our salvation would
lie in the art of measurement?" (347; 356e). It is unlikely that anyone's
"salvation," including our own, is very often at stake in our seminars
and classrooms. And this is fortunate, given the "art of measurement"
that we have for teaching in the contemporary university. It is difficult, for example, for me to think of the many different forms and
practices for "evaluating" my teaching over the past twenty years in
terms either of "art" or of "measurement." On the other hand, we
have very sophisticated and elaborate ways of measuring our accom-
plishments as scholars and researchers. In that disparity—not only in
complexity, but also in kind—we begin to get at the root of the problem we might have in satisfying Socrates' question about the "effect"
of what we do when we "teach." Most of us, most often, simply don't
know—and don't have any good way of finding out or, frankly, any
pressure on us to come up with an answer. It is not merely now a
matter of finding different instruments of measurement. What we
need to do is think much more closely, as Plato does here through his
mouthpieces Socrates and Protagoras, about what it is we want to
find a way of measuring, as we have found very precise ways for measuring our scholarship and research.

166   The structure of any complex system is always most strained at
joints such as these, where contrary pairs are linked and differenti-
ated, mutually enhancing and limiting one another, not to mention
defining the means by which labors will be divided, status accorded
or withheld, relative value assigned. No matter which of these two—
teaching or research—is given greater weight in any particular depart-

ment or institution, we have already proclaimed, by so distinguishing them, that one is not the other. And that, I think, is the problem with many of the current attempts to resuscitate or reclaim something we want to call "teaching": It is by definition not "research." This presents a considerable barrier, to get back to Plato, when it comes to thinking about "what we have for sale" at the graduate level. Almost all approaches to graduate curricula and certification are based on the assumption that we are in the business of producing researchers. And most of the roles and slots available to those who teach graduate courses are based on the premise that we have demonstrated before-the-fact expertise *as* researchers. Teaching, if and when it comes into it at all, is approached more as a craft or an art that may be enhanced (the potential for which is already possessed as a talent) by experience but that cannot really itself be taught. Or even worse, as a kind of drudgery that must be endured in order to allow us to do our "real work," which is research. This leaves teaching vulnerable to the major complaint that Socrates has about the "field" of his contemporary sophists, a position he touches on only briefly with Protagoras, though he devotes considerable portions of other dialogues (especially, e.g., *Gorgias*) to this issue. "On what matter," Socrates asks, "does the Sophist make one a clever speaker?" (312; 312d–e). The implied answer is that there is no "matter" to this profession, at least not in the same sense that other more customary disciplines—medicine, music, painting—have their own bodies of knowledge and specialized discourses. And "teaching" as it is circumscribed by the strictures of the contemporary academy is much like sophistic rhetoric in that respect. Outside of schools of education, in which teaching has been substantiated by a framework of certificatory procedures, it has no "matter," no "field," precisely because we have defined it as not-research, a distinction that most of the arguments on behalf of teaching these days take unproblematically for granted (in some cases by seeking to translate it into the category of "service," an even more feeble counterpart to "research"). By what means then could it possibly accrue the sort of "matter" that we associate with our research areas: the methodological instruments, the specialized discourses, all of which are now prerequisites for disciplinary status in the university? Consequently, and ironically, all of us teach, but none of us ever really *learn* how to teach in a systematic way, nor do we make central to our mission the teaching of teaching.

One of the most significant, and still largely unexamined, effects of the gradual shift over the last thirty years from a teaching- to a research-based economy in higher education (and this is especially accessible to scrutiny at the graduate level, which was always research-based) has been a profound transformation of the dominant figurative relationship between professor and student. For example, in an academic system that defines the classroom as its primary laboratory, the product of one's work, the equivalent of the bottom line, if you will, is going to be the student that such a classroom, or a congeries of such classrooms over a period of years, constitutes or shapes or produces. Here, Socrates could get an answer to his question, if not in advance then at some time after the fact. In such a system, one's audience and one's colleagues are present to one another in most of their interactions and are able to communicate with one another in relatively immediate, informal, and sustained ways. Power, prestige, and reputation are then achieved locally and by means of the pedagogical relationship.

It was quite common in the fifties and sixties for colleges to promote themselves, and compete with one another for prospective students, in such terms, and this same tendency found expression to some extent even at the graduate level, in the development of programs like the Master of Arts in Teaching and the Doctor of Arts, both of which were designed as alternative structures for "professional study." This version of the mission of the university—with teaching at the center rather than the periphery—survives today in some quarters, but for the most part, and especially so for large universities, the primary laboratory for one's work must be outside the classroom, with the only meaningful arena for the disposition of the knowledge thus constructed being by publication for disciplinary peers. In such a system, one's primary audience—one's colleagues or "students" depending on how one looks at it—are generally absent or remote, available to one another only on a delayed basis (often with gaps of years between publication, reception, and response) and only through the highly mediated and severely disciplined publishing marketplaces. Power, prestige, and reputation are, then, achieved extra-institutionally, circuitously, and exclusive of the classroom.

There is little incentive—and little good reason, actually—to abandon this latter set of conditions in favor of the former. We need instead to begin to find better ways to make teaching a fit "field" for the latter kind of professorial activity, reintegrating thereby our professional identities with our local arenas, back to the level of the classroom and to teacher-student interactions and relationships. Let me work through some of the implications of this contrast, using the opportunity both to extend some of the arguments I have already begun to sketch out and to make clear what I want my position *not* to be taken to mean. It might seem on first take, for example, that I am seeking simply to reverse the historical trend to subordinate teaching (as a "measured" credential) to research as the primary index of professorial status, reinscribing the fundamental polarity that divides them and falling prey in the process to an un-de(re)constructed nostalgia for a social system that valorizes orality and "presence" over textuality and "absence." The apparent appropriateness of such a critique is amplified by the fact that I am making my case through a discussion that seems to warrant a Socratic—that is, logocentric—pedagogy. I try to forestall, if not circumnavigate, that critique by stating forthrightly that I am not calling for a simple restoration of teaching, and the professorial personae concomitant with it, to its rightful throne in our disciplinary hierarchy. Nor do I favor a resuscitation of some neological version of the "Socratic method" as a regimen for classroom discussion. On the contrary, I am suggesting that the only way we will ever escape from our comfortable addiction to an even more insidious and simplistic nostalgia—one that constructs our current notions of "teaching" in terms that preclude it from the

169

sorts of "textuality" (and critical inquiry) that poststructuralist criticism recognizes and analyses in almost all other institutional systems—is to destabilize the binary that is at its root. That binary, which regulates more materially than any other I can think of our day-to-day lives, as well as the much broader contours of our "careers" or our "reputations," remains, ironically, out of bounds by its very composition: Teaching is not-research. Research is not-teaching. And that is that.

I open the process of destabilization by asking a fairly matter-of-fact question: On the basis of what terms is this polarity being maintained and enforced? One of them is "knowledge": what counts as knowledge, where and how it is to be produced, accounted for, accorded its status. The generally accepted cliché that governs the economy of our profession—finding its expression both in the way we talk about "our work" and in how we are rewarded for it with money or prestige—is that we produce this commodity, knowledge, generally through individual and private processes of "research," and then we share it in one form (full strength) with our colleagues through publication and in another form (watered down) with our students through classroom interactions. What all of this ignores is the simplistic notion of knowledge upon which such a paradigmatic fiction depends; preventing us, for example, from systematically examining the ways in which knowledge is inevitably regimented by the invisible matrices of disciplinary media (especially academic journals and presses) and professional forums (including, often, quite informal social networks). We might pursue part of this examination by talking about the hegemony of the "article," with all of its attendant characteristics and constraints, about alternative genres, or voices that are thereby excluded or marginalized. Or we might initiate a debate about where we are, or should be, drawing the line between knowledge and not-knowledge. For example, the most simplistic way of reading our current professional strategies is to say that any "work" that finds its terminus in juried publication is, by definition, constitutive of "knowledge," while anything else that we write—say, for example, the kind of material that the first half of this book comprises—or, more to the point, that happens in a classroom, is not. We have all experienced occasions when the pedagogical transaction produces (rather than simply transmits) knowledge, both for us and for our students. That experience is much more common, obviously, in a small, discussion-based seminar than in a large lecture hall. But even that latter, perhaps, could be a site for producing knowledge if we look at it from the right angle, or think about the prospects of such a setting in the right way. I, we, have no way of knowing, mostly because we are not encouraged —by the way the teaching-research binary is posed for us—to look for such a possibility.

And further, if we presume that the primary import of our research-generated knowledge is to influence others, to change the way people or systems function or behave, to have an "effect," then there are clearly ways in which teaching—an activity that puts most of us in sustained intellectual contact with well over one hundred students every year—might also be seen as profoundly productive of certain kinds of "influence," of certain kinds of "change," of certain kinds of "effects," at least as much so as the small-circulation-journal article might. The sort of "influence" that we wield in the classroom is often demeaned in inverse proportion to the degree to which we often exaggerate the influence the average university professor actually wields through publication. These may be unpleasant issues for us to face, both personally and professionally, but any meaningful examination of the currency that drives the economy of our profession must sooner or later attend to them.

Another significant term by which the distinction between teaching and research is enforced is an extraordinarily (for us) naive notion of textuality. Again, the cliché seems to presume that research is textual and teaching is not. Our scholarly oeuvre is static and portable—and therefore eligible for certain kinds of measurement, both quantitative and qualitative—in ways that our pedagogical work is not; and it lends itself to institutional efficiencies in ways that our teaching does not. But to presume that the classroom and the figurative roles that

171

we and our students occupy and play out there are either pre- or post-textual constructions or, even worse, not textual at all, is to fall into obvious contradiction with our current critical biases, a contradiction that happens, at the moment, to allow us to under(deter)mine teaching as we construct the preferred versions of our work, as well as to deploy unselfconsciously an array of pedagogical practices that are directly contrary to our "professed" critical positions.

It is important to recognize and take full advantage of the textuality of the classroom and what we do there, to see that site as eligible for, even demanding of, our most careful, sophisticated, complex, critical scrutiny, not unlike all of the other cultural "texts" we have generally made it our business to write about over the last twenty years or so. In this process—as we begin to find discursive systems for sharing our "work" on teaching through the customary "outside" professional networks (conferences, journals, newsletters, etc.)—we will necessarily be drawn simultaneously more and more "inside," into our own local settings, where we can inquire with some rigor about our own students, the textbooks we are ordering for them to buy, about our collegial relationships, or lack of them, in our department, across disciplines, about our curricula, the administrative personnel and structures that circumscribe their possibilities, and so on—and drawn to all of this in a much richer and more provocative way than we can ever be as long as the teaching/research binary remains uncharted and unchallenged. Such a shift in our angle of vision would open up a new arena for critical scrutiny and potential publication, as well as foster a more self-conscious reference to classroom-specific issues in our other modes of research, an especially crucial matter in a discipline such as ours, which has so few extra-academic outlets. And we will simultaneously be inclined to examine potentially fruitful analogies, or differences, between the sort of teaching we do in our classrooms and the sort we do through juried publication. The real promise of "our work" cannot be fulfilled until we give it a full turn toward this multitude of micro-settings, making legible to ourselves and to our absent colleagues the significance not only of their commonalties, but

172

more importantly of their differences. Then we can begin to get some purchase on what we want to be our version of the question "what effect will it have?"

Realistically, what I have just proposed is not going to happen easily or any time soon, but there are ways in which we can start to think about this matter on a fundamental level. One of them is through the concept of change as it applies to the pedagogical contract, a theme that in one guise or another animates much of the discussion between Socrates and Protagoras. There is, for example, the concern with knowing rather than knowledge that follows almost immediately on Protagoras's first vacuous answer to Socrates' question about "effect," an answer in which he lays claim merely to the cliché of continual betterment. Socrates then follows up, simply, "toward what . . . and better at what" (317; 318d). Inevitably, then, the conversation turns to matters of value, specifically the issue of whether "virtue"—first in its political and later also in its broader moral sense—can or cannot be taught.

At the outset of the argument, Protagoras claims to teach only what his students "come to learn": the "art of politics" (317; 319a),[5] which in Socrates' opinion cannot be taught. By the end of the dialogue, Protagoras comes to think that, well, maybe it can't be taught (at least not when it is synonymous with "virtue"), while Socrates begins to think that maybe it can. The answer to that conundrum is, in large measure, beside the point, if not to them, then at least to me. What is telling is that they are willing to confront it and talk about it, and generally we are not. I don't mean the old bromides about producing better citizens or more decent people, both of which seem to me to be blind alleys for us in ways that they may not have been for Plato's Greece. But more simply and narrowly, what is the "good" toward which our pedagogical activities are driven or directed? Again, the issue is not what is being *ex*changed in the transaction, but how the parties are being changed by it, actively, over time, by some process of interaction. It is not so much a matter of a teacher's having arrived at a position of authority or expertise, of *being* knowledgeable, acquir-

173

ing thereby the right, and the rituals, to determine when a student has done so, but where each of these parties is heading in their institutionally constructed relationship, how they are respectively, and mutually, *becoming* knowledgeable.

This theme is recapitulated in the dispute about Simonides' poem, an arcane demonstration—and spoof—of sophisticated literary criticism, aspects of which I examined in my final missive to the Race and Gender class. Once again: The disagreement between Socrates and Protagoras turns on the question of whether the statement "Hard is it . . . to become/ a good man truly" is fundamentally like or different from the statement "To be noble . . . / Is hard" (333; 339b–c). In short, whether "to become" and "to be" are the same, or different. Protagoras says the same, Socrates different. On one level, the argument seems to be a long and torturous bit of philological hairsplitting, exactly the kind of thing that gives academics a bad name. Even Socrates says, at the argument's close: "Conversation about poetry reminds me too much of the wine parties of second-rate and commonplace people" (340; 347c). But the distinction Socrates has in mind is central both to his critique of Protagoras and to his implicit theory of education. For a conception of knowledge that is based on the economy of "being" will, in effect, exile the process of coming-to-know from the classroom, where teacher and student are present to and engaged with one another. The teacher will have achieved expertise beforehand, usually through hard, private labors, and will then display that expertise— usually in the form of a lecture, an extended disquisition, or questions with prefigured answers. And students will usually use their time in class to take note(s) of what is being said and to display, through various testing devices or written work, the degree to which they have come to "know" the proffered material.

174

The key word here, on both sides of the transaction, is display. Just before the discussion of Simonides' poem, in fact, Socrates and Protagoras have a testy exchange about the ground rules of their dialogue. After a particularly.long "answer" to one of Socrates' questions the following exchange takes place:

. . . I'm a forgetful sort of man, Protagoras, . . . cut down your answers and make them shorter if I am to follow you.

What do you mean by 'make my answers short'? Am I to make
them shorter than the subject demands?

Of course not.

As long as is necessary then?

Yes.

As long a reply as *I* think necessary or *you*?

What they told me, I answered, is that you have the gift both of
speaking yourself and of teaching others to speak, just as you prefer
—either at length, so that you never run dry, or so shortly that no
one could beat you for brevity. If then you are going to talk to me,
please use the second method and be brief. (329–30; 334c–335a)

After several unsuccessful attempts by both parties and other listeners to resolve the dispute, Socrates proposes a reversal of their roles:
Protagoras will ask the questions and Socrates will answer. In the
course of all of this, the issue of teaching—Protagoras's worthiness
to become mentor to Hippocrates—is never directly addressed. Yet
both parties enact for him, and for their larger audience, and then
dispute about, the two primary discursive relationships available to
teacher and student when they interact: one speaks, the other listens,
resulting in a series of "long speeches"; or one asks, the other responds,
resulting in a discussion. The former model, whether it is the teacher
or student speaking or listening, enacts a pedagogy of display. Usually, the speaker is constructed as "full" of knowledge which is being
deposited in the "empty" vessel of the listener (as, e.g., in Paulo Freire's
"banking" metaphor). The latter enacts a pedagogy of construction;
that is, one in which knowledge has the prospect for being constituted mutually in the process of the interaction rather than in seclu-
sion beforehand or afterward.

175

This may seem a superficial observation. Of course, everyone
knows the difference between lecture- and discussion-based pedagogies. Or do we? As I try to piece together and learn something from
this section of the dialogue, I am led to think that, for Socrates at

least, the latter is going to be a legitimate alternative to the former
only if it respects the distinction between being and becoming, only,
that is, if it acknowledges and allows for the hard work of coming to
know to take place in the exchange, both parties equally engaged,
equally at risk, equally authorized.[6] Not all Q and A methods do that,
of course. In Socrates' view the poem argues that "to be a good man
—continuing good—is not possible, but a man may *become* good"
(338; 345c). Likewise I am suggesting by analogy (an analogy I feel is
tacit to Socrates' argument as well by the context in which the dispute about virtue takes place) that to "know"—in some static and
permanent way—is not possible, but one may come-to-know. Thus,
a pedagogy that is premised on the fixity of authorized bodies of
knowledge will differ in much more than technique from one that is
premised on the communal activity of coming to know, a difference
that will show itself precisely at the joints of "at what" and "toward
what" that Socrates starts this all off with. And if teaching is to be re-
constituted as a full partner with, rather than understudy to, research
in our professional lives, we will need to find ways of examining, and
communicating about, in all of our public disciplinary forums, the in-
tricacies of differences such as these. We simply don't yet have such
sophisticated, discipline-specific (rather than generic) discourses for
talking about what it is that we as professors do for at least half of our
living: teach.

I have no prospect, obviously, of developing such a discourse here,
or even I suppose in my whole lifetime. A project of that sort must be
a communal one, driven by individual passions and desires, of course,
but also initiated and sustained by larger forces: economic, institutional, professional. What I can offer are a few "snapshots" from the
conclusion of the dialogue in question, which moves through its cli-
max this way:

176

> To remind you [the "common man," whom Socrates introduces ear-
> lier as an additional foil for his inquiry] of your question, it arose be-
> cause we two [himself and Protagoras] agreed that there was nothing

more powerful than knowledge, but that wherever it is found it always has the mastery over pleasure and everything else. You on the other hand, who maintain that pleasure often masters even the man who knows, asked us to say what this experience really is, if it is not being mastered by pleasure. If we had answered you straight off that it is ignorance, you would have laughed at us, but if you laugh at us now, you will be laughing at yourselves as well, for you have agreed that when people make a wrong choice of pleasures and pains—that is, of good and evil—the cause of their mistake is lack of knowledge. We can go further, and call it, as you have already agreed, a science of measurement, and you know yourselves that a wrong action which is done without knowledge is done in ignorance. So that is what being mastered by pleasure really is—ignorance, and most serious ignorance, the fault which Protagoras, Prodicus, and Hippias profess to cure. (348; 357c–e)

From this point on, the dominoes topple: "To 'act beneath yourself' is the result of pure ignorance; to 'be your own master' is wisdom" (349; 358c). . . . [I]gnorance of what is and is not to be feared must be cowardice. . . . [K]nowledge of what is and is not to be feared is courage" (351; 360c–d).

This brings the argument full circle, both Socrates and Protagoras being forced to change their initial positions on whether or not virtue can be taught, an irony Socrates takes some delight in:

It seems to me that the present outcome of our talk is pointing at us, like a human adversary, the finger of accusation and scorn. If it had a voice it would say, 'What an absurd pair you are Socrates and Protagoras. One of you, having said at the beginning that virtue is not teachable, now is bent upon contradicting himself by trying to demonstrate that everything is knowledge—justice, temperance, and courage alike—which is the best way to prove that virtue *is* teachable. If virtue were something other than knowledge, as Protagoras tried to prove, obviously it could not be taught. But if it turns out to be, as a single whole, knowledge—which is what you are urging, Socrates—then it will be most surprising if it cannot be taught. Protagoras on the other hand, who at the beginning supposed it to be

177

teachable, now on the contrary seems to be bent on showing that it is almost anything rather than knowledge, and this would make it least likely to be teachable.' (351; 361a–c)

What strikes me in this series of moves is not so much the reversal of positions—and the fitting puzzlement it leaves us with about the teachability of virtue—interesting as all that might be; but that as Socrates and Protagoras talk about teaching, they are comfortable using words that we would ourselves find awkward, maybe even embarrassing, to use in our own collegial discussions of teaching—words like *courage* and *cowardice*, for example—as well as words that have become so overwrought with nostalgic connotations that they are stripped of current pedagogical significance—simple concepts like *wisdom* and *ignorance*, for example. These various terms have both meaning and moment, however, in this conversation, and they, or words like them—words that will allow us to talk simply and directly among ourselves about matters of value, of "what effect it will have," about whatever it is that we want to call our equivalent of "virtue"— need to find a way back into our own conversations about what we do when we teach.

I don't mean to propose that finding an answer to the question of "virtue's place" in education is what we need to get about doing in order to restore the status of teaching in our professional lives. The concept of teacherly research that I have in mind would find its realization more in the conversation itself, a conversation in which the everyday desires and needs of teachers and students get addressed, haggled over, as fully and richly, in as polemical and particular terms as they are here in the argument between Socrates and Protagoras. And if in the process we can be, by turns, as eloquent, as comical, as fastidious, as earnest, as persnickety, as wise, as noble, as quixotic as these figures are in the hands of Plato, we will have gone a long way toward finding the sort of "discourse" that any contemporary field requires if it is to serve appropriately those who come to it, with the enthusiasm of Hippocrates, to "study professionally."

178

SOCRATIC METHOD AND
THE ABSENCE OF THE STUDENT

. . . you have not consulted either your father or your brother or
any of us who are your friends on the question whether or not to
entrust your soul to this stranger who has arrived among us. On
the contrary, having heard the news in the evening, so you tell me,
here you come at dawn, not to discuss or consult me on this ques-
tion of whether or not to entrust yourself to Protagoras, but ready
to spend both your own money and that of your friends as if you
had already made up your mind that you must at all costs associate
with this man. . . .

It looks like it, Socrates, from what you say. . . .

So I suggest we give this matter some thought, not only by our-
selves, but also with those who are older than we, for we are still
rather young to examine such a large problem.

"PROTAGORAS" (312–13; 313B–314B)[1]

What promises early on here to be a helpful consultation to
aid Hippocrates in making a responsible decision about his education

turns out, of course, to be both much more and much less than that. On the one hand, Socrates and Protagoras end up arguing at length about a very large question, the teachability of virtue, enacting in the process two quite different pedagogical methods. On the other, it doesn't take long for Hippocrates, and with him the problem that Socrates claims to want to help him with, to be cut off from the explicit agenda of the argument. While neither Socrates nor Protagoras seems to realize the irony of this excision, it is, nevertheless, one that we as readers cannot miss, one that Plato, in a dialogue so rich with turn after playfully ironic turn, keeps nudging us to notice—as for example in Hippocrates' response to Socrates, above, "It looks like it, Socrates, from what you say," if we read it with a little light sarcasm on the words "looks" and "you." Here and elsewhere Plato seems to be calling upon us, as outsiders, to ask the one question that none of the insiders bothers to consider: Why isn't Hippocrates an active participant in this conversation about his future? Indeed, why is Hippocrates —the one with everything, putatively, at stake—an absent figure in this dialogue, excluded almost from the outset through the polite Socratic "we" that concludes my epigraph? And Hippocrates is, to be sure, absent *from* this conversation. He says nothing after the opening setup, and it would be easy for us to forget about him and his predicament entirely as the argument develops, as the two primary contestants seem to. On the other hand, he is not absent *to* the conversation. His position as silent observer affords him a vantage point to see in some detail the range of his options and the prospective courses of his future as a student. Because he is, though, by all overt indications, incapable of accomplishing all of that entirely on his own, it falls to us, as companionable outsiders, precluded ourselves in a similar way from any active role in constructing the specific terms of the debate, to do some of the work for him. By offering his readers this student-function to work through, Plato opens up a critical space for us to explore all manner of possibilities and problems concerning the pedagogical relationship. He becomes thereby a teacher-function far surpassing in complexity the more traditional teacher-*figures*—from among whom Socrates has emerged as the most prominent cultural prototype—that his dialogues portray.[2]

The general contours of Hippocrates' figurative place in this "scene of instruction" can be adapted productively to any number of comparable contemporary scenes. In the last chapter, for example, I used him as an analogue for a graduate student. Here I want to use him to see through much younger and less experienced eyes.[3] Imagine for example a typical high school senior trying to decide where to spend her four years of college. Such a prospective student has far more diverse sources from which to draw information than Hippocrates did. But are they better? That depends on what one presumes are the key voices she needs to be hearing from at this stage of the process. Her school almost assuredly has a guidance counselor and caches of brochures to which she can turn for preliminary and contextual information. She most likely has some family members or friends or acquaintances who have been to, or are now attending, a variety of colleges. There are the numerous independently produced resource manuals that she can use to winnow down a larger number of options to a smaller number. There are the catalogues produced by individual colleges to describe and sell themselves, any number of which she can easily procure. There are a variety of administrative offices to which she can turn for additional information about her finalists. Hippocrates has no such reservoir of information to help him with his choice. But he does have the one thing that is, oddly enough, most difficult for our contemporary inquisitor to gain access to: the faculty itself.

My hypothetical student can find out some important things about a college's faculty by reading the general descriptions of university mission, departmental specializations, and available programs of study that all catalogues proffer, texts that the faculty has a highly mediated voice in casting. And she can examine the specifics of the curriculum, which is almost always a construction that the faculty takes a significant hand in framing. And there are campus visits, during which she might sit in on a class, even chat casually with a professor. She can

181

learn a great deal about a faculty by evaluating this kind of information; although, as was the case with the absent Hippocrates, the degree to which she will be in a position to critically sort through such highly stylized, elliptical, and/or overdetermined texts is open to question. But it is these days a very rare young woman who would be able to sit and listen to someone as smart and artful, as smarmy and cantankerous, as deft and pestiferous as Socrates grill the university's "star" professor about exactly "what effect" he and his operation will have on someone who is interested in "purchasing knowledge" (313; 314a).

Every time I read this dialogue I recall myself, at Hippocrates' age, troubling with his decision, his dilemma—wishing, retrospectively, I had had a way of getting the information that falls into his lap here. Because so few people I knew had actually been to college, my impressions and expectations of that world were largely of my own concoction, a brew of my parents' and townspeople's ambitions and dreams, of my own private desires for a world where the life of the mind was the highest priority, of pictures and sentences from the boxful of high-sounding college catalogs I had read diligently over the previous year and now reanimated piecemeal in my mind. Here finally, I imagined, was to be my utopia, this forum where passionate and brilliant professors gathered to converse and argue with one another in the most rigorously intellectual ways, where vast bodies of knowledge would be mastered through arduous private study and strenuous public debate.

I would be equally hard-pressed, obviously, given these expectations, to overstate the disappointment I felt during my first year of college. Here was a place basically like the other kinds of schools I was familiar with: A lot of students pouring through their courses, going through the motions for a lot of teachers who, smart and well-intentioned as they might be, were, if only for institutional reasons— the nature of the curriculum, the emerging tendency to define the status, and therefore the work, of the professoriate much more in terms of research than teaching—often distracted, frustrated, even sometimes just going through the motions themselves. This was, admittedly, a better place than high school, at least to the extent that I was allowed considerably more discretion in deciding which classes I would attend and when. Much of the time I cut classes, stayed in my room, and read—the ultimate in the "absent" student.

There was a lot of talk in the late sixties about replacing traditional, distribution-type curricula with curricula that were "student-centered," that is, flexible enough to respond to the desires and needs of a wide variety of individual clients with a wide variety of individual plans. During my freshman year, I helped design and then propose to the dean just such a curriculum at my own school, though it never got off the drawing board. My feeling then, as now, about the need to shift the basis of authority in the university away from the institution and toward its clients was premised not on the belief that this was the best way to organize such an enterprise. In some ways, I knew even then, it's one of the worst. It was driven by the sense that the rightful authors of the system in question, the faculty, in the face of over-powering institutional and cultural forces, had simply given up on a central part of their mission, dismissed their quotidian charge to re-animate themselves and their subjects with their students, and turned it over to administrative structures, which were never designed to foster and conserve the life of the mind, and which were, therefore, ill-suited to the job of constructing curricula in general and the class-room arena in particular.[4]

Though it may not sound like it, I mean none of this to derogate the quality of the education I received either in the local public schools as I was growing up or at the university I attended. I was well-prepared for college by my public schooling. And I had some wonderful undergraduate teachers, under whose guidance I learned much of what I had hoped, and needed, to learn. It's not either to argue that colleges should be striving to become the sort of idyllic republic I had imagined mine would be. Such a place is, I know now, not only impossible (there's always some curmudgeon like Socrates deciding who belongs there and who doesn't), but also undesirable (the human tendency in an open scheme to try, and inevitably fail, to do everything at once is reason enough to invent the concept of a curriculum and its attendant

183

administrative apparatus). But it is to say this: Unless to some extent faculty members in a university consider deeply and regularly their obligations—as individuals persistently, as a collective at crucial moments—to the intellectual character of "higher" education, to the intellectual life of their actual students and their immediate institutions, then those matters are not likely to be considered systematically by anyone at all.

What "intellectual" might mean in this context is a highly debatable matter. And that is, of course, the point. Socrates and Protagoras actually argue with some vehemence about it, and in front of a potential student no less. And, well, we don't. Many of the younger professors I had as an undergraduate were basically like, in most respects, the average university professor today. They were conscientious, well-educated scholars. And they understood fully, even if it was never made explicit, that their survival in the academy depended more on what they wrote for their colleagues and peers (and who published it) than on what they taught their students. They could blame the torpor they observed behind their classroom doors on the perpetual, obvious suspects: an outworn or uninspired curriculum; the obligation to teach boring, entry-level classes; the absence of in-house collegiality; the "quality" of students being admitted, or their subsequent inability to satisfy legitimate academic demands; even the agitated political climate of the time. Any one of these was and remains a reasonable, if inadequate, explanation for simply consigning the college classroom to the realm of obligatory routine.

This may be an ungenerous critique, and I may seem by implication to be expecting us as university faculty—and for higher education generally—to be more than we ever really can or should be. But in that regard, to get back to Plato, I'm a piker compared to Socrates and Protagoras. Just look at the hyperbolic (from our vantage point, not theirs) ways in which they cast the enterprise to which Hippocrates is about to commit himself. Socrates, for example, starts talking about high stakes right from the outset, in part, perhaps, to shake up Hippocrates, but mostly because that's what he believes:

184

If then you chance to be an expert in discerning which of them is good or bad, it is safe for you to buy knowledge from Protagoras or anyone else, but if not, take care you don't find yourself gambling dangerously with all of you that is dearest to you. . . . [K]nowledge cannot be taken away in a parcel. When you have paid for it you must receive it straight into the soul. You go away having learned it and are benefited or harmed accordingly. (313; 313e–314b)

"Safety," "gambling dangerously," "all that is dearest to you," "the soul," "harm"—one would think Hippocrates is thinking about becoming a hit man rather than signing up to study with Protagoras, who himself uses a discourse from another part of the spectrum to suggest that something of similar magnitude is at stake in his curriculum:

The very day you join me, you will go home a better man, and the same the next day. Each day you will make progress toward a better state. . . .

What is [my] subject? The proper care of his personal affairs, so that he may best manage his own household, and also of the state's affairs, so as to become a real power in the city, both as speaker and man of action. (316–17; 318a–319a)

"Better state," "better man," "a real power," "man of action": sounds like a lot to gain, again, from "studying professionally" (314; 315a). Neither of these is the most likely first thing we would have to say about our own work in the university—at least not in our professional journals and forums, and probably not to our students. Neither would we, though, dismiss out of hand their underlying sense of urgency about the ultimate "effect" (316; 318a) of education, which is change—sometimes significant change—that can, if we work at it, be calculated, even described, in promotional documents about our institutions and departments.

There are as I see it three quite distinct levels at which Socrates and Protagoras locate the kinds of change that "studying professionally" can effect, each of which derives from a correspondingly different take

185

on what sort of knowledge is being rendered. That they talk so often at cross purposes, especially when they hit their main points of contention, is due in part to a persistent (con)fusion among these three modes of knowledge. The first constructs knowledge-as-information, *what* one learns, for which arguments of more or less are applicable. The second constructs knowledge-as-skill, what one learns *how* to do, for which arguments of better or worse are applicable. The last constructs knowledge-as-value, *who* one is or becomes as a consequence of instruction, for which arguments of good or evil, virtue in general, the main theme of this discussion, are applicable. Information, skill, and value are, most of us would agree, both incommensurable and interrelated as aspects of the educational process. And to prioritize them too rigidly or to discriminate too sharply among them risks falsifying that process as much as presuming there are no such functional distinctions at play in the first place. We can and do, though, pose a variety of stereotypical questions about our expectations and our practices that get at differences along the range of changes our pedagogical transactions promote. For example, at the level of information: "What do we want students to demonstrably 'know' about 'our' 'subject'?" This is the customary way we have for thinking about the "expertise" we bring to our courses, a commodity, in effect, for which we consider remuneration appropriate. Each of the terms I have isolated is marked by an array of ideological assumptions so ingrained in our way of doing business that we simply take them for granted. Or, at the level of skill: "What do we want students to be able to do?" Such a question frames pedagogy in the more practical terms of a "discipline" that can be taught/mastered at the level of technique or method, to be translated ultimately into a job or a career or a profession. Here, tacit connections between the academy and the larger, usually dominant, contextual forces of "society," are foregrounded, with functionality as the keynote. Or, at the level of value: "How do we want students to think?" Such a question, asked quite commonly by those of us who teach writing and reading, elevates the issue at hand to a moral/ethical/political plane, turning our work

186

around terms like *mission* or *agenda*; and it correspondingly makes the transaction potentially more volatile for all parties. Unlike Socrates and Protagoras, we tend to formulate our enterprise in this respect most often at the extremes: when we have to say something bland, impressive, ceremonial, to an "outside" audience—parents, boards of trustees, state legislators—or when we think privately about the ultimate benefits of what we have to offer, through our intercession, to individual students. When an argument over these matters actually erupts in a consequential way, it is most often temporary and isolated —in response to an unanticipated crisis, as in the case of the many recent "PC" interchanges, celebrated or otherwise—rather than sustained and systematic, as an integral part of our professional discourse.

These distinctions are essential to my overall argument, yet I hesitate to make them at all, let alone make them in exactly these terms. As soon as the pedagogical transaction is conceptualized in terms of aspects (like information, skill, and value) it becomes tempting to assume that—or just fall into a way of talking as if—these aspects are fully distinct and separable from one another, can be analyzed or addressed in part, or, worse, *as* parts. There are probably hundreds of other equally useful ways of categorizing "knowledge" to allow us to reflect on it as a set of categories. I mean to compete with none of them. We need plethora not paucity if a serious, systematic debate about "teaching"—in its institutional form as the counterpart to "research"—is to be recuperated from the stagnancy of arguments that are either exclusively ideological or exclusively technical. This dissociation of ideology from technique is one of the fundamental problems that contemporary discussions of pedagogy, and approaches to the teaching of teaching, tend to have at all educational levels; and it is part of the reason I locate my argument here in the framework of the debate between Socrates and Protagoras, neither of whom makes that mistake. While the specific terms I have chosen to extend this analysis may seem nostalgic—in the sense that critics now use the word when they want to be dismissive—I see no powerful alternatives emerging from current critical theory, at least not with any specific

187

application to the classroom. And to some extent I want very overtly to distance myself from poststructuralism at precisely this moment of fulcrum, here, where I originate my discussion of the one venue it has been most inept at recasting.

The terms I offer here have potential application to a variety of pedagogical situations that university professors commonly face. For example, the ambivalence I felt when I agreed to co-teach Race and Gender in Twentieth Century American Poetry was not so much with the matter of knowledge-as-information. I had, after all, already read the "major figures" we would be including in a course of that sort. I had taught many different courses that used authors from this "period" in a variety of ways. And I had written and published several articles in that "area." I highlight these terms to call attention to the very traditional ways in which my expertise had been commodified by disciplinary and professional conventions. It was only in relation to the modifiers—race and gender—that I felt potentially inadequate. But why? To understand that inadequacy, it is necessary to move to the knowledge-as-skill category—which I apply here to the "how" of teaching. I had not, that is, either read or taught or written about this material primarily in terms of race or gender. In some ways—for reasons I have begun to sketch out, though still not fully fathomed—this seemed to me to be a course whose purpose and design required expertise more with the terms of modification than with the body of textual material. And there was a degree to which I deeply felt—and not just for personal but also for disciplinary reasons—that expertise in this "field" needed to some degree to be informed by firsthand "minority" experience, of which I had none. It was not then a matter, for me, of doing a lot of research to "bone up" for the course; and clearly it was impossible for me to become someone else in the meantime. What I needed to do to overcome this lack was what I did: In concert with Toi, I refigured the concepts to fit my identity in such a way that my firsthand experiences were warranted. Once I had done this, I was able to approach and develop my own "bodily" knowledge about both gender (as in my essay of September 14) and race (as in my essay of

188

September 21, in which I discuss this mode of physiological learning in some detail). Further, in my essay of December 7, I analyze the way in which my initial deficit in this part of the course's knowledge base actually allowed me to teach it; and it was, ironically, the acquisition, *through* the teaching, of some modicum of expertise that seemed to me, afterward, to disqualify me from teaching it again. The category of knowledge-as-value is one I address over and over in my essays to the class, most often through the rubric of "the political." Once I had found a way to strategize my "personal" knowledge-as-skill problem, I was able to negotiate with little difficulty the otherwise quite awkward value-related aspects of the knowledge that the course both proffered and generated. I mention all of this mostly to highlight the ways in which even such blunt and simple categories as those I offer here can be quite powerful in allowing us to reflect on the complexities that are inherent to teaching.

All three of these dimensions of the pedagogical e/merge as Socrates and Protagoras begin their debate. And because they tend to couch their respective promises and threats in different discourses—Socrates favoring the moral and metaphysical, Protagoras favoring the civic and historical—they come to an immediate impasse, each one having a fundamentally different take on just what virtue is, where it comes from, what it is for. This conflict is refracted throughout the dialogue as they converse about the particular kinds of change that schooling promotes. When, for example, Socrates asks "what effect" his pedagogy will have on Hippocrates, Protagoras responds initially, and pretty lamely—the "better man," "better state" passage above—as if the question were what kind of status his student will gain as a consequence of his schooling. When Socrates asks "toward what" and "at what," it seems that he wants a much more specific, skill-based answer. But when Protagoras responds in terms of functionality, with the "proper care . . . real power . . . man of action" quote, above, Socrates again foils his answer, even though it is much more responsive on the face of it. When Socrates follows up—in the fashion that is his custom when he most wants to irritate a sophist—with a series

189

of discipline-specific counterexamples, in this case about "architects" and "naval designers" (317; 319b), it becomes gradually clearer the degree to which he imagines both value and skill—relatively separable and commodified entities for Protagoras—as intimately bound up with distinct and proper bodies of knowledge-as-information, a mode of expertise that Protagoras, like most of the sophists, seems ambivalent about at best. By the time that Socrates and Protagoras begin their discussion of virtue in earnest, it is obvious they could not disagree more on how to think about pedagogy on all three of the levels I have mentioned.[5]

For Protagoras, the pedagogical transaction is relatively simple: One is "a good and noble character" (324; 328b) or "a real power" (317; 319a) as a consequence of certain kinds of instruction. The process has a beginning, a middle, and an end; and a specific economic value can be affixed to it. For Socrates, there is no such thing as transmitting goodness or power—or anything for that matter—in such a direct and practical manner. One must constantly strive to approach a goal that seems always to be moving away at precisely the speed one approaches it. One can seek, happen upon, even contract with various kinds of teachers to help with this process. But there is no way to measure the value of any such transactions in material terms. This difference leads to a corollary argument about whether there is any direct and necessary relationship between the "good" one does and how "good" one is. The connection between these is, for Protagoras, like most of the sophists, a highly mediated one, particularly so in matters of rhetoric or pedagogy, for which there are no overriding sets of absolutes to hierarchize "goods." Socrates sees this as a way of justifying an equation between appearing to do/be good and actually doing/being good, and he rails against it less so here than in other dialogues only because Protagoras never expresses this position forthrightly.

Socrates and Protagoras disagree as well about matters of pedagogical practice, as is demonstrated in their argument over Simonides' poem, which revolves, as I indicate above, around a distinction (for Socrates) or lack of one (for Protagoras) between "being" and "be-

coming" "a good man" (333–40; 339a–347b). Their difference of opinion is one that I extrapolate into the pedagogical arena in this way:
Education can be constructed either as an ongoing (and never-ending)
process or as a means to an end, a potentially finished state. Socrates
endorses the former; Protagoras the latter. What is most telling in
that regard, and most applicable to my discussion here, is the difference this makes at the level of rhetorical technique. Protagoras prefers,
and is extremely adept at, one version of the display, or "lecture"
model, presenting in polished, finished form his expertise for his audience to "remember" in its precise particulars. Protagoras expects
his students to learn what he knows, claims that this will make them
powerful (one of the primary indices of "success" in the political terms
of his system), and believes it is worth what they are asked, or are
willing (324; 318b–c), to pay for it. Socrates prefers and is extremely
adept at one version of the dialogical or "discussion" model, probing
and provoking his interlocutor with question after question to "remember" what he already knows. Socrates expects his students, generally, to resist just enough to make it possible to comply with his
overriding moral agenda, wants them to keep searching for "the
truth" (one of the primary indices of "success" in the philosophical
terms of his system), and believes that this process is worth so much
that money is not a fit measure for regulating the transaction.

Positions entrenched so contrarily from the outset—Socrates in the
soul, Protagoras in the polis—will, and do, remain so throughout the
dialogue. The bizarre progression of the specific argument about
the teachability of virtue—each party ending in exactly the opposite
position from which he started—can itself be partially accounted for
by their mutual reluctance to abandon their initial discursive premises,
even when those premises are causing them to "lose" the debate, suggesting the degree to which, from Plato's point of view at least, this is
not by any means a settled matter.

Who "wins" or "loses" this argument—or the one Socrates has
with Gorgias/Polus/Callicles for example,[6] or many other Platonic
debates for that matter—is arguable, and a determination will turn on

191

the pivot of the presumed relationship between what we know and who we are. Socrates poses most concisely the problematic of this relationship at the end of *Lysis*. After a long conversation in which he induces a series of "false reasonings" (162; 218d) about the meaning of the term *friendship*, all parties to the conversation, including Socrates, are so "dizzied by the entanglement of the subject" (160; 216c), so "intoxicated," that they are completely disabled:

> For our hearers here will carry away the report that though we conceive ourselves to be friends with each other—you will see I class myself with you—*we have not as yet been able to discover what we mean by a friend.* (168; 223b, italics mine)

And at the end of *Lesser Hippias* Socrates ends up in much the same position as he does with Protagoras: unable to agree even with himself, simply as a consequence of following the seemingly necessary course of the argument:

> I am all abroad, and being in perplexity am always changing my opinion. Now, that I or any ordinary man should wander in perplexity is not surprising, but if you wise men also wander, and we cannot come to you and rest from our wandering, the matter begins to be serious both to us and to you. (214; 376c)

Serious, indeed. Especially for someone trying to decide who is the better teacher. Which gets us back again to Hippocrates' problem.

One of the questions we're left with is which of these two is a preferable mentor for Hippocrates. In my view, Plato is a lot more ambivalent on that matter than we might be inclined to presume.[7] The general cultural tendency is to construct the relationship between Plato and his principle mouthpiece as both direct and unproblematic, as is, therefore, the relationship between Socrates' pedagogical method and Plato's pedagogical method. But what is this thing that we have come to call so comfortably the Socratic "method"? For those of us schooled in teaching during the 1970s, when the "discovery method" was commonplace, its most simplistic and extreme version is embodied in his conversation with Meno's slave, as "good" a student as any of us are ever likely to find. Taken in isolation from the rest of this dialogue, and from the rest of Plato's work, this instance has some very obvious and transferable parts, which are worth examining closely here first, as a way of creating a backdrop for a more complex notion of what the Socratic system has to offer.

Here is yet another argument about the teachability of virtue. Socrates again contends that it can't be taught; Meno claims that it can. The first part of the dialogue is an elaborate effort at definition, focusing on the part-whole problem of virtue(s). Meno holds his own for a while against Socrates, more irritating here than he was with the more cordial Protagoras. But after a spirited series of thrusts and parries with Socrates, Meno simply gives up in exasperation:

> Socrates, even before I met you they told me that in plain truth you are a perplexed man yourself and reduce others to perplexity. . . . If I may be flippant, I think that not only in outward appearance but in other respects as well you are exactly like the flat sting ray that one meets in the sea. Whenever anyone comes into contact with it, it numbs him, and that is the sort of thing that you seem to be doing to me now. (363; 79e–80a)

Oddly enough, this seemingly devastating complaint becomes, for Socrates, the motive to demonstrate his pedagogical style—in this case, tellingly, with one of Meno's slaves. We're faced with a corollary to the question that faces us at the end of *Lesser Hippias*: How could "numbing" a student into "perplexity" be promoted as a worthy endeavor for a teacher? The conversation that Socrates has with the slave serves as a classic demonstration of this sort of pedagogical transaction, and it offers a wonderful—if highly stylized—version of Socratic technique.

As the exchange opens, Socrates asks a series of six very "leading" questions—such as, "and these lines which go through the middle of [the square figure drawn in the sand] are also equal?"—to all of which the slave answers, slavishly, "yes." Only in the seventh does Socrates ask for a "content" response: "And how many feet is twice two?" he asks. The boy answers, correctly, "four" (all quotes on p. 365; 82c–d).

Since Socrates probably could have elicited this response immediately from any slave "born and bred in the house" (365; 81b) of Meno, he must clearly have another motive in this portion of his pedagogical transaction. This exchange is, in fact, merely a setup, in that it creates in the boy a sense of confidence that he "knows," and in the audience a sense of inclination to believe that Socrates' method actually works. That it accomplishes this with such a trivial outcome suggests the degree to which their conversation is as much psychological and rhetorical in its motives as it is instructional. Socrates then uses a comparable series of more difficult questions to demonstrate that the slave doesn't really know as much as he thinks he might, a pedagogical ploy that works much better, of course, after the proper setup. This is the key move in the progression of his interrogation, putting the slave "in a better position now in relation to what he didn't know" by "perplexing him and numbing him like a sting ray" (368; 84b). Here I think is an element in the "Socratic method" that needs to be highlighted: its reliance on negation as a means of dialectical progression, and negation, often, of a very unpleasant sort.[8] In effect, Socrates is saying here, and many other places as well, not "Here's something I know, let me teach it to you," or even "Here's something you already know, let me elicit it from you," but rather, "Here's something you think you know but obviously don't, and I will prove it to you." Socrates clearly has in mind using this humiliation as a first step in his process, one that creates a context for change in the student. When the ploy works, it does, if only by its shock value, clear out a large empty space within which many kinds of "new" knowledge/skills/values can be deposited or uncovered. But there are risks to it as well, as the remainder of this dialogue demonstrates. Meno's slave for example remains just as mechanical in his responses, as if he wants even less now to risk another such rebuke by taking chances, seeming to sense now that "yes" is almost always the safest response to the long setup questions Socrates poses for him. He does finally come to the "correct" answer, but the interaction sounds to me a lot more like a boring drill than a process of illuminating recovery. And, as with any object-lesson, one can't un-

194

derestimate its effect on the audience that observes it—and, in this case, dreads its repetition on them. We can see this aftershock effect on Meno himself. Resistant and feisty before Socrates turns to the slave, he becomes curt and cursory in his answers immediately after, as if he is perfectly willing to "lose" the argument—he basically concedes every major point to Socrates, even though he clearly doesn't agree with him—to avoid having to endure the rigors of contention with such an obnoxious and intractable opponent.

And we might also take issue with Socrates' claim that for Meno's slave "starting with this state of perplexity, he will discover by seeking the truth in company with me, though I simply ask him questions without teaching him." First of all, seeking the truth about geometrical matters is quite a bit different from seeking the truth about philosophical matters, at least in the manner by which "definitions" are established and deployed, as much of the rest of this dialogue makes clear. In addition, by promising to "simply ask [Meno's slave] questions without teaching him" Socrates seems to be limiting the term "teaching" to various kinds of "instruction or explanation" (all passages from p. 368; 84d) rather than, for example, various kinds of interrogation and debate. If we accede to this differentiation, how can his method then serve as a pedagogical model? If we don't accede and assume that his method *is* a mode of teaching, what happens to the foundation upon which this whole argument rests: that learning is a process of recollecting what one already knows, having learned it before birth? This underlying conundrum becomes fully operational when Socrates turns back to Meno, asking, "let us do the same about virtue" (372; 87b). When Socrates tries to enforce this analogy across what we would these days consider some pretty tall disciplinary boundaries, a host of problems comes up. They may not be intractable, but they are formidable. For example, if the analogy is to be carried out in terms of learning-as-recollection, what "knowledge" does one recollect when one "recalls" the meaning of virtue? Surely it is not in the form of a "solution" to a "problem," as is the case with geometry. Socrates himself both here and elsewhere claims that such an "answer"

195

is impossible for a concept like virtue, though he clearly knows the answer to the mathematical problem he induces Meno's slave to "solve." And if these two types of unteachable knowledge are to be elicited by the same modes of interrogation, why does Socrates always succeed in "finding" an answer when it comes to things like geometry and never when it comes to matters like virtue? Indeed, he himself argues over and over again that the latter intellectual enterprise is a process of never-ending "wandering" (*Lesser Hippias*, 214; 376c).

The remaining portion of Socrates' conversation with the slave is really just a routine lesson about squaring and the meaning of the term "diagonal" (370; 85b), which Socrates concludes with another version of his "I didn't teach him anything, just helped him remember what he already knew." This position depends on the assumption that knowledge precedes birth, that it is "always in our soul." Very few of us are likely to assent to this assumption in terms of professional practices (there is as far as I know no contemporary pedagogical theory or approach, though there are psychological ones, that rely on the process of recollecting what one knew before one was born). Meno, as I note above, so contentious as this conversation opened, just concedes Socrates' point, behaving in his brief, perfunctory responses exactly as his slave did, benumbed it seems both by his prior conversation and by the exemplar of the slave. And by the time Socrates says to Meno, "let us do the same about virtue," reasserting the identity between geometry and philosophy" (372; 87b), Meno is really as absent a figure from this transaction as either Hippocrates or the slave are from theirs.

Whether or not then this "numbing process" is a "good" (368; 84c) pedagogical ploy is certainly open to question. It elicits very little consequential "knowledge" from the slave, it shuts down almost entirely an otherwise potentially productive argument with Meno, and it even provokes a harsh, foreboding warning from Anytus about his tendency to "run people down" and to do more "harm than good" (379; 94e). And what about the role of memory, recollection, in the pedagogical process, a theme that crops up over and over again in Plato's

196

dialogues, suggesting the degree to which it was a serious concern of his?[9] Where exactly he wanted to stand on the matter is, to me at least, not at all apparent. One version of the problem is the one that Socrates raises quite bluntly here: If certain things cannot be taught, like virtue, then they must already be known, inborn at least, if not actually learned in previous incarnations. Learning is not a process of acquisition, of supplementation, of adding what is new, of filling up a space *with* these things; but rather of uncovering, of exhuming, of sub-tracting barriers and impediments, of emptying out a space *for* them.

Just what approach Meno would specifically oppose to this is never made clear here, though Protagoras offers a more explicit alternative.[10] The best way to see this difference between Socrates and Protagoras is to look at how they seem most comfortable in presenting their positions. Socrates, as usual, tends to prefer the role of questioner; Protagoras, as is the case with many of Socrates' interlocutors, prefers longer displays. The first portion of their argument proceeds in such a fashion, Socrates asking brief questions, Protagoras supplying long, sometimes very long, declamatory "speeches," until, finally, Socrates demurs:

> I'm a forgetful sort of man, Protagoras, and if someone speaks at length, I lose the thread of the argument. . . . [S]ince you find me for-getful, cut down your answers and make them shorter if I am to fol-low you. (329; 334c–d)

What is key to note here is that Socrates seeks to shift the structure of Protagoras's mode of argumentation—from longer to shorter speeches—on the basis of forgetfulness, a transmogrification of mem-ory. He seems again to be suggesting that remembering what some-one else has said, particularly if it is a long and elaborate display, is at least difficult, probably impossible, and perhaps useless as a way of coming to know.

The latter pedagogical implication, though only tacit here and in the *Meno*, is worked out in more detail in the *Phaedrus*, where Socrates speaks again about "forgetfulness" in his famous speech about the "old

197

gods" Theus, the inventor of calculation and writing, and Thamus, who criticizes writing, especially, in just these terms:

> If men learn this, it will implant forgetfulness in their souls; they will cease to exercise memory because they rely on that which is written, calling things to remembrance no longer from within themselves, but by means of external marks. What you have discovered is a recipe not for memory, but for reminder. And it is no true wisdom that you offer your disciples, but only its semblance, for by telling them of many things without teaching them you will make them seem to know much, while for the most part they know nothing. (520; 275a–b)

This is not only a general indictment of the "majestic silence . . . [of] written words" (521; 275d) but also a much more specific, retrospective critique of Phaedrus's presumption that he has "learned" something from Lysias by memorizing his speech. More a propos to my argument here, the distinction between "telling . . . things" and "teaching" serves to amplify and clarify, in terms of its magnitude at least, the seemingly minor complaint Socrates has about *how* Protagoras is talking to him.

Socrates goes on in this vein:

> [N]othing that has ever been written whether in verse or prose merits much serious attention—and for that matter nothing that has ever been spoken in a declamatory fashion which aims at mere persuasion without any questioning or exposition—that in reality such compositions are, at the best, a means of reminding those who know the truth. . . . (523; 277e–278a)

The analogy between the impotent written text and the declamatory speech is especially telling, reinscribing in epistemological terms his objection to both Phaedrus's method of "learning" (from Lysias) and Protagoras's method of "teaching" (either Hippocrates or Socrates).

The alternative that Socrates offers is perhaps his most concise description of his own preferred method:

> The dialectician selects a soul of the right type, and in it he plants and sows his words founded on knowledge, words which can defend both

themselves and him who planted them, words which instead of remaining barren contain a seed whence new words grow up in new
characters, whereby the seed is vouchsafed immortality, and its pos-
sessor the fullest measure of blessedness that man can attain unto. . . .
[L]ucidity and completeness and serious importance belong only to
those lessons on justice and honor and goodness that are expounded
and set forth for the sake of instruction, and are veritably written in
the soul of the listener, and that such discourses as these ought to be
accounted a man's own legitimate children—a title to be applied primarily to such as originate within the man himself, and secondarily
to such of their sons and brothers as have grown up aright in the
souls of other men. (522–23; 276e–277a, 278a–b)

The elaborate array of metaphors of fertility, procreation, and pater-
nity suggests the degree to which Socrates does believe that knowledge
can be engendered, not just recalled, that "memory" can function as
more than just "reminder" or regurgitation. And more specifically, as
the "father" of his students in these various interactions, we begin to
get a clearer image of the manner in which he, as teacher, controls
these interactions at their most "seminal" level.

But even given all that, questions remain about the degree of his
success in this endeavor, specifically the degree to which his interaction with Phaedrus—or Hippocrates, or Meno's slave—has effected
any significant change in his "student." Phaedrus, frankly, seems as
flat and docile at the end of this piece as at the beginning. He may not
be as captivated by Lysias's rhetoric and pedagogy, but it is not at all
clear that he wouldn't be likewise swayed by the next powerful orator
that came along. Neither is Meno's slave much changed by his encounter with Socrates. He may now know the difference between
sums and squares. He may be miffed enough about his embarrassment
in front of his master that he will be a little more careful in his claims
about what he knows. But has he changed in any fundamental way? I
don't think so. And we can tell even less about what Hippocrates has
learned by sitting in on the debate between Socrates and Protagoras.
He may, for all we know, go right out and sign up with Protagoras or,
having failed to observe any measurable difference between two dis-

199

putants who end up concluding exactly the opposite of what they started out claiming, give up entirely on the idea of "studying professionally." The figure of the student in these various scenes—and in so many other of Plato's dialogues—is so weak, so mechanical, so "absent" in the broadest sense of that word, that we must begin at least to wonder whether Plato intends to recommend the Socratic method un(equ)ivocally.[11]

Just what, then, if anything, has been "taught" or "learned" in these conversations, and by whom? Ironically, as I see it, it is often the most absent "students" who have the greatest prospect for real change in these interactions, but only to the extent that we, as readers, can retrospectively perfect their role as listeners, critics. Hippocrates is emblematic in this regard. Precisely because he is forgotten, set aside by the major players, he has the opportunity to grow, to learn. It is exactly to the extent that the various parties to these disputes, including Socrates from my point of view, get "written into" rather than written out of the texts that they become impotent, their positions more and more paralyzed. This might seem on the surface to be then the ultimate proof for Socrates' critique of written discourse: it is static, degenerate, dead. But that would be to disregard the position and status of the most important function in the dialogues: the author, Plato. Surely Plato is smart enough to be aware of the irony that arises when he uses his primary mouthpiece to render a devastating critique of written discourse, while he, as author, is writing it out for us to read. It would be patently absurd for him to be writing at all if he identified exactly with Socrates' position in this instance. And if he doesn't here, he probably doesn't elsewhere, at least not in a simplistic, unmediated way. From his consequent position as "outsider" to these arguments, a whole range of readings becomes possible, for him at least.

200

And he opens up the same possibilities to us, his readers, by offering us silent vantage points, "absences" that we can inhabit, work in, see through, "read" along with. Hippocrates is one of the best because he allows us—if we identify with his lack of place in the scene—both to concentrate entirely, in a critically sophisticated way, on what is transpiring, and to bridle, even fester, with resentment, with impatience, with a frustrated desire to get a word of his/our own in edgewise. Through this medium of the absent Hippocrates, we become the only legitimate student-function, much as Plato, as author, becomes, through his own agency, the only legitimate teacher-function, who must himself be absent if the logic of the relationship I have sketched out is to be kept intact. Plato: the puppeteer, the ventriloquist, in whose hands, from whose throat, this elaborate cast of marionettes comes to life for us. To the degree that we choose to translate his method into our own pedagogies, our own classrooms, it is only, as I see it, with a proper respect for its fundamentally prosopopoeic character that we will be effective.

The temptation at this point, following the formulaic of an "essay on teaching," would be to describe, in terms of technique, a properly "prosopopoeic" pedagogy and leave it at that. I want to resist that move, not so much because I feel that such a pedagogy cannot be specified at the level of technique—any pedagogy can—but because I believe that matters of technique are not in this instance, or in most instances when pedagogy is the subject, what we need first to be thinking and talking about.

Let me return to my earlier discussion about the three kinds of knowledge—as-information, as-skill, as-value—that Socrates and Protagoras seem to be (con)fusing. These categories offer one locus for us to reflect on pedagogy as, at least to some extent, necessarily discipline-specific. For example, if a discipline tends to construct its knowledge primarily as-information the professor will be inclined to see his mission primarily as a process of "telling them what we know." If a discipline tends to construct its knowledge primarily as-skill the professor will be inclined to see her mission primarily as a process of "showing them what we do." If a discipline tends to construct its knowledge primarily as-value the professor will be inclined to see her mission primarily as a process of "teaching them how to think." Again, I don't

201

want to suggest that there is some essential hierarchy among these options or that they are ever functional in one-dimensional forms. All professors do some of each in every course they teach. But clearly there are important differences among us. Each discipline has certain in-built assumptions about the form of the knowledge that is proper to its field; and such assumptions play both a medial and a structural role in regulating how the disciplinary "subject" will be conserved and transmitted, both in the classroom and among professional peers. The hegemonic effect of these assumptions will be stronger, and less visible, obviously, in disciplines that are homogeneous; weaker, and more visible, in disciplines that are heterogeneous. To the degree that we make ourselves conscious of the shape of these forces in our own professional venues, to the degree that we locate ourselves critically in relation to the framework they preconstruct for us, that is the degree to which we free ourselves from the illusory belief that effective teaching is a matter of talent and/or technique, that is the degree to which we can begin to reinvest the concept of "professor" with its intrinsic pedagogical imperative.

Which is to say that these are, at least initially, local matters that need to be attended to in terms of a particular disciplinary history. My discussion here for example will focus on "composition," my own primary field; and I'm especially interested in its "service-function" aspects. Another discipline would of necessity take a different tack on these matters. The larger form of the question—"What is the pedagogical mission of the American university at the end of the twentieth century?"—is I believe impossible to answer from any one disciplinary site. It requires instead a larger-scale, *inter*disciplinary—in the sense that I used that term in the introduction to this half of the book —dialogue. That is, we need to be able, ultimately, to engage one another on terrain we carve out between and among our individual disciplinary turfs. Certain sites in the university happen to be better adapted than others to moderate such a dialogue—precisely because of their specific disciplinary histories. Composition, in my view, is one of them, in part because its own history is so deeply vested in the

202

forum of the undergraduate classroom, in part because it is a field with unusually vexed proprietary relationships to the three kinds of knowledge I have specified.

Composition has for example a fairly small reservoir of knowledge-as-information that it can claim as its own (rather than as appropriations from other disciplines). It is also riven by persistent internal contention about what, if any, set of methods are appropriate both for teaching writing and for generating "new" disciplinary knowledge indigenously. And problems of "value," of political and ethical influence, are endemic to work in composition, particularly in the classroom, in ways that they are not for most other disciplines, which don't routinely choose to promote, or need to defend, their enterprises in such ideological terms. Each one of these conditions tends to reinforce the traditional role of composition as a "service" function to the rest of the curriculum, a means by which non- or pre- or extra-academic work can be efficiently accomplished. But one could argue equally well that it is precisely because of these "problems" that composition is so well-positioned to initiate and orchestrate discussions about teaching in the university. All educational enterprises devolve, as I said, from some set of assumptions about what knowledge is, where it comes from, and what it is good for. In disciplines with long-standing institutional histories, these issues have become so settled, so reified, that debate about basic epistemology is effectively decommissioned. Not so in composition, where little is settled, or likely to become so very soon.

The easiest way to get at the two faces of the paradox I have just sketched out is to turn to Socrates' aggressive questioning of Gorgias about his "field." Driving this dialogue is Socrates' firm belief that rhetoric has no "field," at least not in the practical senses that other branches of inquiry have their own respective "subject matter" (233; 449d–450b), actual bodies of knowledge that can be codified and transmitted in measurable ways. Rhetoric is therefore both specious and corrupt. Gorgias basically assents to this line of attack, reversing its momentum to support his counterargument for the *privileged* status of his field, one which absent a prescribed territory can roam any-

203

where, absent a prescribed method can borrow whatever it needs from wherever it wants. At the center of this dispute about the relative merits of the field is, then, the most basic sort of disagreement about what is knowledge, how it is to be produced, and what are its ultimate "effects." The emergence of composition over the last generation or so can be construed, by analogy to this dispute, in either Socratic or Gorgianic terms: as a systematic search to acquire a proprietary disciplinary territory and apparatus, to become a distinct and self-generating field in all the ways that Socrates (and the contemporary university) would recognize and respect; or, as a progressive excursion through and among a wide range of other fields, appropriating from each what is useful, but never originating a method of its own, seeking ultimately not to reside among but to stand in a critical, even supervisory relationship with the rest of the disciplines. In the first of these scripts, composition seeks to escape from its low-status disciplinary betweenness; in the second, it makes betweenness its defining function.

Both of these scripts can be read as alternative responses to the contentlessness of composition, its paucity of knowledge-as-information, a condition that influences the "work" of the discipline in profound ways. Consider the composition teacher, for example. Just what knowledge-as-information does she have to offer in her classrooms? Composition has no textual canon in any of the customary, artifactual senses that characterize most other disciplines, or the other branches of English studies, like literature or criticism. The composition classroom tends to be constructed around less monumental kinds of texts than these. There are the ubiquitous text*books* for example, which lack the historical durability and intellectual standing we customarily accord to literary or even scholarly works. Or there are the "readers," with assortments of texts that can range anywhere from a John Donne poem to an article on DNA to a business letter, none of which "belong to" composition in any necessary way. Such unbridled discretion about materials is atypical in the university, especially in English departments where most courses are habituated to the disciplinary constraints that

204

preselect what students will read and write about. Because composition has no such obvious constraints, the subject of such a course can be really "anything," which makes it appear to other specialists to be insubstantial, even irrational, in precisely the ways that rhetoric appears to be insubstantial and irrational to Socrates. Oddly enough, even texts that would be accorded considerable status on their home terrain—a Donne poem in a sixteenth-century literature course or an article on DNA in a biology course—somehow lose their cachet by the translocation to composition. Or there are, finally, the essays that students are producing, which, again, can be *about* anything at all that a particular student or professor or program happens to choose. In this instance, the subject is nominal and the texts that comprise the "canon" for the course are by long tradition predefined as arbitrary and unimportant. It seems then that no matter which text one chooses for a composition course—textbook, reader, student writing—it brings with it no essential or self-sustaining body of knowledge-as-information. Then again, taking Gorgias's tack, one could argue that it is precisely because no texts belong intrinsically to composition that all texts become available for its use, and to a large extent for use on its own terms.

The lack of a canon creates a considerable problem for the composition researcher as well. Because compositionists have no prescribed subject, they also lack a prescribed object, a predefined something to investigate, to write about. Thus, research in composition is quite unlike research in most other fields. Composition has had to turn to other disciplines for most of its research apparatus, appropriating their various techniques for producing recognizably academic discourse(s). Rhetoric has offered one especially generative focal point for this kind of work, with Aristotle the most common ur-text. One needn't read far into his *Rhetoric* to see why this book has attracted a lot of interest among compositionists: Aristotle carves off a broad and substantial territory for his field. He begins with the assumption that effective persuasion is more a matter of "knowledge" (a term he uses over and over again), and of various kinds of quite teachable knowledge, than it is of instinct or innate talent. There is the knowledge of

205

the various kinds of public discourse, of their proper forums and formats, of human emotion, of intellectual processes, of content-laden
topoi, of political systems. All of these are, from his point of view, appropriate for and indigenous to the teaching of rhetoric in ancient
Greece. The degree to which they are transferable to twentieth-century America is arguable, for a variety of obvious cultural and institutional reasons. As is the degree to which they are transferable from
the (non?) field of rhetoric to the (non?) field of composition. But,
while compositionists might not be able to transport the actual content of Aristotle's "field" directly into their own projects, many have
emulated his ambition and/or borrowed his terminology.

Process theorists, for example, chose early on to abandon Aristotle's
specific litany of human emotion(s)—which are difficult to translate
into contemporary psychological systems—and sought instead for a
set of procedures (a mode of research, to use the parlance of the university) that would disclose for academic purposes the contemporary
equivalent of such suasive entities and forces. To enact this project,
investigators borrowed instruments and techniques for "discovering"
knowledge from disciplinary areas as various as cognitive psychology,
computer science, and sociology. Such borrowings allowed some compositionists to become for the first time researchers in a manner that
the university recognizes as reputable. That composition has not been
able to reach consensus on this particular way of defining its disciplinarity, or even to establish an indigenous methodological hybrid for
research from this cross-disciplinary mix (as, for example, a field like
artificial intelligence has) serves merely to aggravate, by fragmenta-
tion, the problem that motivated the moves in the first place. In effect,
while a large part of the discipline has staked a claim to a particular
body of knowledge-as-information, as well as to a "means of production" for generating additional knowledge (both of which are pre-
conditions for disciplinarity in the modern university), another large
part of the discipline considers this project ill-founded and alien. The
basic structure of this disagreement is repeated in ongoing arguments
about the proper place of qualitative research (which derives mostly

206

from education), or ethnography (which derives mostly from anthropology), or discourse analysis (which derives mostly from rhetoric), to name just a few of the most obvious trouble spots on the current landscape. Disciplinary integrity—and the consequent benefits that accrue from it in the economy of the contemporary university—is unlikely under such circumstances. On the other hand, one can, following *Gorgias*, argue that such seemingly irreconcilable differences are what make this *particular* discipline so potentially powerful in relation to its more staid and opaque academic counterparts, any of whose instruments can be borrowed or retooled to serve new and different purposes. Which is to say that *settling* these arguments may be more injurious to the identity of the discipline than sustaining them; for such arguments are what define an essential part of the *work* of the discipline, distinguishing it not only in matter but in kind from most other areas of academic specialization. From this vantage point, composition can be construed as one of the best sites to begin an interdisciplinary conversation about the academy's pedagogical structures and practices.

We compositionists tend to have a much easier time understanding ourselves, and being understood, in terms of the knowledge-as-skill that is proper to our domain. Reading and writing are to a large extent culturally self-defined as skills that are negotiable at the level of technique. And our historical lineage as a "service" function of the academy is, again, skill-grounded by its nature. The odd duality of our cultural constructions of literacy is reified quite precisely in the institutional apparatus that contains work in composition, which is simultaneously so crucial that no other work can be properly carried out without it, and so inconsequential that almost anyone is considered capable of doing it. This particular conundrum has been reenacted in its most basic form in the Writing Across the Curriculum (WAC) movement that has dominated writing instruction in the university for the last generation. There are, in effect, two primary models for the implementation of such a program, each of which answers the question "Who knows how to teach writing?" in a different way.

207

In one version, the answer is "the faculty of the English Department, especially those in the Composition Program, who will be happy to set up workshops and seminars to share their expertise with other faculty, and to provide ongoing support to other departments as they seek to execute this mission." While the position of privilege associated with specialization is not in this case equivalent to that of other disciplines—can we likewise imagine the faculty of, say, the Biology Department setting up a few workshops to teach us to teach biology in a writing class?—it is still a position of privilege in that it allows the "experts" to retain substantial control over the procedures, discourses, and practices that will implement the WAC initiative. In its opposite version, the answer is "anyone who writes for publication in any disciplinary discourse is, by definition, a writer and can therefore teach writing." Almost every professor in a research university becomes then a potential "expert" on the teaching of writing, at least, or especially, in his own field. In this format, writing generally remains in the province of the English Department, under the rubric of composition, only in its mode as a set of generalizable skills and techniques that need to be mastered prior to, or in concert with, this other, more specialized, disciplinary writing. In other words, it stands in a relationship of service to the rest of the curriculum.

There is very little prospect for the knowledge-as-skill function, in and of itself—especially at the service level—to support disciplinarity. While adequate skill with language might be a prerequisite for advanced study in any field or for a job or profession, it is not what that study or job or profession is about. By the same token, to recall *Gorgias*, the absence of such knowledge-as-skill is widely acknowledged to be a significant cultural and institutional problem, and in moments of crisis or need, the effective practitioner is a powerful, even valuable (if not highly valued) commodity. What I am suggesting is that compositionists may stand on much the same sort of ground in relation to pedagogy. Precisely because we are charged to teach a prerequisite skill, we are constantly being forced to consider the relationship of our work to that of the other disciplines. And, in the case of WAC we

208

are often called upon to teach teachers in other disciplines how to use writing to teach what they know. Again, this positions us at a fulcrum that we can use to leverage interdisciplinary conversations about teaching.

The knowledge-as-value aspect of our educational enterprise has been so much to the forefront lately in both our disciplinary discourses and in our general news that it is hard to imagine there are practitioners left unaware of the degree to which their work is politically/ ethically volatile. Whether the argument is over the ideological imperatives of "race/class/gender" for both the writer and the teacher of writing, or over the oppression that the "political correctness" of such discourse induces; whether the argument is over the students' "right to their own language," or over the need for a standard of "correctness"; whether the argument is over the mission of the university to produce literate workers and citizens, or over its obligation to instill a subversive critical reflexivity; we are faced daily with the issue of not just *what* we are teaching students to know or do, but *who* we are teaching them to become. From this point of view, students are constructed as "subjects" for our disciplinary work in a mode quite different from the one quantitative researchers use. Via this angle the classroom itself becomes a dense and provocative text, about which we can write credibly for publication, whether we deploy the discourses of the "right" or the "left" to do that work. The very fact that such political terms are a propos to our arguments suggests the degree to which what we do is inevitably value-driven, whether we want it to be or not. While other areas and disciplines surely deal with consequential value-related matters, I can't think of another that must deal with them so persistently and so integrally, as a daily matter of course. Here again, the field is well-positioned to orchestrate, in our time, the sort of conversation about a university's mission—both in the presence of and on behalf of students—that Socrates and Protagoras had in theirs.

209

I return to *Gorgias* to bridge this discussion, finally, to the figure(s) of the teacher. Let me begin by positioning myself in the most commonplace of our cultural stances toward Socrates: that he is right (from Plato's standpoint) and his antagonist, Gorgias, is, therefore, wrong. From such a vantage point, rhetoric becomes deeply suspect as an intellectual enterprise (as does its contemporary replica, composition.) But if this were Plato's agenda, why doesn't Socrates win this argument, as he clearly does not? He and Gorgias/Polus/Callicles argue more and more vehemently as their dialogue proceeds, and neither one flinches from his position. It is almost as if they choose, mutually, to give up the fight before they come to blows. In effect, Plato offers us, through Gorgias, a view of the nature and status of rhetoric that is as compelling and as powerful as Socrates'. We can, then, simply choose to endorse Gorgias's position at the expense of Socrates', as certain theorists have, thereby retaining the binary economy of the traditional way of reading Plato. Or we can abandon entirely our cultural compulsion to valorize Socrates (or his interlocutor) and see what Plato allows us to see here: a wonderful, double-faced, conundrum that captures perfectly the in-built contradictions of any enterprise, including our own, that seeks to address matters of public literacy. In other words, it is because of the defect that Socrates ascribes to rhetoric—its lack of any specialized content—that it can become powerful in the way Gorgias describes. And, in a further irony, it is because of this kind of almost ubiquitous power, that the field is so invisible and weak in the broader contexts of more rigid and traditional institutional hierarchies, like for example the contemporary university. These two are so inextricably bound to one another, I believe Plato is saying, that neither case can be made independently.

210   Assuming such a Platonic, rather than exclusively Socratic, vantage point helps to explain any number of other anomalies in the dialogues. These include the otherwise ludicrous reversal of positions in *Protagoras*, for instance, which draws attention, through its irony, to the mutual inattention of the two antagonists to the real audience of and purpose for their conversation, draws us ultimately to the prospect

that questions about the teachability of virtue are not answerable in yes/no terms; or the long, figurative display in *Phaedrus* in which Socrates criticizes long, figurative displays, calling our attention to the centrality of figure in all discourse; or the critique of writing written out in the *Phaedrus*; or the slavish conversation with Meno's slave.

And why does Plato choose to depict Socrates-as-teacher in so many different, even contradictory guises and modes? With Meno's slave, he is the master of the "leading question," exhuming the inbred knowledge of his subject. With Meno himself, and even more so with the irascible Anytus, these same techniques blow up in his face. With Gorgias, Socrates is more aggressive, overtly positional, relying often on extended rebuttals and attacks. With Protagoras, he is the obsessive questioner, deploying almost every kind of interrogation technique imaginable over the course of his debate, unable to resist this stance even when he assigns it to his antagonist, ending up, in part because of that inability, arguing on behalf of the opposite claim from which he started. With Phaedrus, he uses long, elegant speeches—a habit he abhors in Protagoras—to rebut Lysias's long, elegant speech, insulating himself from ultimate critique by claiming he is only repeating someone else's long, elegant speech, the self-contradiction of both his position and his pedagogical technique highlighted and evaded through the dissimulation of a displaced voice.

Every dialogue seems to show us a different teacher at work, as if Plato is saying that what makes Socrates an interesting and effective pedagogue is his mutability, his adaptability, not his consistency. But there are also many places where Plato, at least as I read it, is making as much fun of Socrates as he does of everyone else, or where other contenders get to display their pedagogical moves, often very effectively, particularly if we imagine ourselves into the silent places of their "absent" students, who are surely being "educated" and changed, even if Socrates is not. Socrates, Protagoras, Gorgias, Lysias, all of them, offer us a great deal to think about and use as we construct our own teacherly personae, ideologies, and practices. It is even possible to imagine the most docile of their students—Phaedrus and Hippocrates come first to mind—as redoubtable teacher figures in their own right, precisely through the generative possibilities opened up for us by their creative absences. It is tempting to think about how they, too, can be translated into our practices. As it is tempting to imagine a pedagogy modeled on Plato himself, who never gets to "speak in his own voice" and is therefore absent himself from these arguments.

Where might I begin to constitute a pedagogy premised on such "absences"? I wrote in "Race, Gender, and (Teaching a) Class" about how some kinds of learning are as often fostered by a teacher's silence as by his words; about how one of the functions of a good teacher is to open spaces for certain kinds of work to get done right there and then by others and not to fill those spaces up with his own thinking, especially that part of it that was "done" last semester or last year or for the last book; and about the odd and generative disembodiment that seemed to accompany both the presentation and the reception of the texts, mine and others, during our class-opening read-arounds. I wrote about the difficulties that arise when one wants, or tries, to speak on behalf of, or through, "others"; about the inevitable cultural con-structedness even of what we imagine to be our most authentic per-sonal voices; about how a general selflessness—in ways that include but surpass what a poststructuralist might mean by calling the self into crisis—in the face of large and important questions provides the oc-casion for certain kinds of dialogues to transpire, not perhaps as ex-tensive and sophisticated as the ones Plato facilitates, but often just as substantial, just as interesting, sometimes even just as strange. All of these are specific instantiations of the sort of pedagogical "absence" I am interested in exploring. I think as well about the clumsy distinc-tions we rely on to choose our pedagogical techniques, assuming that the proper means will somehow magically get us to a proper end even when we haven't given much thought to what that end is. The line we draw between the lecture and discussion "methods" is a good example. Even Socrates seems sometimes to teach just as well through his long displays as he does through his elaborate interrogations. Cer-tainly his second speech to Phaedrus is more pedagogically effective—

212

in both manner and effect—than his boring drills of Meno and his slave, in part because it is *not* "his own" speech. This raises an even more particular question about modes of questioning themselves. There is a general professional tendency, especially among those of us who teach small classes, to presume that the question/response format is more conducive to active learning than more declamatory approaches. And that is probably so in most cases. But this position fails to account for the many different kinds of questioning techniques that are available to teachers, each of which produces a different kind of "effect" and leads to a very different end. There is for example a huge difference between the sort of technique that Socrates uses with Meno's slave and the several different ones he uses with Protagoras. And these are not merely stylistic differences—they reach to the very core of the epistemic transaction. I can even imagine an argument in which Socrates' second speech to Phaedrus is promoted as a more effective mode of interrogation—of both the absent Lysias and of Phaedrus—than many of the actual question/answer exchanges he has with Phaedrus at other points in the dialogue. Again, this requires a construction of Phaedrus as a generative absence that may seem to be stretching the limits of his express characterization. But I can still imagine having that argument. And enjoying it. Even if it's one I am destined to lose on semantic grounds.

The classroom is that arena in which we are both called upon and allowed to bring into voice(s) a conversation—a conversation, when it all works, that has a life of its own, to the extent at least that its primary participants, the agents by which it is made audible, are as much constructions of the exchange and its context as it is of them, as much spoken *by* as speaking; a conversation that includes in very important ways all of those present to but absent from its actual expression, the nonspeakers, the listeners, the "silent participants" I talked about in my final Race and Gender postscript. I imagine Plato's figures in this way, as instruments through whom a particular argument is given its necessary voices—and its necessary absences, vehicles through whom we can sit in and listen, come ourselves to the verge of our own voices

213

over and over again, only to be returned again to silent attention, participating thereby in a process of inquiry through which Plato, without uttering a word in "his own voice," teaches us something even he cannot fully fathom, nor would ever need to. To the extent that we too can function in this manner, at least sometimes, in our classrooms, to the extent that we too can bring into play, or resist, as the occasion demands, the full range of "our" voices—which are after all given us to speak by surpassing cultural and institutional forces, from Plato to the arguments that dominate our specific departments—to that extent will we begin to understand the pedagogical potential that "absence" affords us; to that extent will we assume a measure of control again over our proper role in the intellectual life of the university.

AUTHOR/ITY IN THE CLASSROOM: QUESTIONING THE SOURCE

Socrates: I can't tell you offhand, but I'm sure I have heard some-thing better, from the fair Sappho maybe, or the wise Anacreon, or perhaps some prose writer. What ground, you may ask, have I for saying so? Good sir there is something welling up within my breast, which makes me feel that I could find something different, and something better, to say. I am of course well aware it can't be any-thing originating in my own mind, for I know my own ignorance; so I suppose it can only be that it has been poured into me, through my ears, as into a vessel, from some external source, though in my stupid fashion I have actually forgotten how, and from whom, I heard it.[1]

As a set of power relations, the typical pedagogical transac-tion in a university classroom is much more complex than it might at first appear. From a cultural and institutional standpoint, the domi-nant figure seems obviously to be the professor, whose authority—in its commonplace sense as a combination of credibility and control—

is sanctioned by prior processes of certification and reinforced by the ongoing privilege to assess performance. When the classroom is construed along these lines—as a scene, say, for the brokerage of valued commodities (credentials)—the professor clearly controls both the inventory (knowledge) and one of the main instruments by which its value is regulated (grades).

Anyone who has taught for very long knows, though, that the power that derives from this control is highly mitigated and easily overridden. The university is, after all, a marketplace of many different sorts, and it is therefore subject to a variety of market forces. Students for example are more and more these days construed as customers, and, as in any potential "purchase," to recall the Socratic term, the customer ultimately controls what matters most: money. While university professors are not, like the sophists, in the business of selling services in one-on-one negotiations; while we can even ignore most of the time the degree to which our paychecks derive in part from tuition collected; we all understand and must respect the ways in which considerable powers adhere to the role of the consumer in our institutions. Our daily lives—what courses we teach and to whom—are impacted, for example, by enrollment levels. At the entry level, we must consider, at least tacitly, matters of retention, especially if and when our local institution has an ongoing initiative in that regard, either for certain types of students or for general enhancement on a percentage basis. In certain kinds of introductory courses, we must consider matters of recruitment into the major, whether we imagine this in broad terms as a means of perpetuating our species or in narrow terms as a way of guaranteeing a clientele for our expertise. From an economic standpoint, then, the student is the dominant party in our transaction. A variety of tensions arise at the intersection of these two quite different modes of power, tensions that can enliven or disrupt the relationship they preconstruct.

We can see a similar dynamic in the more idealistic aspects of higher education. Most of us, I presume, are motivated to do some sort of "good" through our work, whether or not we want to declare those

216

intentions publicly, whether or not we can even formulate clearly what they are. And most students are similarly motivated by a desire to "better" themselves somehow through the educative process, whether or not that desire is strategized, whether or not its material conditions can be specified. Again, a variety of tensions arise at the intersection of these two, often quite different, ideas of the good, and they likewise can enliven or disrupt the relationship they preconstruct.

I could extend this inventory to more and more specific aspects of the power relations in the classroom: using the concept of the will, for example, to borrow a term from philosophy; or of *ethos*, to borrow a term from rhetoric; or of personality, to borrow a term from psychology. And the same dynamic would be replicated on a smaller and smaller scale: the potential for confluence or conflict that arises from the different economies that govern the roles of teacher and student in the classroom setting. It would be useful, obviously, to have a fully evolved taxonomy of such analyses, rather than the bits and pieces currently available to us—I think, for example, of the concept of resistance, which has been fairly well documented in teacher-student interchanges. But even that would get us only part of the way along the route of understanding the mechanisms that regulate classroom teaching. For what all of these approaches to the pedagogical dynamic have in common is the assumption that professor and student inhabit their positions relatively straightforwardly, deploying the discourses available to them with relative integrity (in its practical sense, as a self-consistency, as well as in its legalistic sense, as an accounting for sources).

Both the concept of prosopopoeia that I discuss in "Socratic Method and the Absence of the Student," and the term *duplicity* that I use from time to time in "Race, Gender, and (Teaching) a Class" to characterize the ways in which the work of writing and/or teaching is multiply layered—not to mention the above epigraph—suggest that such integrity, at the discursive level, is in certain crucial respects alien to the university classroom, an arena in which all parties operate as much as functions and fields as they do as individuals, giving voice to words and positions that are not their own—sometimes consciously, and with adequate acknowledgment, sometimes haphazardly and inaccurately, often at so many removes from the "source" that it is impossible to trace, let alone be aware of, genealogy. And both teacher and student often do all of this with varying degrees of earnestness and irony, complicating the ways in which author/ity is being vested in any particular utterance. I use this familiar slash-marked version of the word here to suggest a different kind of authority from the one we usually presume for ourselves by dint of our professional status and institutional position. I want to conserve and foreground the active function of the author that stands at the base of the concept, suggesting thereby how difficult it often becomes to determine who exactly is author-izing, even in some instances actually author-ing, what gets said in a university classroom. And it is often equally difficult to know the extent to which the various parties to a pedagogical transaction are assuming their available voices and playing their prescribed roles straight or with tongue in cheek, when they say what they mean or mean what the say, even who can properly be said to be speaking, and with what degree of deference to, or displacement from, the stated position, at any given moment.

There is no better literary display of the dazzling effects of this sort of deference and displacement than the *Phaedrus,* in which neither of the parties ever seems to be saying something in his own words, choosing instead to read from or quote from or render simulations of or just plain invent a panoply of dead/absent/imaginary "sources" to aid them in their struggle to control the conversation.

218
SOCRATES: No, my friend, . . . we must not just rely on Hippocrates; we must examine the assertion and see whether it accords with the truth. (516; 270c)[2]

One easy way to open a discussion of "authority" in the *Phaedrus* is through an examination of how Socrates chooses to stand in relation to the various authors he both defers to and challenges as the argument proceeds. I take my cue along these lines from Socrates' chronic urge to "examine assertion[s]," to interrogate them in a wide variety of ways in order to elicit the degree to which each "accords with the truth," a process that raises a perplexing array of questions about the status and function of the "sources" of Socrates' knowledge, not to mention our own. The pattern is established early in the elaborate dance that Phaedrus executes to avoid having to read-from-document the text of Lysias's speech, which Socrates finally forces him to extract from under his cloak. It is hard to know exactly why he is so reluctant to do that, though part of it must be his desire to impress Socrates with his memory and skill with elocution, if only as a step in the seduction that this conversation represents. But that Socrates insists on making overt the artifactual aspect of the text becomes quite crucial later in the argument, when he assails writing, vis-à-vis speech, as a pedagogical instrument. More immediately, it allows Socrates both to blame Phaedrus for the position that the speech represents—which he does by blaming his own first speech, an effort to best Lysias at his own game, on Phaedrus—and to forgive him for endorsing it, which he does by seeking to dissuade him of its efficacy. Just from a rhetorical point of view, a sharp distinction between rhetor and speech facilitates that kind of subtle discrimination. And it allows what could otherwise be a testy conversation to proceed in an amicable way, which is fairly important for a seduction.

Socrates offers an alternative to Lysias's argument, and along the same lines. That he decides to "cover my head before I begin; then . . . I can rush through my speech at top speed without looking at you and breaking down from shame" should offer one good signal that Socrates might not want to stand entirely behind this "tale" that he claims is being told "under compulsion by my good friend here" (484–85; 237a) and by various "muses," "divinities," and "nymphs." Socrates immediately disavows this speech as "foolish" and "blasphemous," "pernicious rubbish" (490; 242e), offering in "recantation" (502; 257a) his famous second speech, a direct contrary to the argument of his first speech.

So why bother delivering the first speech, when the second one declares his intentions on the subject? A good question. Part of the answer seems to me to have to do with this issue of authority, in its mode as control, as power. It's not enough for Socrates as peda-(phile)gogue simply to supplant Lysias's position with his own. He needs to demolish his competitor in the process. And part of the way he does that is proving that he can compose a better "evil" speech than Lysias. What happens here is that Lysias's seduction—in a figurative and perhaps also a literal sense—of Phaedrus is taken over by Socrates. We work now in a cultural and legal climate that proscribes many of the commonplace ways in which pedagogical relationships have, historically, been sexualized, so the metaphor of, and the practices associated with, Socratic seduction are quite problematic.[3] But certain parts of the analogy clearly apply to the contemporary academy: One of the ways in which the ground for professorial authority is prepared is by disestablishing the authority of others. This is, obviously, a key move for many of us in our research/scholarship modes. How and why we similarly endeavor to change, by disrupting, the affiliations, commitments, and allegiances of students—and we do it all the time, especially in our discipline, which is so clearly driven by ideological motives—is a matter of some consequence.

This strategic move of usurping the authority that Phaedrus has already invested in someone else is one way Socrates goes about controlling his relationship with him. He does it in smaller-scale ways by undermining the status of other "experts." In the portion of the conversation for which he personifies the discipline of rhetoric in order to question Phaedrus, for example, there is this exchange:

> SOCRATES: What? Are you acquainted only with the 'Arts' or manuals of oratory by Nestor and Odysseus, which they composed in their leisure hours at Troy? Have you never heard of the work of Palamedes?
>
> PHAEDRUS: No, upon my word, nor of Nestor either, unless you are casting Gorgias for the role of Nestor, with Odysseus played by Thrasymachus, or maybe Theordorus.

SOCRATES: Perhaps I am. But anyway we may let them be. . .
(506–07; 261b–c)

Here Socrates first renames his apparent sources as cultural proto-
types, dissociating them thereby from their authorial status. And
when Phaedrus calls him on this ploy, he basically dismisses them altogether, in their role as personal authors, as inconsequential to his
argument. What other purpose could Socrates have in obfuscating the
genealogy of his position than in maximizing his own authority at his
sources' expense?

This exchange immediately precedes Socrates' critique of Lysias's
actual speech. He has Phaedrus repeat for him, twice, the opening
sentences of the speech—"Read it out, so that I can listen to the author himself," he says before the second repetition—in an obvious en-
actment of the later claim that "if you ask [written words] anything
about what they say, from a desire to be instructed, they go on telling
you just the same thing forever" (521; 275d).[4] But Socrates does question those very words very aggressively and at a close level of detail,
concluding finally that Lysias "goes about it like a man swimming on
his back, in reverse, and starts from the end instead of the beginning"
(509; 264a). That Lysias's words are written, unchanging, makes them
much more vulnerable to precisely the sort of criticism that Socrates
is adept at deploying. Not only is this move crucial to the advance-
ment of his argument about "true" discourse, it really is "instructive,"
at least for Phaedrus, perhaps even, ultimately, for Lysias, to whom
Phaedrus promises to report. And, in point of fact, Lysias's words do
not say "the same thing forever." They say something quite different
to Socrates in each of their renditions here, as they said something
different to him in the first presentation to us through Phaedrus's rendering of the whole speech. So, in the very process of preparing for
his climactic argument on behalf of "living speech," Socrates inad-
vertently demonstrates one of its inadequacies. For, unless a position
can be reified, fixed, "written," it can't be properly interrogated at the
most basic level: as a position, declared, believed, authorized. The ul-

221

timate irony of this contradiction, while it may be invisible to Socrates, is not, to my way of reading, invisible to Plato or precluded for us.

Problems with re-presentation are endemic to pedagogical transactions. For example, in the forum of the classroom, spoken discourse can be so evanescent, so provisional in nature that it is sometimes difficult even to remember exactly what gets said let alone to trust that it accurately declares the position of the speaker. This poses significant difficulties when we try to write about what goes on there. For example, with a couple of minor exceptions, I chose not even to try to re-present, verbatim, actual classroom discussions in the postscripts I wrote for "Race, Gender, and (Teaching) a Class." The fact that I was writing these pieces so long after the fact and had no transcript to work from was one significant limiting factor. Absent this sort of documentation, we must depend on notes or memory—which can be quite unreliable by comparison—when we report to others on what went on in a classroom.

Unlike Socrates, who often plays it pretty loose with his "sources," we generally hold ourselves to a high standard of accuracy when we use one another's published work as a "source" for our own. And we have the means by which that standard can be applied: comparison to the "original" text. But when the "source" is remembered oral discourse, who is to say whether or to what degree it represents anything but a self-centered/interested (mis)take on what actually got said? Let's say, though, that I had a transcript of our proceedings. Would it solve my problem? Not entirely, for such a text is not equivalent to, say, a published article, in much the same way that Phaedrus's comments, and even Socrates' two speeches, are not equivalent to Lysias's speech in this dialogue. While Socrates can treat Lysias's speech as a fixed, durable expression of its originator's position (even if it is not)—much as we treat our colleagues' articles—both Phaedrus's comments and Socrates' speeches remain provisional; under (re)consideration, under revision, or even, in the case of the first speech, under erasure; throughout the dialogue.

I wrote to the Race and Gender class, in the essay of November 16,

222

about my sense that nothing anyone says or writes in an academic setting is ever fully "off the record." But that doesn't necessarily mean that everything is equally "on the record." While it is probably fair that we, as paid professionals, be held accountable for our classroom discourse, all of us I'm sure can think of times when we would have liked to have had an almost immediate chance at least to revise, if not to retract entirely, some of those "texts." Students, however, are positioned "provisionally" in relation to their discourse in the classroom —and most especially in a classroom of the sort that Toi Derricotte and I sought to construct in our course—in a much more vulnerable way. They are being chronically invited/required by us to speak extemporaneously, to try on or try out their positions in an atmosphere of both conciliation and contest. Under such conditions, they might well say things that, before the class is even over, they decide to drastically revise, if not disavow entirely. What then is to be the authority we accord to such pronouncements? This problem is complicated by issues of privacy, again especially in the sort of course Toi and I were teaching, where the declaration of "personal" information was a prescribed feature of its method. The expectation of some degree of confidentiality in such a setting seems to me to go without saying— to recall the metaphoric way in which I used this expression in the essay I've been indexing here. All of this is to say that even if I had had transcripts of our discussions, I most likely would not have used them in writing the essays that compose the first half of this book.[5]

When the "transcript" of the conversation between Phaedrus and Socrates returns to rhetoric, Socrates uses exactly the opposite strategy from the one I described above, perhaps because his initial ploy wasn't sufficient to fully undermine his sources. This is the one place in the dialogue where Socrates seems to be entirely scrupulous in specifying accurately the authors and texts he alludes to. And he proceeds in a perfunctory manner through his summary, and tacit dismissal, of sophistic rhetoric. Here, when he's asked by Phaedrus whether he's referring to Theordorus he says "[o]f course" (512; 267a), rather than, as above, "perhaps." Gorgias, Prodicus, Hippias, Polus, Protagoras, all are noted exactly, along with, in some cases, the titles of their "manuals." Socrates no longer either wants or needs any of the "authority" vested in these sources to accomplish his purpose in the dialogue, whether that purpose is presumed to be the elaboration of a properly "dialectical" rhetoric or the continued seduction of Phaedrus. What he needs to do is attach them firmly to positions he finds so trivial he can dismiss them from the scene once and for all, which he quite assiduously goes about doing.

Socrates uses another familiar strategy to chide Phaedrus when he gets feisty about his own knowledge of the "authorities." A good example of this is in the opening stage of his argument about the inadequacies of writing. After Socrates tells the fable of Thamus and Theuth, Phaedrus becomes dismissive: "It is easy for you, Socrates, to make up tales from Egypt or anywhere else you fancy." Finally, we might think, Phaedrus is beginning to question the "authority" of the primary "source" for these arguments about love and rhetoric. Socrates recovers quickly and decisively:

> Oh, but the authorities of the temple of Zeus at Dodona, my friend, said that the first prophetic utterances came from an oak tree. In fact the people of those days, lacking the wisdom of you young people, were content in their simplicity to listen to trees or rocks, provided these told the truth. For you apparently it makes a difference who the speaker is, and what country he comes from; you don't merely ask whether what he says is true or false. (520; 275b–c)

Phaedrus backs down immediately and is led docilely through the remaining steps of Socrates' argument.

But there's a contradiction at the heart of this rebuke that Socrates needs to keep Phaedrus from noticing: The only way, he says, to judge the "authority" one should ascribe to a rendered position—recalling the interrogation of Hippocrates I discuss in chapters above—is to know beforehand the truth to which it can be compared, like a model to its template. And this whole conversation is based on the premise that Phaedrus, like Hippocrates, does not, and perhaps cannot at this stage of his life, at least not without a lot of overt guidance, know

224

what the template of the truth is. Paying attention to, and taking to heart, the mandates of "trees and rocks," let alone the fanciful musings of this beguiling "lover of wisdom," is all well and good for those "authorities" who can distinguish unfailingly between the ones that tell truth and the ones that lie. For those who can't, making a distinction between the authority they ascribe to "tales from Egypt" and those they ascribe to more obviously sanctioned "experts" might be a useful strategy. That Phaedrus does not see this fissure in the argument is not surprising. By this point, Socrates has him entirely under his spell. Surely Plato sees it and intends us to see it as well, opening another space for us to examine the manner in which authority is marshaled to serve very specific ends in the pedagogical transaction.

> As to the soul's immortality then we have said enough, but as to its nature there is this that must be said. What manner of thing it is would be a long tale to tell, and most assuredly a god alone could tell it, but what it resembles, that a man might tell in briefer compass. Let this therefore be our manner of discourse. Let it be likened to the union of powers in a team of winged steeds and their winged charioteer. (493; 246a)[6]

The "briefer compass" of this metaphor of the charioteer goes on here, in Socrates' second speech, for many pages, as elaborate and extended a figure as you're likely to find anywhere in Plato. There is much that is odd and improbable about its placement in the context of an argument that Socrates, while attributing it to Stesichorus, seems in all overt ways to be endorsing. I begin with what this passage seems to me to be saying: When it comes to the most crucial question of this dialogue, perhaps even of the whole Socratic ethic— the question of nature of the soul—Socrates must rely on metaphor, on poetry, for his answer. Only a god could "tell" what the soul is; a man must "feed upon the food of semblance" (495; 248b).[7] This is a remarkable concession for someone with Socrates' contempt for poetical discourse. Later in this very speech, for example, he places the figure of the poet, as a possible human fate in the cycle of life that starts after the fall from the heavenly circuit of being, at the sixth level down from the "seeker after wisdom and beauty" (495; 248d). The only lesser fates are artisan or farmer, sophist or demagogue, and tyrant. In his closing to the speech, Socrates tries to distance himself from his reliance on figurative discourse by blaming it on Phaedrus—much as he blames his first speech, at least initially, on Phaedrus—suggesting in both cases that it is Phaedrus's faults and weaknesses that precipitate his. Still, if we are to take the preamble to the analogy of the winged charioteer at its face value, it seems inevitable: When "a man" wants to tell the tale of the nature of the soul, figurative language is his *only* available option.

That startling admission would be hard enough to comprehend in the context of Socrates' discursive system. But the distinction he draws between the short and the long here is equally puzzling. While divine discourse could render the nature of the soul directly, that would be a "long tale to tell." Human discourse, on the other hand, which is inevitably figurative when it confronts the ultimate questions, can somehow accomplish its goal in "briefer compass." One of the chief attributes of metaphor in Western epistemology is its brevity, its compactness, its capacity to render more economically, if not more lucidly, than "literal" discourse what something "is." We must, after all, especially in the Socratic epistemic, operate at several removes from the truth of being. To the degree that we can achieve through language a representation of the nature, the "form," of any aspect of being, it is only either (1) through "resemblances," which via the process of simulation introduce inevitable *dis*simulations—the main reason why Socrates can't abide poets in the utopia of his Republic—or (2) through the awkward machinations of literal language, which, because it seeks to avoid semblance, would require infinite extension to render form. But why, I wonder here, would the same limitations apply to the gods, who seem to hold an advantage over us in the capacity to perceive reality quite directly? Why can't they therefore render it both straightforwardly *and* economically? That they seem in this statement to be

226

afflicted just as we are by the limitations of literal discourse raises a very fundamental question about either the degree to which Socrates wants to stand squarely behind the assertions of his second speech or the degree to which he wants to stand squarely behind his express contempt for poetic semblances. Socrates' attribution of the whole of this second speech to Stesichorus (491; 244a) and his disclaimer about its central figure—that it "was perforce poetical, to please Phaedrus" (502; 257a)—are two indices of his apparent desire to distance himself from the above declaration. He can, then, both aver and disavow the elaborate figure that is so pivotal to his argument—which is one of the primary advantages of the duplicity that inheres to prosopopoetic discourse.

But where can we say that Plato stands on this basic epistemological question? No matter how I go at this passage—or many others in the Socratic dialogues—it is hard for me to see identity between the inherent duplicity of Plato's author/ity and the inherent duplicit*ies* of Socrates' authority. And all of this has a profound effect on what I presume to "learn" from Plato in this dialogue. When I imagine Socrates as the central teaching "voice" here—in his mode as the straightforward mouthpiece for an unironic Plato—this move in Socrates' second speech is, really, little more than a slick rhetorical trick, grander and more impressive than those of the sophists that Socrates goes on to critique in the latter part of the dialogue, but a trick nonetheless. The sanction against poetical discourse is sustained in the very act of its violation. What could be more impressive, rhetorically speaking, than that? When, though, I imagine Plato as the absent and ironic author, as the central teaching figure, an additional level of deference is introduced and Socrates now becomes a potential object of his own critique. In that framework, it becomes possible to see poetical discourse, metaphor, as the only legitimate discourse for rendering, even apprehending, "reality," the "truth." It even opens up the prospect for thinking that human discourse itself—as distinct from divine discourse—is in fact fundamentally figurative, poetic, in its "nature." Literal discourse ends up as a very weak, almost illegitimate alternative to

227

the figurative, a degraded mode of figurative discourse rather than its predecessor and parent. We may have devoted millennia to the perfection of its capacity to render "reality" precisely, but that project, in the imperative of this figure, is inevitably doomed. Even the prospect of a pure literal discourse available to the gods, one that can render reality immediately, seems to be foreclosed by the fact that their literal renditions of the truth involve "very long" tales, at least by comparison to their figurative, human, counterparts.

One could, then, as a "student" of this dialogue, choose to hear Plato in many different ways. That is one of the inevitable consequences of prosopopoeia. When Plato chooses to render this second speech at two removes from himself—from Stesichorus, through Socrates—he introduces considerable play into the potential pedagogical transaction. He makes it difficult, at the most practical level of "reading" the lesson of his text, to determine what authority we should ascribe to the statement I quoted. Why would a teacher do this? Why not just say straightforwardly, as, say, Aristotle does a few years down the philosophical line, "This is this and that is that," as if the matter is already resolved, settled. Well, perhaps because settledness is not Plato's pedagogical ambition, as it is clearly not Socrates'.

I offer this snapshot to suggest that the manner in which any teacher inhabits and deploys his or her authority can be quite difficult to pin down, that there is a wide range of alternatives available to us in that regard, and that each constructs the end of the pedagogical transaction in a different way. Aristotle is a good example of a teacher who speaks unambiguously, almost always in the declarative mode, as if matters of speculation are taken care of beforehand and need not be readdressed. Authority is conserved almost entirely on the teacher's side of the relationship. Knowledge is fixed and extant and can be transmitted efficiently in quite literal ways. Aristotle is the lecture-method personified. Socrates is a good example of a teacher who *leads* by questioning, who knows where he wants to go with his argument and with his student; who wants—generously, I think—to authorize his student to come to know what he wants him to know—

228

and not what he doesn't. To the degree that he is strategically hegemonic in his method, it is through his earnest desire to ensure the former and prevent the latter. One can take serious issue with the sort of
unsettledness that results from his interrogations—as Meno does in
complaining that they effect a mind-numbing "perplexity" rather than
productive change. But Socrates usually does everything in his power
to control the process. Plato is, at least as I read him, much harder to
pin down. In this small instance, for example, which I think is emblematic of his method, he really does allow us either to identify with
Phaedrus and to allow Socrates' trick to work, or to be much more
aggressive in calling Socrates' bluff, which immediately transforms
his argument into sophistry—of a very impressive sort, but sophistry
nonetheless. As Plato's "students" we are to some extent free to choose
both the nature and the significance of the lesson we will learn. There
is some play in his system, which allows us to engage in a much more
thorough-going reexamination of the role and status of metaphor, of
figure, of poetry, in human discourse, than either Socrates or Phaedrus
seems to be aware of. And that, I think, is a worthy project indeed.[8]

For example, I end up reading this whole second speech, from the
Platonic point of view, as a witty and devastating critique of the
Socratic attitude toward poetical discourse. At the most basic level
here, we have an argument *against* poetry being made *with* poetic
devices—because they are at least the best, if not the only, devices
capable of making that argument. The irony is inescapable. Socrates
does make a few very clever moves to try to avoid the apparent self-
contradiction in which he is caught here. They work quite well on
Phaedrus, but a more forceful contestant would have a field day at
Socrates' expense. I'm not willing to argue that Plato's position is exactly the opposite of Socrates' on the role of the status of figure in a
linguistic sense (that it is essentially and by definition what language
is and does), and of poetry in a cultural sense (that it is the highest and
most truth-laden rather than one of the lowest and most untrustwor-
thy modes of human discourse). I am saying that he makes a very good
joke here at Socrates' expense. He allows Socrates to backpedal from

229

its impact by attributing his speech to Stesichorus, which allows him as well to stand a couple of removes from these problems with the "author/ity" of the position. But by that act of deference he allows the contrary to the Socratic attitude toward figure to emerge as a fully author/ized alternative. That is an awful lot to accomplish pedagogically without ever uttering a word in your own voice.

⟡

>PHAEDRUS: . . . But now by what means and from what source can one attain the art of the true rhetorician, the real master of persuasion?
>
>SOCRATES: If you mean how can one become a finished performer, then probably—indeed I might say undoubtedly—it is the same as with anything else. If you have an innate capacity for rhetoric, you will become a famous rhetorician, provided you also acquire knowledge and practice. . . .
>
>All the great arts need supplementing by a study of nature; your artist must cultivate garrulity and high-flown speculation; from that source alone can come the mental elevation and thoroughly finished execution of which you are thinking, and that is what Pericles acquired to supplement his inborn capacity. (515; 269c–270a)[9]

I am not interested in endorsing, or even engaging really, Socrates' critique of the way rhetoric got taught and learned in his time. Contemporary rhetoric, while it may retain all of the elements that Socrates found shallow and potentially pernicious in sophistic rhetoric, has not only come to embrace the whole of the sophistic/Socratic/Platonic/Aristotelian system but also has extended the range of its province by appropriating texts and issues and problems that originate from many different disciplines: philosophy, biology, psychology, linguistics, literary criticism, cultural studies, et al. One could argue that rhetoric has become, in many respects, precisely the sort of "field" that Plato, if not Socrates, would approve of.

I want instead to transfer the terms of his critique of rhetoric to teaching, and especially the teaching of teaching, which as it stands in our profession right now is much like rhetoric was to Socrates: "no art, but a knack that has nothing to do with art" (506; 260e),[10] a general professional imperative fleshed out unreflexively with a disparate array of conventions, traditions, and techniques. What sort of endowed abilities, if any, are essential for competent teaching? What is it that we actually understand about "how to teach" that might legitimately be called a form of "knowledge" that we could share with one another professionally? And what is it that constitutes a suitable and instructive form of "practice" at teaching? Beyond a few palliatives and clichés, we have no answer to any of these questions.

I taught our department's Seminar in Teaching Composition ten times during the 1980s and early 1990s.[11] We offer this course in concert with the first-term teaching assignment—a section of freshman composition—of our new TA/TFs. Most of the course's participants are teaching for the first time in their lives. I had some of my most exciting and rewarding experiences as a teacher in that venue—and some of my most painful and depressing. Every year I asked myself the same question both before the course started and after it was over. And I find myself asking that question yet again here: What do I have (in both its proprietary and its imperative senses) to teach when I teach teaching? What does any of us have to teach one another about teaching? I've used a variety of structures and formats for exploring that question, and I still haven't found a satisfactory answer. Here I'll start with the set of categories—innate capacity, knowledge, and practice, a fairly ordinary and innocent group—that Socrates offers as a way of getting at one part of the problem that faces us when we must purport to teach teaching.

In our culture the general assumption seems to me to be that while "innate capacity"—what I call talent earlier in the book—is a prerequisite for one to become a "finished performer" as a teacher, it is neither a rare nor a singular endowment. Most people, in other words, following this cultural bias, could become teachers if they had the desire, and spent the time, to get the necessary credentials. For most K–12 teachers in the public schools this "innate capacity" needs to be "certified" through various kinds of instruction and assessment before any actual "practice" can begin. At the university level, oddly enough, this prior certification is generally not required. Anyone with a college degree can begin teaching a university class during their first term as a supported graduate student. And most of those graduate students will be asked to devote no more than a few credits of their academic time to "teaching" during their long progress toward the Ph.D. In other words, the vast majority of university professors have never "learned" to teach in any measured and systematic way, and they rarely teach teaching in any measured and systematic way. They must, and do, rely largely on their "innate capacity" to perform the pedagogical part of their academic mission in an expert and professional manner. Again, this is not to say that we would all be better teachers if we had been "taught" how to teach. It is only to say that, as a form of knowledge upon which we can rely to guide our work and specify its nature and consequences to others, "teaching" is very superficial and inchoate by comparison to its professional counterpart, "research."

This is not a problem for most of us—nor for most of our students —most of the time. But it does become a very big problem when one is called upon to teach teaching in the context of a graduate program. One can't, obviously, rely on "innate capacity" to generate a set of required readings or to guide assessment. It becomes necessary to confront the question of what, in fact, is the "knowledge" that constitutes, or is pertinent to, this thing we call "teaching." There seem to be two quite distinct kinds of knowledge at play in the Socratic system, one having to do with the legitimate "content" of a prescribed "field," which he often calls "facts," and one having to do with the mechanism by which those facts are sorted and marshaled toward a given, and greater, usually morally driven, end, which he generally calls "truth." This is as good a place as any to start thinking about what we have to teach about teaching. The first assumption—that one must actually know something prior to the pedagogical transaction—is one we take for granted. Our way of figuring the nature and role of disciplinary

232

knowledge is pretty much like Socrates': a body of related information about a prescribed part of "nature." The vast majority of our current certificatory procedures are geared around the assumption that mastery of this body of knowledge is the primary purpose of graduate education. We marshal this initiative under the aegis of "research," and we have extraordinarily demanding and sophisticated ways to warrant this sort of disciplinary knowledge. The assumption here is much like Socrates' in relation to good speaking: One must know one's subject before one begins to teach it.

That is all well and good, except when we think about those new teachers in my Seminar in Teaching Composition. They haven't, first of all, had time to "master the subject" they are in the midst of teaching. But to say that this is simply an unfortunate but necessary flaw in the economic structure of the contemporary academy is both inaccurate and unfair. How many of the rest of us, for example, have a cogent idea of the "subject" we need to have "mastered" when we talk about teaching composition, where, most often, we are relying in pretty standard ways on textbooks and approaches of someone else's design? And many of us would even be hard-pressed to specify in any great detail, let alone justify, the underlying ideology that drives the textbook or approach of our choice. Arguable, as well, is the degree to which we consider ourselves entirely "knowledgeable" in the areas of many of our teaching assignments on the literary side—where it is much easier, by dint of long-standing scholarship and tradition, to know just what it is we should know before we are deemed expert enough to teach it—a problem with *my* "authority" on the "subject" of the course that I wrote from in the first half of this book. Like the first-term teaching assistants in my seminar, we quite often best "learn" the subject we are teaching through the activity of teaching. So, while knowledge a priori may be a useful criterion for determining good classroom teaching, it is by no means a sine qua non, especially in a field like composition, for which even knowing what "knowledge" *is* can be problematic.

We have an equally hard time negotiating this problem in terms of

Socrates' notion of "truth," even at the most practical level of the "truth about his subject," a mode of knowledge that "successful discourse presuppose[s]" (505; 259e). Most would accede to the generalization that the "truth" about, say, Shakespeare is not, should not be, and never will be, settled in many areas that are of great import to our discipline. And an area like composition makes Shakespeare studies seem quite static and tame at that epistemic level. There is, of course, an obvious disciplinary "body of knowledge"—a canon of "approaches" for construing what good writing is and how it is accomplished—that constitutes the "field" of composition. One of the ways of designing a course to teach teachers of this discipline is to introduce and discuss, as an array of comparable alternatives, a selection of those approaches. To some extent, we could argue, all of these approaches are "true" parts of the discipline of composition, and it is important to acquire a knowledge of them to claim "mastery." But as Socrates complains, along these lines, about the teaching of rhetoric: "And so they teach these antecedents to their pupils, and believe that constitutes a complete instruction in rhetoric; they don't bother about employing the various artifices in such a way that they will be effective, or about organizing a work as a whole; that is for the pupils to see to for themselves when they come to make speeches" (515; 269c). Or, to extend my analogy along these lines, when they come to teach their classes.

There is, then, this other level of truth that concerns Socrates, the only level that concerns him ultimately, one that may have application to the project of teaching teaching. When Socrates talks about the "truth of his subject," what he really means is the right and wrong, the "good and evil" (505; 260c). This highly moralistic discourse is quite awkward in, even alien to, the context of the contemporary research university. But we do I think have comparable, more comfortable ways of talking about this level of "truth." Almost all of us for example would concede to having a preferred set of ideological "positions" that precede and inform our choices not so much of course material and day-to-day pedagogical technique as of critical "method." This facet

234

of the "truth" of our work is much more visible, almost unavoidably so, in an area like composition, for which "method" is nearly everything. We sort through and choose from the array of competing, even mutually contradictory methods, by making decisions about our own sense of their relative "truth." We may do this fairly casually, by simply deferring to a method that a trusted colleague or a famous author or a prominent program endorses; we may do this grudgingly because our own program or department requires it; we may do this viscerally or intuitively on the basis of the right "feel"; or we may do this in a very rigorous and highly conscious way, as a sort of "moral" obligation.

The teaching seminar I refer to tends to be constructed along these lines. We have, as a program, a method that we both develop and endorse. Its ideological aspect is made quite visible and overt. All first-year teaching assistants are required to use it. While this is often perceived as a mode of indoctrination or oppression, it is intended as quite the opposite. For a teaching seminar designed under the aegis of this way of thinking about the truth must not simply offer its preferred method, it must interrogate it in the framework of its ambitions and its alternatives. This is, then, quite a different way of thinking about teaching the canon of a discipline. Here we have not simply a congeries of approaches from which one can select this one or that one as relative co-equals. We have an argument with and among a number of mutually exclusive, incommensurable methods, each of which is informed and motivated by an ideology that will be expressed in certain of its aspects and tacit in others. The process of exploring in a reflexive way that ideological initiative becomes the "subject" of the course.

It would seem, then, that the approach I'm recommending is essentially a Socratic one. I say, however, any number of times in these essays, and I'll say it again, that I have no interest in recommending a Socratic solution to problems that belongs to our culture and our time. I actually believe that his solutions are not particularly good ones. That makes it imperative in this instance that I try to specify the ways in

235

which my version of the role of the "truth" in teaching teaching is different from his version of the role of the "truth" in teaching speaking. One way at this is to acknowledge that while there are advantages to teaching method-as-ideology through an approach that one endorses wholeheartedly and has a voice in formulating, one could just as well do the same with any method, even a disagreeable one. That we choose our own approach as the central text in the Seminar in Teaching Composition is more, to my way of thinking about it, because we care about, and are accountable for, the instruction that large numbers of our undergraduates are getting as a consequence of the work of the seminar—and we, as a program faculty, are lucky enough to stand in concert on many basic assumptions about what literacy in the university is and is for, on what "effect" (recalling *Protagoras*) we want to achieve—than because we feel a need to indoctrinate our graduate students in the "truth" of our approach. That may seem a weak, even specious argument, given the power relations that regulate relative authority in a context like this, which, unlike other graduate seminars, puts directly at stake not only the intellectual but also the economic condition of its "students." But it is an argument that mitigates the degree to which the teacher in this framework is compelled to function with a Socratic single-mindedness. It introduces play to the system. At the level both of day-to-day pedagogical practices and of ultimate effect that makes a great deal of difference.

Another analogy I want to draw between the teaching of teaching in the contemporary academy and the teaching of speaking in ancient Greece derives from the notion of "practice" that Socrates specifies as an essential prerequisite for the "finished performer." Just what sort of "practice" is he talking about here? Initially it seems to be merely the relatively trivial sort of practice involved in having to plan and deliver a number of different speeches under a number of different kinds of conditions. But he seems almost immediately to call into question, if not dismiss entirely, the ultimate efficacy of this kind of practice—"the line of approach adopted by Lysias [the villain of this whole dialogue] and Thrasymachus" (515; 269d). He then offers a strange kind of "practice"—though some readers may choose to place this under the heading of "knowledge"—as an alternative: "garrulity and high-flown speculation" (515, 270a), what Helmbold and Rabinowitz translate as "leisurely discussion, stargazing," and Nehamas and Woodruff as "endless talk and ethereal speculation."[12]

The conversation drifts almost immediately away from this odd sort of practice/knowledge into a much more rigorous, and boring, analogy between medicine—the science of "the nature of body"—and rhetoric—the science of the nature "of soul" (515; 270b). I think we see in this momentary flash and retreat a perfect example of the contradictory intellectual inclinations that afflict Socrates, making his "method" impossible to specify and difficult to replicate. On the one hand, he seems in love with, even addicted to, conversation for its own sake, and the theme and progress of this dialogue are rife with the playful sort of "madness" that carries the "lover of wisdom" through the pleasures of witty repartee and poetic displays. On the other hand, he is equally in love with, or addicted to, the rigors of the dialectic. As he says himself, after a long critique of Lysias's speech: "I am myself a lover of these divisions and collections, that I may gain the power to speak and to think" (511–12; 266b). Like the two steeds pulling his proverbial charioteer, these contrary inclinations work sometimes in concert and sometimes at odds with one another. Then there is Socrates-as-charioteer—compelled by an obsession for the "truth" that he seems quite often to have a very clear notion of, though he refuses to disclose it. This is the Socrates that makes me most uncomfortable. Perhaps because I am like him in that respect or am often misunderstood to be like him when I'm not. Perhaps both. I tactically diminish the "oppressive" threat of this irritating ideologue by deferring, or retreating, (depending on how you look at it) to Plato, whom I always imagine as having a good sense of humor about the excesses of his primary mouthpiece, as I always, in my professional life, try to imagine "myself" as having a good sense of humor about the excesses of my "self." Finding a way to add this last layer of irony to the teaching, especially to the teaching of *teaching* is, I think, the key. It is im-

237

portant, crucial even, to have a set of strong beliefs about what good teaching is and is for at this level, in this culture, at this time. It can be extremely difficult to "remember" that it's the process of thinking the matter through, from the level of first principles to the level of minute technique, that most matters, that is the "subject" of such an enterprise, and not the specific "answers" that emerge at any given moment. But it is essential nonetheless, for me at least, if I'm to avoid disliking about my "self" the things I most dislike about Socrates.

All of this raises an ancillary set of questions about the notion of "practice," which is so endemic to contemporary critical discourses— in its mode as *praxis*, for example—that its meaning is overdetermined for us, as it was not for Socrates, who seems above to be using the term in a relatively straightforward and "untheorized" way. We, of course, have the prospect for construing practice in a much more aggressive manner, as a mode of knowledge in its own right, or at least a means by which various kinds of knowledge can be generated and revised. It is this form of knowledge—not the one that derives from having done the same thing repeatedly thereby feeling qualified to tell someone else how to do it; but the one that derives from having done something in many different ways thereby feeling qualified to call them similarly into question—that constitutes a good part of the domain proper to "teaching." The teaching of teaching, therefore, must to some extent involve the systematic discussion of, and reflection upon, the ongoing, actual "practices"—from the implementation of course materials to comments on student writing to the details of personal interaction in the classroom—of the participants in the enterprise. By that means these practices can be theorized in the context of both the prescribed method and the broader disciplinary matrix of which it is a part. This becomes, to my way of thinking about it, the contemporary equivalent of the "study of nature" with which, according to Socrates, the "great arts" need to be supplemented.

Socrates even offers us one set of metaphors for construing how a part of that study might proceed: what he calls "high-flown [or ethereal] speculation," "stargazing." But just what are these, as modes of discourse? My gut feeling is that while Socrates may—like Pericles—have spent much of his apprenticeship cultivating his "garrulity" in "leisurely conversation" with someone like Anaxagoras, Pericles' "teacher," he is not doing that in most of the extant dialogues. If this one for example is, in one of its modes, a "seduction," it is a seduction by domination. Look at what happens to Phaedrus, as a figure in this romance, as the dialogue proceeds. At the outset, he is "my friend" (476; 227a) and "my dear fellow" (477; 228d). Socrates repeatedly addresses him in a collegial, even deferential, way, as if he might be his equal. By the beginning of Socrates' second speech, however, through a series of very delicate put-downs, Phaedrus yields to Socrates' power. "Where is that boy I was talking to?" Socrates asks. "He must listen to me once more, and not rush off to yield to his nonlover before he hears what I have to say." To which Phaedrus answers: "Here he is, quite close beside you, whenever you want him" (491; 243e).[13] While this might appear on the surface to be merely another form of the rhetorical deference I have been talking about—Phaedrus agrees to function as the audience that Socrates' speech seems to need—I think the analogy to sexual seduction is useful: Phaedrus is now Socrates' "boy." As the dialogue continues, the relationship degrades even further, until, in its final stages, Phaedrus's contributions are little more than robotic tics necessary for Socrates to move from point to point, speech to speech. From colleague to beloved to lackey, the domination is complete. I can't imagine a worse progress for a pedagogical relationship, most especially at the graduate level, where the ultimate ambition is to create full-fledged colleagues, not drones. No, there's not much stargazing going on here, except in the sense of Phaedrus gazing at the "star" professor, ending up starstruck rather than enlightened.

239

But it is possible to see this dialogue—all of them really—as Plato's stargazing, as speculative in the most playful sense of that word, a process of looking closely at something, sort of for the fun of it, which is basically what Socrates thinks that writing—and that's what Plato is obviously doing—is best suited for. Again, this sharp distinction between author and character offers Plato as a different kind of pedagogical model from Socrates. In a sense, Plato gets to try on, without acceding entirely to the consequences of, his character's compulsions. It is this layer of remove that marks the distinction I have in mind between what I am calling authority (which belongs to Socrates, as a mode of self-identity) and author/ity (which belongs to Plato, as a mode of self-reflexivity).

> SOCRATES: . . . And once a thing is put in writing, the composition, whatever it may be, drifts all over the place, getting into the hands not only of those who understand it, but equally of those who have no business with it; it doesn't know how to address the right people, and not address the wrong. And when it is ill-treated and unfairly abused it always needs its parent to come to its help, being unable to defend or help itself.
>
> PHAEDRUS: Once again you are perfectly right.
>
> SOCRATES: But now tell me, is there another sort of discourse that is brother to the written speech, but of unquestioned legitimacy: Can we see how it originates, and how much better and more effective it is than the other? (521; 275e–276a)

This other discourse is "living speech" (521; 276a), the currency of most kinds of "teaching," not only for Socrates but for us as well. This writing/speech dichotomy, despite our extended disciplinary critique of the philosophy of "presence" that supports its otherwise arbitrary conceptualization of textuality, remains for the most part intact in the research/teaching binary that defines the most practical elements of our work in the university. Research is written, permanent, univocal, artifactual, portable, and most often broadcast in our absence. Teaching is oral, perishable, multivocal, evanescent, ad hoc, and most often immediately social. We in the contemporary research university, though, have obviously inverted the hierarchy of importance that Socrates establishes here, choosing to valorize our textual credentials and to minimize our pedagogical credentials. This is a perfectly "legitimate" inversion, though it has one striking problem in our discipline in particular, where the vast majority of our research generates very little capital, either cultural or economic. Most of us, frankly, myself included, are simply not brilliant or generative enough as scholars to warrant our positions solely on the basis of our historical contribution to the body of knowledge that comprises our field. And our disciplinary research is simply not practical enough to earn our way in the world on the basis of the knowledge we "invent" or even the texts that we publish. Unless we author a popular textbook or are among the tiniest upper echelon of the elite (in which case we can command, ironically, significant recompense for our public speaking) the money we get paid derives mostly from our capacity to teach—either directly through tuition or indirectly through state and federal funding. The fact that we are rarely called upon to demonstrate that we merit those expenditures is, as far as I can see, mostly the result of the inertia of historical precedent. The figure of the classroom teacher personally present in a public room with a group of students collectively present for and involved with one another has served as a commonplace in our profession for generations, for centuries even. And the economy that supports that commonplace on its current large scale is so deeply entrenched both in the academy and the culture that we tend not to be aware of it, let alone question it.

It is really only in the last forty years or so, with the advent of technologies like television, then interactive video, and more recently computers that alternatives to that traditional classroom have become available: the absent professor teaching remotely to separate students, clearly a more economical strategy for accomplishing the teaching-related business of a university, primarily because in such a format, one teacher can do the work of many, and he can do it over and over and over—sort of like Socrates' nightmare vision of written texts—without any additional expense for salary.[14] But is it as effective? So far, it has not proven to be. Otherwise many of us would already be out of work. But it remains unclear whether that derives from the impossibility of the mission or from temporary inadequacies with currently available technology.

You will note, above, that there are three distinct kinds of "presence" that characterize the traditional classroom: The teacher is present to the class, the class is collectively present to the teacher, and all parties are individually and simultaneously present to one another. At least until now, the extant technology cannot duplicate this level of interactivity very predictably or very efficiently, not by comparison to the much more labor-intensive practice of placing many teachers in many classrooms with many small groups of students. "Educational TV," for example—with various "programs" widely available to anyone at home through normal broadcasts—had problems with *any* kind of interactivity, not to mention with the matters of assessment necessary for credentialing. The teacher can, through such a medium, be made virtually present to vast numbers of individual and separate students. But there is no possibility for attention to, feedback from, or intervention for the individual student, let alone any prospect for the existence of a "class." And assessment, credentialing, is extremely difficult. In a culture like ours, where it might be accurate to say that "higher" education has been commodified in very specific ways, such problems are devastating. Videotapes of "expert" teachers essentially delivering lectures that can be viewed remotely by individuals and groups have the same problems with responsiveness to audience, making them a similarly unsuccessful alternative, despite significant investments of energy and capital by numerous universities. Interactive video-teaching, in a format where a professor teaches his course "live" to a remote audience of separate classes or students, each of whom can, with some degree of immediacy, engage actively in the work of the course, is somewhat more effective in this regard. But the intercessory technology makes it much more time consuming for individuals to "contribute" to the discourse of this sort of class—usually it's only in a question/answer format. And it is extremely difficult for discourse to be generated among several parties in anything approach-

242

ing "real time." In a purely material sense (ignoring the portability of students, that is) such a classroom is, then, less efficient, and probably even more expensive, than just scheduling a large lecture section on campus. CD-ROM teaching was the next step along this path, solving through hypertextuality many of the space/time problems associated with more primitive media. In this interactive format whole courses can be designed in such a way that the consumer may access the material in the manner best suited to her learning needs and style. Assessment can be accomplished quite easily via Internet hookups. Still, though, it is extremely difficult for the student to be "present" to the teacher, or vice versa; nor is it possible for anything we might recognize as a class, conceptualized as a simultaneously engaged collective, to emerge.

It is probably only a matter of time before some combination of technologies—Internet, holography, virtual reality, robotics, artificial intelligence, whatever—makes it possible for a "teacher" to be virtually present to members of a class who are virtually present to her and to one another. Then there *will* be an alternative delivery system capable of competing with what we do now. Classrooms, campuses even, would become anachronistic. And so would most of us. Instead of a herd of faculty teaching personally in their separate spaces, a few "experts" working with a technical staff could generate the material for a whole curriculum. And why not? Is anything really lost in such a transition? That, I think, is the question. Socrates asked it quite aggressively in response to a much less threatening technology—the written text, which has proved to be a generally weak educator absent an actual "teacher" to mediate and evaluate its effects on the "student." Whether or not we want to buy the Socratic argument about the soul-to-soul relationship between teacher and student—and I'd wager most of us don't, at least not if it means carrying along all the paternalistic baggage of his figurative demonstrations—there has until now been something about such an arrangement that seems necessary for most people to "learn" what teachers have to "teach." Are we about to reach the limit of that necessity? Will our "presence" soon be duplicated

243

adequately by technological means? The question we are faced with, then, that needs addressing, is: In what manner and to what degree is it necessary, or even useful, for a teacher to be actually rather than virtually present with her students—and in what specific ways—for certain parts, or kinds, of learning to occur? If we believe that actual presence is important, I think we had best be preparing arguments on behalf of what we have to offer through classroom teaching. If we believe it is not, I think we had best be preparing for the demise of our kind.

CONCLUSION

"... the demise of our kind." There's an ominous phrase to end a book with. Or maybe just melodramatic. I'm of both minds about this, as I am about most things concerning change. It seems inevitable that the figure of the professor as we know "him" will ultimately become anachronistic unless we dramatically reconfigure the manner in which "his" work is constituted. I foreground these masculine pronouns intentionally here to indicate that despite the various and laudable ways in which our profession has been diversified over the last generation or so, the manner in which we measure the relative merits of our work, the means by which power is accrued and wielded, even the instruments by which status is regulated remain, in my view, essentially as they were a generation ago, at least at the level of given structural assumptions about what and who matters and what and who does not in the economies of our workplace. I've used the term inertia a number of times to describe the general drag of the invisibly entrenched familiar against the force of individually initiated changes; and I am often astounded, retrospectively, by how little things actually do change at a fundamental level, even over generations, in our discipline, in our institutions, in our culture, no matter how dire the circumstances.

If this book could be said to have a theme, this one, *change*, which has been a recurrent motif, would be a good candidate. I've been specifically interested in the kinds of change that a professor is capable of achieving, for himself and for others, through classroom teaching. I believe we underestimate both the range and the potential consequence of those kinds of changes. The process of demise that I allude to above, if it actually occurs, is a change of a different order of magnitude from these, in that many of the forces that might impel it are out of our control. At the same time that competition among colleges and universities is increasing, the commodity they offer seems to be becoming more and more expensive. When these two factors get stretched too far out of whack, technological solutions to the problem of "delivery"—our current function in the system—will become even more attractive alternatives than they are now. And the outsourcing of certain parts of the general instructional function to institutions outside of the free-standing university, which has already started, will increase, perhaps exponentially. All of that's inevitable. It's just a matter of whether, in the long run, the professoriate retains its primacy in this economy.

One way we can influence the outcome of this process is to begin to think strategically about what we are, and have to offer, that cannot be replicated in either the virtual or the corporate university. We can start this process of (re)definition by (re)examining that aspect of the work of the university over which we properly wield considerable author/ity: its academic mission. If there is one thing that I want to emphasize in this regard, it is that the central defining constituency in the university—when it is construed broadly as a cultural force with a coherent intellectual agenda—must be the faculty. Not in the highly personalized terms of the current "star" system, which is, in my view, one of the worst ways to concentrate power in the professoriate. But in a more general way, as a function, through which the work that is proper to the university—which I continue to characterize as "intellectual" for lack of a more specifically conceptualized term—gets defined in our classrooms. We need to find better ways to make our "presence" felt there, to figure out what makes the classroom setting —where everyone is physically there in real time—a unique venue for teaching and learning, difficult, perhaps even impossible, to replicate electronically.

One reader of this text asked me, "So what *do* you think we should we be doing to accomplish all of this?" I drafted several responses to that question, to use right here in my argument. And they all sounded exactly like the ones we read all the time, approvingly, and then don't pay attention to: high-sounding, vague, forgettable. This is not, as I said early on, a book that purports to offer big answers. Still, I can't in good conscience leave that question unaddressed. So let me offer two starting points.

The first is, in keeping with the tenor of the book, quite "personal." About ten years ago, in the midst of what looks to me now, in hindsight, like a necessary, even predictable, gender-related passage in my career as a teacher—when the roles appropriate for me to play were shifting from the fraternal to the paternal—I was standing in front of one of my composition classes, just before it started, pacing around, which is what I usually do, preparing to do my job, to the best of my ability, as I always had. I suddenly realized in a conscious way what I had been aware of in my nervous system for a couple of years: The teacherly personae and pedagogical techniques that had worked so predictably for me during the first decade of my career were not working with the same efficacy any longer, or were producing entirely different, and often quite troubling, effects. I had been struggling for some time to cope with this apparent failure of the causal relationships I had come to take for granted in "my" classroom. But I too often felt like I was performing surgery in the dark. My frustration in response to this meant that, quite often, I was doing my work more and

247

more on the strength of sheer will and less and less for the great pleasure and satisfaction that it gave me. This, it struck me, was a serious problem, not only for the students in front of me but with my life. And I knew I needed to do something about it. At that moment, a question lurched forward with an unusual force: "What am I doing here?" I remember mouthing its words beneath my breath. The effect this question had on me was more like waking up from a coma in an alien place than like "what's my plan for today?" That question has dogged me ever since, and I have tried over and over again to address it respectfully.

But its mode keeps changing. In one of its guises it asks me to explain "What am I doing *here*?"—a compositionist, teaching General Writing at the University of Pittsburgh, in front of a particular class, when this locus is imagined as the terminus of an almost infinite series of prior choices, some quite mindful, others entirely accidental. Why for example wasn't I setting up an experiment in a physics laboratory or selling a hammer in a hardware store, or any number of the other worthy jobs that I had seriously considered in my time? And who exactly were these people in front of me? What did I, or could I, presume to know about them? Where should we start? And where should I expect us to finish?

In another of its guises it asks me to explain "What am I *doing* here?" —in vocational terms, as in actually accomplishing, making a contribution, serving the world. What is the ultimate worth of this work I continue to perform with such apparent urgency? How does it relate to my wider sense of what work is and is for in a broadly moral or historical sense? Is it what I should be using my "talents" for right now? Are there ways I need to be redefining that work for myself, for my profession? How do I go about doing that in a way that fits my temperament and my principles?

In another of its guises it asks me to explain "*What* am I doing here?"—as in teaching, with this "subject," at the level of practice, in terms of the knowledge or skill I, as a function of my discipline and my institution, purport to provide. What *is* my "discipline" at this point in my career? What do I want it to be or to become? How can I contribute to that process? What effects do I want to achieve by means of it? What are the value(s) of writing and reading as I am trying to teach them? Do I really have something of consequence to offer my students, and is that what I really am offering them?

In another of its guises it asks me to explain "what am I doing here?" —as opposed to, say, someone else, one of the many excellent colleagues I have met along the way for example, who are now, for no good reason, out of the profession or working in marginal positions. What, further, am I doing here in a selfish sense, in terms of what I really want and need out of my life? And, more importantly, who is this "I" that I imagine to be "there" in the first place? Is "he" properly integral with the "I" of my life, this white male moving through his fatherly forties, a transition I have always dreaded and now am about to achieve; or is he an empty and anachronistic figurehead who needs to be recast, or even cast out?

So, "What am I doing here?" I keep asking myself that question. I have spent a lot of time living in the shadow of its imperative, so it doesn't scare me now quite the way it did for the first couple of years. On the basis of this experience, I say: If you are looking for a place to start thinking about teaching, ask yourself that question while you're standing in front of a class, just before it starts. And don't settle for the answers that are always already there for us, the answers that the profession at large offers us, clichés so easy to mouth, to believe, to pretend are our own. They are it seems to me designed to keep that question from having a "personal" import. In part, then, what I have to offer is that question. And this book, which is a first installment on certain parts of my answer to it.

My second starting point is "practical." Above, I posed a very simple, even trivial, question for myself, and it has taken me years now to answer it even partially. That question, like the two parts of this book, opened up—or more accurately exposed—a rift that I cannot seem to fill. I think we underestimate the number of our questions that have that potential. So we don't bother to wait for, and then listen to, the responses they elicit, even when they are our own. Anyone who teaches "discussion" courses regularly knows just how hard that is to do in a routine way in the classroom, let alone in our own intellectual life—to listen, I mean, with patience and attention. We pose a question, call on someone, and before she starts to talk we're (1) filling in the answer we expect or hope for; (2) planning what the next question might be; (3) remembering what we said ten minutes before, with an eye toward expanding it; (4) thinking about the last class or the next one, trying to gear this moment to that longer narrative; or (5) just trying to find the chalk—almost anything but preparing ourselves to listen to exactly what is about to be said. We do much the same thing in our collegial meetings: planning our interventions, taking notes of what we intend to say, getting bored or frustrated or irritated; almost anything but preparing ourselves to listen. And we often do the same thing when we read, whether it's our students' work or our colleagues': filled up with our own ideas, our own desires, our own expectations, we are unprepared to listen to what has been written, on its own terms rather than ours. We read and are read in these ways all the time. It's an occupational hazard.

So I want to focus here on this very small and specific kind of a "between," that concept I borrowed above from Donna Qualley. In this case, it's that silent space between the question's having been posed and the answer it is about to elicit. Perhaps more than any other space, this one defines the position of the teacher. We stand in front of our classes day after day in exactly that position. The question is posed. That's the easy part. It's what comes next I'm interested in. And I don't mean the answer—we always get answers to our questions: good ones, bad ones, partial ones. What we can turn them into is what matters. And it's in that first second or two after the question is posed where that gets determined.

I have three modes of behavior in relation to the questions I ask in the classroom. The first is basically Socratic: I have a prefigured plan that has a kind of loosely scripted role for student response. In this mode, I am prepared to hear the degree to which the response fits with my expectation. If it doesn't I have work to do, and I set about doing it. This is a very reputable mode of teaching. In the second, I'm filled with my own thoughts, my own knowledge maybe, or with meta-pedagogical planning, or just some distraction. I'm unprepared to hear anything but myself. This is a mode of listening that can lead to various kinds of pedagogical display, which can be quite useful, or down a side track toward a dead end, which usually is not. In the third, I actually wait with an open mind prepared to hear what is about to be said. I feel as if I am empty of "myself," as if I have a lot of available space just waiting to become occupied, and a lot of available time, to accept and engage with and learn from whatever is coming my way. Oddly enough, having spent all of these years accumulating the stores of knowledge that I have now to share, it's when my mind is "empty" in this way that I feel I do my most important work as a teacher. It's not that what I know is irrelevant to that moment. It's more like it's held in abeyance, prepared to advance if it's called up, but willing simply to wait. And it's not that what I might say in response to what I am about to hear is brilliant or profound. Mostly, it's just ordinary. I might ask another question—but it's one that derives from and is pertinent to what I just heard. I might make an observation or comment—but again, it's one that arises out of that moment. And from there a conversation emerges. Sometimes I will talk back and forth like this with a student for a few minutes, or more. Sometimes I will turn to other students and get them involved as respondents. Then I'll go back to the "source" again for a while. I find myself in these exchanges working to perfect what that student has to offer in response to the question, working with what she gives, pushing to the next step, trying hard to understand on her terms rather than mine what her "answer" is. I feel fully engaged, excited even, as if I'm learning something myself, as her comments make me think and speak in response. It is as if I have no voice of my own but have put my considerable resources somehow in the service of hers.

Now, everyone who teaches has these experiences, I know. They are not unique or even extraordinary. My point is simply that they are made possible by what I do in that moment *between* my asking of the question and the first word of response. If I can properly clear a space from which I can hear another voice, I become "open" not only to what is going to be said, but also to my own prospect for change in response to it. Even when I don't end up saying anything in my own voice. Or at all: That is the position I was in chronically during the Race and Gender read-arounds, and during much of the final class session. It is the position I imagine Plato in as he listens to his dialogical voices, fully prepared to say something of his own, but never needing to. It is the position I was in as a seventh grader reading Poe at night in my room. It is the position of the teacher when he knows enough to listen to something "other" than his own voice. This space between question and answer is filled with possibility. It is where my hopefulness about teaching begins, and where I try to return when I've lost it. That space is very much like the position of the writer, just before he starts to write, except here there are many authors present. From the "text" that is about to issue from this collaboration, changes of consequence may be effected, for all the involved parties. Here writing and teaching might be said to (e)merge toward a new kind of research.

Just by coincidence, I finalized the contract for this book on the same day I delivered my paper at the 1999 CCCC in Atlanta—for a round-table on "authenticity" with four graduate students from Pitt's English Department: Lisa Schwartz (who organized the panel and invited me to participate), Linda Huff, Cherise Pollard, and Patricia Sullivan. I want to close with what I had to say that day:

> Room 512 in Pitt's Cathedral of Learning is long and narrow, maybe fifteen by forty feet. It's dominated by a semi-elliptical wood conference table that can seat about 25. This is the room where our annual Seminar in Teaching Composition is scheduled every fall, Tuesday and Thursdays, 11–12:15. I've taught the seminar, in that room, somewhere between ten and twelve times—I lost accurate count back in the early nineties. Among those experiences are both the best and

the worst of my pedagogical times. I have eight minutes today to say something about the work I try to do in that room. So I need to get focused fast. Let me start with what it must seem like to at least some, if not many, of our first-year teaching assistants and fellows when they start in our program.

Typically, about half of the group are creative writers pursuing the M.F.A. Given a choice, they would prefer to be teaching creative writing. The other half of the group are pursuing either the M.A. or Ph.D. in critical and cultural studies. Except for the two or three among them who come expressly to specialize in composition, they would prefer to be teaching literature and theory. All twenty-something of them are, though, required to teach composition during their first year. Long before they arrive, we tell them what books they will be teaching with. We send them the exact assignments they'll be teaching from. We require them to attend a three-day introduction to teaching in our program, scheduled the week before classes begin. We assign them an advanced graduate student as a mentor. We arrange for each of them a mandatory class observation schedule and, for the group, biweekly staff meetings. And then we require this very demanding 3-credit seminar in teaching composition. In the face of that overwhelmingly institutionalized apparatus, they often, and quite legitimately, must be asking themselves: Where am *I* in this picture? This question is obviously a vexed one for these new teachers. But I want finally to suggest that what applies to them at the outset of their graduate study applies to all of us, and it applies throughout our academic careers, at least in relation to our work in the classroom.

So: Where am I in this picture? There are of course many levels of picture involved here, some of which must at least appear to most of these new teachers already to be finished and framed: The classroom, the roster, the syllabus, the course, the program, the university, the discipline, they are all always already there. One might legitimately ask: If I could scratch my "I" into any or all of these pictures, what difference would it make? Which brings us to the equally complex set of questions concerning this "I" who hopes to find a place there. It can, for example, be construed as individualistic, independent, relatively small, but at least within one's own control and therefore strong enough to find a ground for its own expression; or,

253

if not, at least for sustained resistance. Here, of course, is the intellectual dynamic of the authenticity model that dominated so much disciplinary thinking in composition pedagogy a generation ago. And it is often the intellectual dynamic that animates the creative writers in the group, who have absorbed this expressivist ideology from a much longer and stronger (and in some respects more venerable) cultural tradition. Or this "I" can be construed as socially constructed, implicated already in the ongoing cultural and academic conversations within which it is being inscribed. This is the intellectual dynamic of contemporary critical theory, the one generally shared by the Ph.D. and M.A. candidates in the group. But I have become convinced over my years of working to negotiate the arguments (and they can be intense) that inevitably arise between these two ideologies of the "I," that neither, taken in its ready-made form, is adequate to the task at hand, at least as it applies to work in the classroom. Teacherly identity is never simply a matter of being oneself, just as it cannot ever simply be the robotic ventriloquizing of disciplinary and institutional discourses.

From the time I taught my first composition course as a teaching assistant, back in 1972, students in my classes have been saying: "My high school teachers told me never to use 'I' in my writing. Now you're telling us that's OK. Why?" I had been teaching for quite a while before I fully realized how different the "I" that these anonymous high school teachers had exiled from my students' writing was from the "I" I was inviting them to try out, or try on, in my assignments. I came to understand that it's not enough just to permit, or even solicit, this "I." I needed also to conceptualize it, to offer opportunities both for talking about and critiquing it, to sanction it. Gradually I developed vocabularies for making clearer what I had in mind. Right now, I use the terms *position*—which I differentiate from *belief* or *opinion*—and *project*—which I define not in terms of "task" but as "ongoing intellectual enterprise"—to familiarize my strategy to them.

I tend to teach primarily by asking questions, trying to tease out more and more extended or complex responses from specific students. One day, maybe ten or twelve years ago, in the middle of a discussion of this sort—me poking and prodding about something or other—a student asked me: "We keep having to tell you what *we*

254

think. Why don't you ever tell us what *you* think?" My immediate response—though I don't think I expressed it this way—was that in the classroom, I don't "think" anything, at least not in the sense of having pre-cast opinions or answers. I want to engage in an open inquiry. I ask questions because I don't have the answers. Or the questions themselves have no answers. That sounds nice, but I was wise enough even back then to realize it wasn't an adequate answer to my student's question. If it was necessary for them to put their "I" at stake in my classroom, it was necessary for me to do it as well. Ever since, I've made a conscious effort to be more declarative in my teacherly mode, to disclose more, or more fully, what my own "position" is, what my "project" is, both for myself and with them.

I'm teaching Bakhtin's *Problems of Dostoevsky's Poetics* in another graduate seminar this term, one in which we are focusing on the concept of "voice" as a medium for contemporary composition theory and pedagogy. As I reread part of the book for class a few weeks ago, the following passage just leaped out at me, offering another angle on this question of teacherly identity:

> A man never coincides with himself. One cannot apply to him the formula of identity $A \equiv A$. . . . [t]he genuine life of the personality takes place at the point of non-coincidence between a man and himself. (59)

The problem Bakhtin is getting at here is one that has troubled me since I was a child. I remember back in the fifties watching Popeye cartoons every afternoon before supper. I loved Popeye. I wanted so much to be able to say as confidently and repeatedly as he did: "I am what I am and that's all what I am." I knew I couldn't say it back then and I assumed that growing up would give me that clear identity, that $A \equiv A$, my own "I," and I really looked forward to it. I remember in college when I first read Descartes' meditations, how he gradually and deftly strips away all his biases and opinions and attitudes and judgments; until he gets to the jewel of absolute identity at the center: "I think therefore I am." I envied Descartes in exactly the same way I envied Popeye. But I knew I still didn't have that $A \equiv A$, that "I," he was talking about and I was looking for, and I was beginning to fear that maybe I'd never get it.

When I started to teach, I found myself over and over—and still

255

do—in a position not much different from my students. What was happening in the classroom was changing *me*—both in who I was and what I knew—at least as much as it was changing them, sometimes more. I thought there was something wrong with me. That I lacked authority. Or knowledge. Or confidence. Some necessary tooth in the gear that turned the teacher wheel. I seemed, unlike my image of what a professor should be, to have no stable, durable, version of my "subject," whether that term is applied to the material of the course (and wasn't I after all supposed to already know what I was trying to teach, which is not so easy to presume when one's subject is composition or, even more so, teaching itself?); or whether that term is applied to a sense of myself, my "I" (as a figure of authority, to be sure, but also as a person, a soul, whose real life was, in some significant part, getting defined by, and played out in, this arena).

My sense now—and I'm hoping as time goes on not simply to re-endorse this truth for myself but to revel in it—is this: We are never who we are when we teach. Nor should we try to be. We are something always verging on the more, the better, the greater than this "I" who is trying to find its place in the picture. Teaching is in fact the means by which we may become *other* than ourselves: at the hands of the material we are teaching, which teaches us as well, in the hands of the people gathered with us in the room we share, who can teach us as well.

Bakhtin says about some of Dostoevsky's characters, the ones he most admires:

> They all acutely sense their own inner unfinalizability, their capacity to outgrow, as it were, from within and to render *untrue* any externalizing and finalizing definition of them. As long as a person is alive he lives by the fact that he is not yet finalized, that he has not yet uttered his ultimate word. (p. 59)

256

"Inner unfinalizability." That is as close as I can come right now to a version of a teacherly "I" I think I can live with. And one of the things it compels me to do, repeatedly, before I teach, as I teach, after I teach, and most especially when I teach the teaching seminar, is exactly what Bakhtin says: to outgrow from within and render untrue any externalizing and finalizing definitions of me—whether they are good or bad, whether they originate with me or from others. As long as I can do that, I feel I can stay alive to myself *as* a teacher; and, as a teacher of teachers, I can continue to resist the great teacherly temptation to utter my ultimate word.

NOTES

Preface

1. Kathleen Blake Yancey, *Reflection in the Writing Classroom* (Logan: Utah State University Press, 1998), 204–05.

Interchapter

1. Walt Whitman, *Leaves of Grass: Original 1855 Edition* (Santa Barbara: Bandana Books, 1992), 69.

2. Donna Qualley, *Turns of Thought: Teaching Composition as Reflexive Inquiry* (Portsmouth, N.H.: Heinemann, 1997), 159.

3. Mikhail Bakhtin, *Problems of Dostoevsky's Poetics,* ed. and trans. Caryl Emerson (Minneapolis: University of Minnesota Press, 1984), 59.

4. Mariolina Rizzi Salvatori traces out a part of this history in *Pedagogy: Disturbing History, 1819–1929* (Pittsburgh: University of Pittsburgh Press, 1996).

Introduction to Part Two

1. Jasper Neel, *Aristotle's Voice: Rhetoric, Theory and Writing in America* (Carbondale: Southern Illinois University Press, 1994), 197.

2. Maurice Blanchot, *The Step Not Beyond,* trans. Lycette Nelson (Albany: SUNY Press, 1992), 39.

3. Bakhtin, *Dostoevsky's Poetics,* 164.

4. See Susan Jarrett, *Rereading the Sophists* (Carbondale: Southern Illinois University Press, 1991); Sharon Crowley, "A Plea for the Revival of Sophistry," *Rhetoric Review* 7 (1989): 318–34; Victor Vitanza, "Taking A-Count

of a (Future-Anterior) History of Rhetoric as 'Libidinalized Marxism' (a PM Pastiche)," *Writing Histories of Rhetoric*, ed. Victor Vitanza (Carbondale: Southern Illinois University Press, l994).

5. John Poulakos, *Sophistical Rhetoric in Classical Greece* (Columbia: University of South Carolina Press, l995), 102. Poulakos is representative of the extraordinary work in recuperating the sophists that is ongoing in departments of rhetoric and communication. His research is grounded less in the contemporary critical theory that animates that of the compositionists I mention above than in the historical/philological procedures that govern more traditional scholarship. Poulakos seeks more to bring forth an accurate historical picture of the sophists and their rhetorics (thereby restoring their status and credibility) than to dislodge the hegemonic Socratic/Platonic/Aristotelian paradigm from the contemporary academy, though this is also part of his agenda.

Protagoras and Pedagogy

A version of this essay appeared as "Studying Professionally: Pedagogical Relationships at the Graduate Level," *College English* (April 1995): 448–60.

1. Plato, *Protagoras, Collected Dialogues of Plato*, trans. W. K. C. Guthrie, ed. Edith Hamilton and Huntington Cairns (New York: Pantheon Books, 1961), 314; 314e–315b. All page numbers following refer to this text, which, for consistency's sake, I rely on almost exclusively for my quoted passages throughout these essays. I also include in every case the standard passage numbers for comparison to other translations. Since I do not read Greek, I have consulted, comparatively, at least two other translations for each of the dialogues I write about in a major way—*Protagoras* and *Phaedrus*—and at least one other translation for the other dialogues I quote from more than once—*Meno, Gorgias,* and *Laches*. There are of course numerous differences among these various versions of the texts. Where those differences are of some potential consequence to the terms of my argument, I call attention to them in notes. In the case of the *Protagoras*, the other two translations I consulted are Stanley Lombardo, Karen Bell, and Michael Frede, *Protagoras* (Indianapolis: Hackett Publishing, 1992); and R. E. Allen, in *The Dialogues of Plato, Volume 3* (New Haven: Yale University Press, 1996).

2. Lombardo, Bell, and Frede also use the same expression here as Guthrie—"studying professionally." Allen uses "learning the art."

3. Allen translates this passage as "what will result for him." Lombardo,

Bell, and Frede use "what he will get out of it." While there are different implications to each of these, they all focus attention on potential change in the student.

4. For a fuller discussion of the application of a "science of measurement" to ethical matters, see Martha C. Nussbaum, *Love's Knowledge: Essays on Philosophy and Literature* (New York: Oxford University Press, 1990), chapter 3. Nussbaum devotes the first part of her argument to an examination of the *Protagoras*, "investigating the connection between the adoption of a quantitative measure of value and eliminating the problem of akrasia" (107).

5. Lombardo, Bell, and Frede translate this as the "art of citizenship." See their page xii for their rationale for this choice.

6. I'm not at all convinced that Socrates himself is capable of doing this very often, if at all. He deploys many quite different sorts of question/ response techniques in these dialogues but is rarely able to abdicate his own desire for control—one that usually derives from a profound sense of self-righteousness—long enough to actually listen in a way that might open *himself* up to the prospect for change, which is what Simonides' notion of "becoming" seems to me to require. As I have indicated, it is only by turning to Plato, as an extrinsic teacher-figure, that I can find a way out of this conundrum—at least in terms of its potential application to my own teaching.

Socratic Method and the Absence of the Student

1. Plato, *Protagoras*, trans. W. K. C. Guthrie, in *Collected Dialogues*. All passages cited by page number from this text. The other two translations of the *Protagoras* I consult comparatively are listed in note 2 in the previous chapter. I quote *Meno* from the Guthrie translation in the *Collected Dialogues*. In this case, I also consulted comparatively the G. M. A. Grube translation (Indianapolis: Hackett Publishing Co., 1976). *Lysis* is quoted from the J. Wright translation in the *Collected Dialogues; Lesser Hippias* from the Benjamin Jowett translation in the *Collected Dialogues*. In this case, I consulted comparatively the R. E. Allen translation, *Hippias Minor*, in *The Dialogues of Plato, Volume 3*. I quote *Phaedrus* from the R. Hackforth translation in the *Collected Dialogues*. For the two other translations I consulted, see note 1 in "Author/ity in the Classroom," the next chapter.

2. For background on the sophists as teachers see Jacqueline De Romilly,

The Great Sophists in Periclean Athens (Oxford: Clarendon Press, 1992), especially chapters 1 and 2, which develop the contrast between Socratic and Sophistic methods and suggest some connections between the ways in which pedagogy was institutionalized in Periclean Athens and the ways it has been institutionalized in the contemporary academy. See Poulakos, *Classical Greece*, chapters 1–3, for a discussion of the context for and reception of sophistical rhetoric. See H. D. Rankin, *Sophists, Socratics and Cynics* (Totowa, N.J.: Barnes and Noble Books, 1983), especially chapter 2, for a historical account of some of the sophists who engage Socrates in the dialogues I discuss here. See chapter 8 of Nussbaum's *Love's Knowledge* for a sharp critique of sophistry in both its ancient Greek (particularly Gorgias and Protagoras) and contemporary academic (particularly Stanley Fish) manifestations. See *Theory, Text, Context: Issues in Greek Rhetoric and Oratory,* ed. Christopher Lyle Johnstone (Albany: State University of New York Press, l996), for a detailed examination of the issues related to the emergence of rhetoric as a body of knowledge and field of study from the pre-Socratics through Aristotle.

3. Such a stretch is to me justifiable precisely because there is no exact identity between Hippocrates' experience and that of any particular kind of contemporary student. In some structural respects, his dilemma resembles that of a graduate student in our educational system, seeking the proper forum for "studying professionally," a forum in which one is willing to submit to the mentorship of individual "professors" in a disciplinary way. In other respects, he is very much like a novice to "higher" education, one just entering the path of professional training, not quite certain what he wants to do and who he wants to become. Ultimately, in each of my two arguments, I am not much interested in Hippocrates as a "presence" in the dialogue—in who he was or what happened to him in the framework of his own personal, or even generically cultural, experience. I use him primarily as an "absence," through which any number of points of view can be taken in relation to the explicit argument between Socrates and Protagoras.

4. The concept of "student-centeredness" in pedagogy has had a variety of incarnations since the late l960s, when it gained currency through the work of James Moffett, especially his *Student-Centered Language Arts Curriculum: A Handbook for Teachers* (Boston: Houghton Mifflin, 1968), which was re-edited periodically with Betty Jane Wagner from the mid-1970s on. The discourses of "collaborative learning" and "peer-tutoring" arise out of that framework, as do a host of other theories, approaches, and stratagems

for teaching reading and writing. Student-centered pedagogies inevitably raise the question of the degree to which it is possible/appropriate for students to "teach" their colleagues. And such a discussion gets us pretty quickly to the heart of our notions about what schooling is, and is for, in our society.

5. When Socrates is involved in discussions of this sort, as he often is with the sophists, he most often draws his examples from the practical disciplines: sculpture, music, gymnastics, architecture. While method or technique might be generalizable or transferable from one discipline to another, it cannot be taught, he would argue, as a generalized form, in isolation from its application. Socrates develops this critique of sophism much more explicitly and aggressively in *Gorgias*, where he insistently challenges Gorgias to define and describe his "field." Like most of the sophists, and many of us, Gorgias argues (as Protagoras would) that he has none, at least not in the restrictive sense that Socrates is using the term, and he argues further that rhetoric is so powerful a discipline precisely because it is not tied to any specific discipline or discourse but can function in a supervisory capacity toward all of them, in its mode as the "discourse about discourses." Much of what Gorgias (and Protagoras, and many of us for that matter) would claim to be knowledge, Socrates would discount as specious, even corrupt, in that it is not grounded in the certainty of either fact or principle.

6. Gorgias himself is the primary interlocutor only in the first part of this dialogue. The argument he initiates is thereafter taken up, in the terms that he sets, by his supporters/followers—first Polus and then Callicles. Elsewhere in the essay I use the name *Gorgias* as a kind of shorthand for this univocal triumvirate.

7. Drawing such a distinction between Plato (as author) and Socrates (as either a historical figure who is being replicated or a fictionalized character/voice who is being invented and deployed) is relatively commonplace to contemporary critical and rhetorical studies, and there are several ways of going about it. One derives from the poststructuralist gambit of figuring authors as written by rather than simply writing their texts. Derrida's deconstruction of the "Phaedrus" in "Plato's Pharmacy" (*Dissemination* [Chicago: University of Chicago Press, 1981]) is perhaps the most notorious and seminal extension of this project to Plato's work, complicating not only the relationship between Plato and Socrates, but more fundamentally the relationships between and among the various Platos who are written into this text. John Sallis, in *Double Truth* (Albany: SUNY Press, 1995), borrows Derrida's figure of "the double" to examine various aspects of the re-

263

lationship between image and object, author and voice, using Plato as one of his focal points. *Plato and Postmodernism,* ed. Steven Shankman (Glenside, Penn.: Aldine Press, 1994), offers a postmodernist counterpoint to the Derridean/deconstructionist approach to this problem, seeking to reauthorize in certain ways the relationship between Plato and his various characters and voices.

Contemporary rhetorical theory tends to come at this issue of the status of Socrates through the history/fiction conundrum, seeking to examine and, if possible, figure out in what dialogues and at what points Plato's version of Socrates can be said to function relatively straightforwardly as a "historical" voice. In *Socrates, Ironist and Moral Philosopher* (Ithaca: Cornell University Press, 1991), especially chapters 2 and 3, Gregory Vlastos gets at the problem of historicity by distinguishing between the "Socrates" of Plato's earlier period (which would include all of those dialogues I discuss here except for the *Phaedrus*), and the "Socrates" of Plato's middle period (including the *Phaedrus*). Vlastos sees an "irreconcilable difference between" (53) these two Socrates, and he uses this "difference"—in quite another sense, to be sure, from Derrida's *différance*—to get at the variety of distinctions among author, character, voice, and person that inevitably confront a reader of Plato's work. He wants ultimately to argue that through Plato's "Socrates," "we can come to know the thought of the Socrates of history" (81). Terry Penner uses a similar method to examine this same set of issues in "Socrates and the Early Dialogues," *The Cambridge Companion to Plato* (ed. Richard Kraut. Cambridge: Cambridge University Press, 1992), 121–69. Penner differentiates between the early, "Socratic" dialogues, "where the character Socrates speaks for the historical Socrates," and the later, "Platonic" dialogues, "where the character Socrates speaks rather for Plato" (124). The category of earlier dialogues includes, again, all of the dialogues I discuss in detail here except the *Phaedrus*. In *Plato's Socrates* (New York: Oxford University Press, 1994) Thomas C. Brickhouse and Nicholas D. Smith come at the distinctions between Plato and Socrates more directly and matter-of-factly, designating Socrates as a "character" with enough historically accurate aspects to make matters of contemporaneous fact consequential in comprehending the philosophical system Socrates proffers. They remain "agnostic about whose philosophy (if anyone's) is accurately represented in Plato's early dialogues" (viii). Edwin Black, in "Plato's View of Rhetoric," *Landmark Essays on Classical Greek Rhetoric,* ed. Edward Schiappa (Davis, Calif.: Hermagoras Press, 1994), 83–100, suggests that "it is inevitable that any expositor will approach a work from a certain point of view." He then proceeds to declare his own "critical presuppositions . . . that Plato was both a subtle and disciplined thinker and a subtle and disciplined writer, that he would not have allowed patent inconsistency and contradiction into the constantly revised body of his work, and that the dialogues, as speculative inquiries, must explain and justify themselves independent of any circumstances impinging on their composition" (83–84).

My own formulation of the disjunction between Socrates and Plato is relatively straightforward, and in that respect more closely resembles the rhetorical approach than it does the deconstructionist, although, as I have explained, I am not much concerned with the problem of Socrates (or the sophists he argues with, or even Plato for that matter) as a historical figure; and I do conserve the deconstructionist habit of destabilizing the relationship between author and text, primarily by using the prospect of authorial irony to draw a sharper line between Plato and Socrates than most rhetoricians might.

8. For a sophisticated discussion of the "negativity" of the Socratic method see Gregory Vlastos, *Socratic Studies* (Cambridge: Cambridge University Press, 1994). Vlastos examines Socrates' "elenctic method" in detail, looking specifically at some of the dialogues I discuss here, those that depict the Socrates of Plato's "early period" (see note 7). Vlastos argues that the Socratic elenchus is better seen as a mode of "searching" than a habit of refutation by negation. Victor Vitanza's *Negation, Subjectivity, and the History of Rhetoric* (Albany: State University of New York Press, 1996) offers, in part at least, both a response to and an alternative for Vlasto's position. Gail Fine, in "Inquiry in the Meno" (*The Cambridge Companion to Plato* [Cambridge: Cambridge University Press, 1992] 200–226), explores in detail the Socratic elenchus in its relationship to Socrates' theory of recollection, as it is outlined in the *Meno*. She argues that "although the Socratic dialogues typically end aporetically, elenchus need not end in aporia; the elenctic method can take one all the way to knowledge" (208). She sees the latter part of the conversation between Socrates and Meno's slave as evidence that the elenctic method can "go beyond the exposure of ignorance to the articulation of true beliefs" (209), suggesting that the slave comes to know not because of Socrates' leading questions but because of his own "capacity for reflection and revision" (211). She also argues for a direct analogy between the search for truth about a geometrical figure and the search for truth about moral concepts.

265

9. For a discussion of recollection and memory in the *Meno* see chapter 2 of John Sallis's *Being and Logos: The Way of Platonic Dialogue* (Pittsburgh: Duquesne University Press, 1975).

10. I recognize the hazard of conflating these various dialogues as if they were contemporaneous statements on the same theme, virtue. Socrates and his position(s) obviously change in response to different sorts of interlocutors and, as Gregory Vlastos and Terry Penner outline (see note 7 above), over the course of Plato's career. There are dangers as well in treating these discussions of virtue in relative isolation from their conceptual context in ancient Greece and in treating virtue itself in relative isolation from its context in the history of philosophy generally. And there are, as well, dangers in relying largely on translations for my specific language; interesting and problematic ambivalences arise, obviously, at that level of diction that can have a big effect on what Socrates/Plato have been taken to "mean." That I have not attended to these issues at the level of detail that a philosopher, classicist, translator, or philologist might is not to suggest that I am either unaware, or dismissive, of their importance to a full understanding of the Platonic epistemology/metaphysics. But, again, my interest here is not primarily in rendering a reading of Socrates/Plato in their contexts and on their terms. I am interested in exploring the ways in which our contexts and our terms can be informed by some of the characters, arguments, and themes that these dialogues happen to proffer.

11. Certainly there are dialogues in which Socrates' efforts at inducing "perplexity" lead to better results. In *Laches*, for example, he is extraordinarily deft and amiable as he orchestrates the conversation, manipulating the two primary interlocutors, Laches and Nicias, to persuade one another that neither knows what he was so self-assured about as the conversation opened: the meaning of courage, or once again in its most ultimate (Socratic) terms, "the nature of virtue" (133; 190b). That Socrates dismantles their certainty here—by, characteristically, dismantling their definitions— opens up the prospect for continuing dialogue, continuing education, some of it possibly at Socrates' hands. Even here, though, the likelihood that such education will even occur, let alone generate the sort of knowledge Socrates seems to be seeking, is open to question. He continually demurs in the face of their requests to engage him as a teacher for the various "sons" in question here. Nicias is inclined to take his own "ignorance" immediately to Damon, a disciple of Prodicus, a sophist, after which he promises to come back and "freely impart my satisfaction to you . . . [who] are very much in want of knowledge" (143; 200b–c). And both Nicias and

Laches behave at the most crucial portions of the discussion much the way Meno and his slave do, allowing Socrates' "leading" questions to dominate their brief, almost perfunctory replies.

Author/ity in the Classroom

1. Plato, *Phaedrus*, *The Collected Dialogues of Plato*, 483; 235c–d. All page numbers refer to this text, unless otherwise noted. I have used this translation primarily, to maintain consistency throughout this half of the book. I have also consulted comparatively two other translations of the *Phaedrus*: the W. C. Helmbold and W. G. Rabinowitz translation (Indianapolis: Bobbs-Merrill, 1956); and the Alexander Nehamas and Paul Woodruff translation (Indianapolis: Hackett Publishing Co., 1995). Where there are differences of consequence among them about the passages I quote here, I outline them in my notes.

2. Here Helmbold and Rabinowitz use "statement" instead of "assertion." Nehamas and Woodruff use "argument" instead of "assertion" and "that view"—in retrospective reference to Socrates' previous question implying that it is necessary to understand "the nature of the world as a whole" in order to understand the "nature of the soul"—instead of the "truth." Just after this passage, they have Socrates say: "Consider, then, what both Hippocrates and true argument say about nature." This is their only use of the word "true" in this brief portion of the text, but it seems to sustain the general distinction I am trying to draw here.

3. I say "perhaps" in the previous sentence to indicate that there is disagreement about whether this dialogue represents an actual sexual seduction or uses that discourse to sustain an intellectual seduction (see note 13 below, for example.) Determining exactly what Socrates' and Phaedrus's intentions are is not essential to my purposes here. At the most basic level, a pedagogical relationship can be read as sexualized without its necessarily being (or hoping to become) physically sexual in nature. The September/October 1998 issue of *Academe* is devoted entirely to matters—intellectual, legal, and pedagogical—related to sexuality in the contemporary academy.

4. Nehamas and Woodruff translate this passage this way: "if you question anything that has been said because you want to learn more, it continues to signify just that very same thing forever." (80–81) In the reader-oriented economy of our current critical systems, we are intensely aware of exactly the opposite status of written texts: their incapacity ever

to repeat themselves exactly, even to the same reader at different times, let alone to multiple readers across generations.

5. There are two ongoing and interrelated disciplinary conversations that broadly address matters of this sort. One is among ethnographers, and it involves issues of method. The basic question animating this debate is: What is ethnography and what is not? For an excellent introductory survey of this contended space, see *Voices and Visions: Refiguring Ethnography in Composition,* ed. Cristina Kirklighter, Cloe Vincent, and Joseph Moxley (Portsmouth, N.H.: Boynton/Cook, 1997). This book also provides a context for understanding my decision not to name what I do in this book's first half as ethnographic.

The second concerns the matter of student confidentiality, which influences many modes of research in composition, including the ethnographic. Now that actual student discourse—verbatim transcriptions of what students write in their essays or say in class—is entering our professional discourse to demonstrate something other than comic errancy (which was never, in my view, a legitimate use of that discourse), issues of propriety, privacy, and authorial prerogative come to the fore in all of their vexatious complexity. Paul V. Anderson's "Ethical Issues in Composition Research" (*College Composition and Communication* 49, no. 1 [February 1998]: 63–89) offers an excellent starting point (including sample consent forms and bibliography) for inquiry on matters of this sort.

6. Helmbold and Rabinowitz translate this passage—which I was tempted to use here and elsewhere because it is more colloquial and figurative at key moments—as follows: "As for the soul's immortality, enough has been said. But about its form, the following must be stated: To tell what it really is would be a theme for a divine and very long discourse; what it resembles, however, may be expressed more briefly and in human language. Let us say that it is like the composite union of powers in a team of winged horses and their charioteer" (28). Nehamas and Woodruff translate the passage this way: "That, then, is enough about the soul's immortality. Now here is what we must say about its structure. To describe what the soul actually is would require a very long account, altogether a task for a god in every way; but to say what it is like is humanly possible and takes less time. So let us do the second in our speech. Let us liken the soul to the natural union of a team of winged horses and their charioteer" (30–31).

7. Helmbold and Rabinowitz use "illusion" here instead of "semblance." Nehamas and Woodruff use "opinions." All of these carry the implication

of speciousness in the Socratic system. *Semblance* and *illusion* are more strongly in concert with my general argument here, since they implicate figurative discourse directly.

8. In "Metaphor and the Order of Things" (*Audits of Meaning,* ed. Louise Z. Smith [Portsmouth, N.H.: Boynton/Cook-Heinemann, 1988], 125–37) I develop this alternative way of construing the function of figure in more recent rhetorical theory. I am especially interested in opening up a critique of the transparency of literal discourse. Lombardo, Bell, and Frede (see note 2, "Protagoras and Pedagogy") suggest the possibility of a similar kind of pedagogical enterprise on Plato's part in the *Protagoras*: "By having Socrates put his questions and draw his conclusions in a way which raises, but does not settle, the question of the unity of the virtues, Plato may have made the point precisely to encourage us to pursue for ourselves the different possibilities" (xxiii).

9. The Helmbold and Rabinowitz translation of the passage is as follows:

> PHAEDRUS: . . . Yet how and from what source may one acquire the true art of rhetorical persuasion?
>
> SOCRATES: The ability, Phaedrus, to become a finished performer is probably, or perhaps certainly, like everything else: if it is in your nature to be a speaker, an eloquent speaker you will be if you also acquire knowledge and practice. . . .
>
> Every great art must be supplemented by leisurely discussion, by stargazing, if you will, about the nature of things. This kind of discussion seems somehow or other to be the source of the characteristic we are looking for: that loftiness of mind that by all means and at all times strives to attain perfection. (60)

The Nehamas and Woodruff translation is as follows:

> PHAEDRUS: . . . But how, from what source, could one acquire the art of the true rhetorician, the really persuasive speaker?
>
> SOCRATES: Well, Phaedrus, becoming good enough to be an accomplished competitor is probably—perhaps necessarily—like everything else. If you have a natural ability for rhetoric, you will become a famous rhetorician, provided you supplement your ability with knowledge and practice. . . .
>
> All the great arts require endless talk and ethereal speculation about nature: This seems to be what gives them their lofty point of view and universal applicability. (70)

269

10. Instead of "knack," Helmbold and Rabinowitz use "endless routine" and Nehamas and Woodruff use "artless practice." Any of these terms could sustain the application I want to make of this passage.

11. Mariolina Salvatori and I, who team-taught this seminar on four occasions, have reported in more detail on our work in this course in "The Teaching of Teaching: Theoretical Reflections," *Reader* no. 33/34 (spring/fall 1995): 85–124. I also taught this course on several occasions with David Bartholomae and on several occasions by myself.

12. Here I chose to introduce the alternate translations to the text of my argument, primarily because I felt in this instance that the metaphors of "stargazing" and "ethereal speculation" added a figurative dimension to the more conceptual "high-flown speculation" that Hackforth chooses.

13. Nehamas and Woodruff do not see this as a stage in the seduction of Phaedrus by Socrates. They say: "We have no reason to think that Phaedrus is representing himself as courted by Socrates. Socrates favorite is Isocrates (279b2); and Phaedrus is crazy about Lysias, as we already know" (26 n). This position is elaborated in more historical terms in note 9 on page xiv of their preface, where they suggest, on the basis of certain internal evidence, that Phaedrus "cannot be a very young man" at the time of this discussion, and that Socrates' references to him as "child" or "youth" or "young man" are simply common "terms of intimacy" rather than factual references. To the degree that this dialogue might be construed as Socrates' seduction of Phaedrus, it is primarily to convince him "that philosophy is life's most serious activity" (xv).

My own argument here does not necessarily depend on whether Socrates is explicitly seducing Phaedrus sexually. I am more interested in examining their discourse as an analogue for certain kinds of pedagogical transactions in which teacherly "mastery" gradually leads to silence, or its equivalents, as response.

14. Nehamas and Woodruff offer an interesting structural comparison between Socrates' critique of writing vis-à-vis speech and our own contemporary critique of "the visual media, especially television" vis-à-vis writing. This position emerges in the context of their offering "two alternative interpretations" to Derrida's way of reading Socrates' critique of writing as, inevitably, a simultaneous critique of speech (xxxiv–xxxvii).

INDEX

271